Media Access to the Family Court:

A Guide to the New Rules and their Application

Media Access to the Family Court:

A Guide to the New Rules and their Application

Iain Goldrein, QC
Visiting Professor (the Sir Jack Jacob Chair) Nottingham Law School

Fellow of the Royal Society of Arts

Companion of the Academy of Experts

Family Law

Published by Family Law
A publishing imprint of Jordan Publishing Limited
21 St Thomas Street
Bristol BS1 6JS

British Library Cataloguing-in-Publication Data

A catalogue record for this book is available from the British Library.

ISBN 978 1 84661 200 8

Typeset by Letterpart Ltd, Reigate, Surrey

Printed in Great Britain by Antony Rowe, Chippenham, Wilts

PREFACE

The access of the media into the family courts throws into sharp relief the issues of open justice, privacy and confidentiality.

The new rules as to media access – and communication as to information – require focus on three distinct and separate areas of family law practice:

(1)   The extent and limits of the right of the media access to the courts and to watch.

(2)   The extent of what can – and cannot – be reported in relation to cases involving children, with particular reference to the inter-action of the following statutes (see Appendices 3 and 4):

   (i)   Administration of Justice Act 1960, s 12;

   (ii)   Contempt of Court Act 1981, s 11;

   (iii) Section 97 of the Children Act 1989 as interpreted in *Clayton v Clayton.*

(3)   The extent and limit of the right of a party (or legal representative) to communicate information for purposes connected with the proceedings.

Whilst the new statutory dispensation provides a very restricted access, and intimates an agenda more in the nature of permitting debate as to the 'system' of justice rather than the reporting of the individual case in the court room, the very fact of legislative change casts a stone into the mill pond and must necessarily ferment debate with the potential for further change.

One may anticipate that increasingly, application will be made on behalf of the media to be permitted to do more than just sit and watch.

Against that backdrop, the purpose of this book is to provide in one compendium, commentary and source material which brackets the three foci set out above, in anticipation that in any such application time will be of the essence.

The simpler and easier the corpus of knowledge is capable of ready assimilation, so the greater will access to justice be secured.

This need for immediate accessibility to source material is accentuated in the context of applications vis a vis media exclusion not necessarily being made on notice, and one may equally expect such applications to be made in very difficult pressing circumstances, as evidenced in the case of *Re Child X*.[1]

Such access in this arena is so very critical, given the interests of children.

One not infrequently sees pervading the cases in this arena, a suggestion of local authority inadequacy, if not worse. This book should not be interpreted as other than seeking to strike the fairest of balances between all stakeholders in this area of law. Against that backdrop the following dicta of Munby J in *Re B; X Council v B*[2] bear repetition:

> 'There is one further observation I wish to make. As McFarlane J said in *Re X (Emergency Protection Orders*[3]*)* at para [6]:
>
> "The ordinary experience of the family courts is of social workers and social services departments whose professional work is both valuable and appropriately targeted to meeting the particular needs of children and their families."
>
> I agree with that view, which accords entirely with my own experience in the family courts. But too often this experience goes either unremarked or recorded in judgments where the local authority is not named. If local authorities which merit criticism are to be named then so too surely should those which deserve praise. If the public interest is a reason for naming the incompetent then surely the very same public interest requires the naming of the competent. Otherwise the public may have a seriously distorted impression of the family justice system – and that is very certainly *not* in the public interest.'

It is appropriate that dicta of Munby J should feature in this Preface, given the quite profound contribution he has made to the jurisprudence in this field.

Iain Goldrein, QC
7 Harrington Street
Liverpool; and
7 Bell Yard
London
1 August 2009

---

[1]   [2009] EWHC 1728 (Fam).
[2]   [2007] EWHC 1622 (Fam), [2008] 1 FLR 482.
[3]   [2006] EWHC 510 (Fam), [2006] 2 FLR 701.

ACKNOWLEDGMENTS

Dedicated to Lilo de Haas and the memory of Josef de Haas.

CONTENTS

TABLE OF CASES

References are to paragraph numbers.

TABLE OF STATUTES

References are to paragraph numbers.

TABLE OF STATUTORY INSTRUMENTS

References are to paragraph numbers.

TABLE OF PRACTICE DIRECTIONS
AND PRESIDENT'S GUIDANCE

References are to paragraph numbers.

TABLE OF ABBREVIATIONS

AJA 1960	Administration of Justice Act 1960
CA 1989	Children Act 1989
CMC	Case Management Conferences
CPR 1998	Civil Procedure Rules 1998
CYPA 1933	Children and Young Persons Act 1933
ECHR	European Convention on Human Rights
FDR	Financial dispute resolution
FPR 1991	Family Proceedings Rules 1991
FPC(CA 1989)R 1991	Family Proceedings Courts (Children Act 1989) Rules 1991
IRH	Issues Resolution Hearings
MCA 1980	Magistrates' Court Act 1980
MoJ	Ministry of Justice
NYAS	National Youth Advocacy Service
PD	Practice Direction
PG	President's Guidance
PGN	President's Guidance Note
PLO	Public Law Outline

1

WHAT HAS CHANGED?

THE EXTENT AND LIMIT OF THE MEDIA'S RIGHT OF ACCESS

1.01

(a) 'Duly accredited' media representatives have the right to attend at 'hearings of family proceedings which take place in private' subject to the discretion of the court; see FPR 1991, r 10.28. As to overseas journalists, see below at para **7.06**. As to the meaning of 'discretion' see *Re Child X (Residence and Contact – Rights of Media Attendance)*[1] at paras [48] and [56].

(b) The rules are to be applied on the basis of a right to attend throughout, save to the extent that the court exercises its discretion to exclude them on the grounds specified in the rules; the test is 'necessity', see *Re Child X*.[2]

(c) The court has the discretion to exclude such representatives from the whole or any part of any hearing on specified grounds; see FPR 1991, r 10.28, paras (4)–(6). In other words the court's discretion can be exercised in relation to:
(i) the proceedings;
(ii) a particular hearing; and
(iii) to part of the proceedings or hearing.
As to the standard of proof, see *Re Child X*[3] at para [57].

1.02 Thus, save for excepted cases or in defined circumstances, accredited representatives of the media are as of right allowed access to the following courts:

(a) Family Proceedings courts;

(b) Family Proceedings in the county courts; and

(c) Family Proceedings in the High Court.

---

[1]   [2009] EWHC 1728 (Fam).
[2]   [2009] EWHC 1728 (Fam).
[3]   [2009] EWHC 1728 (Fam).

WHAT DOES 'HEARINGS OF FAMILY PROCEEDINGS WHICH TAKE PLACE IN PRIVATE' MEAN?

1.03 The media have a right of access to the following:

(a) Hearings to consider applications brought under the CA 1989, Parts IV and V, including Case Management Conferences (CMC) and Issues Resolution Hearings (IRH);

(b) Hearings relating to findings of fact;

(c) Interim hearings; and

(d) Final hearings.

1.04 This includes:

(a) private law CA 1989 cases;

(b) proceedings for non-molestation and occupation orders;

(c) proceedings for forced marriage protection orders; and

(d) proceedings under the Matrimonial Causes Act 1973, Part 2 – Financial Relief for Parties to Marriage and Children of Family – this being subject to the exception at para **1.06** below.

1.05 In this context, the Explanatory Note to the Rules provides:

> '"in private" meaning when the general public have no right to be present: it is to be noted that because proceedings are in private, reporting restrictions will apply by virtue of section 12 of the Administration of Justice Act 1960 in addition to the restrictions which will apply by virtue of section 97(2) of the CA Act 1989 where the proceedings concern children'.

Also see para **1.20** et seq below.

EXCEPTED CASES TO WHICH THERE IS NO RIGHT OF MEDIA ACCESS

1.06 Subject to any order of the court to the contrary:

- Adoption (including placement order) hearings, but:
  - (i) in the High Court and county court, there is a discretion to permit the media to be present; see para 5 of the President's Guidance (PG) of the 30 April 2009 (see para **A1.15** in Appendix 1); and

(ii) the position of placement proceedings when heard with care proceedings is specifically catered for in the PG, see para 7 (at para **A1.15** in Appendix 1).

- Judicially led conciliation and mediation. This will include an IRH if it is to be used as a process of conciliation. Thus, an IRH and a CMC will *not* be regarded as a conciliation opportunity unless a judge rules to the contrary. See FPR 1991, r 10.28(1).

- Financial dispute resolution (FDR) appointments (as contrasted with financial ancillary relief cases). See para 2.1 of the Practice Direction (PD) of the 20 April 2009 below at para **A1.14**.

DO THE MEDIA HAVE TO GIVE NOTICE OF ATTENDANCE?

1.07 No; they are allowed in as of right, save for the above exceptions.

IS THERE A FORMAT FOR REPRESENTATIONS AS TO MEDIA ACCESS?

1.08 No, but:

- The judge will pause the hearing, for representations to be made.

- The judge's ruling can relate to the whole of the proceedings or any part of the proceedings or hearing.

- Representations are **oral**, rather than in writing from the parties and the media (unless the court directs otherwise, see para 6.2 of the PDs of 20 April 2009, below at paras **A1.13–A1.14** in Appendix 1.

- If the hearing is before a legal adviser of the Family Proceedings Court, he/she will have to refer the case to the magistrates' bench if the media is to be excluded at a legal-adviser-run hearing (directions).

As to exluding the media *ab initio*, see *Re Child X*[4] at paras [83] and [87].

---

4   [2009] EWHC 1728 (Fam).

IS THERE AN APPEAL FROM A JUDICIAL DECISION ON MEDIA ACCESS?

1.09 No, the hearing will proceed. But judicial review proceedings are a recourse (Civil Procedure Rules 1998, Part 54).

HOW DO THE MEDIA PROVE ACCREDITATION?

1.10 The prescribed scheme is the UK Press Card Scheme. The media representative must wear and show the card issued by the UK Press card Authority; see para 4.1 of the PDs of 20 April 2009, at paras **A1.13–A1.14** in Appendix 1.

COURT LISTS

1.11 In family proceedings concerning children, no information should be published that could lead to identification of the child. Thus:

- the cause lists that are printed for display must not show the names of the parties in any proceedings involving children; and

- in adoption and placement proceedings, the cause lists should be edited clearly to show that the hearings are not open to media.

DOES THE MEDIA HAVE ACCESS TO COURT DOCUMENTS UNDER THE NEW MEDIA RULES?

1.12 No, but this is not to be confused with new rules as to disclosure, which is a separate issue entirely from attendance of the media at hearings; see para **11.01** below (and see FPR, rr 2.36(4) and (5); 3.16(1) and 10.20). In this context, see also the PG of the 22 April 2009 at paras 15 and 16 (see para **A1.16** in Appendix 1) for the anticipated opposing arguments. Also see *Re Child X*[5] at para [84].

DOES THE MEDIA HAVE ACCESS TO A TRANSCRIPT OF THE JUDGMENT?

1.13 No; but the media representative is entitled to apply for a transcript of an anonymised judgment.

---

[5]   [2009] EWHC 1728 (Fam).

POST-HEARING RESTRICTIONS ON REPORTING

1.14 The prohibition on reporting, flowing from the CA 1989, s 97 does not apply after the end of a case (*Clayton v Clayton*[6]). Post-hearing restrictions are to be determined on a case-by-case basis by reference to 'welfare' criteria and managed through the use of a prohibited steps order and/or injunctive relief as appropriate. Thus, after the end of a case:

- unless otherwise ordered by the court, publication may be made of the fact that a particular child, or parents, have been involved in children proceedings.

- the AJA 1960, s 12 continues to make it potentially a contempt of court to communicate information about the substance of what was put before the court and what happened in the court room with respect to a child in proceedings brought under the High Court's inherent jurisdiction or under the CA 1989.

NOTE 1

Cases will be rare where an application to extend the CA 1989, s 97(2) prohibition is made: In *Re Webster, Norfolk County Council & Ors,*[7] Munby J said:

> '**[63]** Before passing from this topic it is worth noting the views expressed both by the President and by Wall LJ in *Clayton v Clayton* as to the likely need for specific orders protecting a child's identity beyond the conclusion of the proceedings. Both were sceptical. The President at para [51] said this:
>
> > "Given the existence of section 12 of the Administration of Justice Act 1960 which is apt to prevent publication or reporting of the substance of, or the evidence or issues in, the proceedings (save in so far as permitted by the court or as revealed in any judgment delivered in open court), I do not think that, as a generality, it is right to assume that identification of a child as having been involved in proceedings will involve harm to his or her welfare interests or failure to respect the child's family or private life."'
>
> '**[64]** Wall LJ said, at para [145]:
>
> > "My impression is that there are unlikely to be many cases in which the continuation of that protection will be required."'

THE ESSENCE OF THE NEW PROVISIONS

1.15 The primary machinery to achieve media access are:

(a) access to 'accredited representatives' of the media;

---

[6] [2006] EWCA Civ 878, [2007] 1 FLR 11. Any relief sought beyond the jurisdiction of s 12 or s 97(2) must be founded on Convention rights; see *Re Child X* at para [11].

[7] [2006] EWHC 2733 (Fam), [2007] 1 FLR 1146.

(b) greater use of anonymised judgments and/or summaries of decided cases (to be taken forward through pilot areas in the course of the next six months from April 2009). The pilot areas will have to address:

(i) the need for anonymised versions of judgments in the majority of cases – or at least, a carefully worded summary;

(ii) the preparation of a suitable summary to accompany a consent order.

NOTE 2

(a) A Family Courts Information Pilot is being launched, to be run in three areas: Leeds, Wolverhampton and Cardiff.

(b) The cases falling within the scheme will primarily be public law cases in the family proceedings courts, county courts and the High Court. Some private law cases may be included.

(c) The Government hopes that judgments will be given for the purpose of publication in contested residence or contact cases where the issues are in dispute and the outcome is unusual.

(d) The pilot areas will routinely produce, for county court and High Court cases, a written record of the court's decision, ie a hard copy of the judgement. Family proceedings courts will continue to provide written reasons.

(e) All anonymised judgments and written reasons will be placed online.

NOTE 3

Such an anonymised judgment would in turn be available to the relevant child later in life, explaining the circumstances in which he/she was brought up; in this context also see *Re Child X* at para [15].[8]

THE ESSENCE OF THE CHANGE

1.16 The Secretary of State explained in *Family Justice in View*[9] (this being the backdrop against which the amended Rules can be understood):

'1. To improve confidence

We will:

- Change the law so that the media will be able to attend family proceedings in the courts, unless the court decides otherwise.
- Improve and increase the amount of public information accessible to all who want to know more about the way the courts work and how decisions are made.

And [we will] pilot:

---

[8] [2006] EWHC 2733 (Fam), [2007] 1 FLR 1146.

[9] *Family Justice in View* (dated 16 December 2008) can be accessed at: www.justice.gov.uk/news/announcement161208a.htm; and see *Re Child X* at paras [42]–[43].

- Placing anonymised judgments on-line from some typical family cases from local Family Proceedings Courts and County courts, so that the public can see how decisions were reached;
- Giving the parties a copy of the judgment at the conclusion of their case so that they have a record of what was decided and why.

The pilot will also look at the practicalities of retaining judgments for children who are the subject of proceedings so they can access it when they are older, should they chose to do so.'

HOW SHOULD THE NEW RULE BE APPLIED?

1.17 FPR 1991, r 10.28 anticipates, and should be applied on the basis that, media representatives have a right to attend family proceedings throughout save and to the extent that the court finds it 'necessary' to exclude them from the whole or part of any proceedings on one or more of the grounds set out in paragraph (4) of the rule (see PDs of the 20 April 2009, para 5.1). See paras **A1.13–A1.14** in Appendix 1.

THE OVERRIDING JUDICIAL CONTROL

1.18 During any hearing, courts should consider whether the exception in FPR 1991, r 10.28(1) becomes applicable so that media representatives should be directed to withdraw (see PDs of the 20 April 2009, para 2.2 at paras **A1.13–A1.14** in Appendix 1).

SUMMARY THUS FAR

1.19 The new provisions do *not* provide for the public being allowed *into* the family courts; rather it provides for information as to the system/'gist' in relation to the family courts being allowed *out*. To give effect to this policy change, there can be perceived three categories of hearing in the family courts:

- Open ('O') as under the existing law;

- Confidential ('C') (to which the existing law applies); and

- Private ('P') (to which the new law applies).

HOW DOES THE OLD LAW AND THE NEW LAW INTERACT?

1.20 Para 2.4 of the PDs (20 April 2009) says:

'The question of attendance of media representatives at hearings in family proceedings to which rule 16A/rule 10.28 and this guidance apply must be distinguished from statutory restrictions on publication and disclosure of information relating to proceedings, which continue to apply and are unaffected by the rule and this guidance.'

See paras **A1.13–A1.14** in Appendix 1.

1.21 This is perhaps best expressed in tabular form:

Type of proceedings	Court	References
Adoption Act 1976	C	
Child Abduction and Custody Act 1985	C	
Child Support Act 1991 – appeals	C/P	See Note 4
Committal for breach of court order or undertaking	O	
Children Act 1989	C	
Domestic Proceedings and Magistrates' Courts Act 1978		
(1) Finance	C	See Note 5
(2) Personal protection	P	See Note 5
Family Law Act, Pt IV	P	See Note 5
Family Law Act 1986, Pt III (e g parentage declarations)	O	FPR 1991, rr 3.16(12) and 2.28 (1)
Inheritance (Provision for Family and Dependants) Act 1975	C	
Civil Procedure Act 1997: search orders; freezing injunctions (s 7(1))	P/C	See Note 6

Type of proceedings	Court	References
		P: If no disclosure ordered.
		C: If application in civil proceedings (CPR 1998, Pt 25) and involves e g personal financial matters (CPR 1998, r 39.2(3)
Married Women's Property Act 1882	C	
Matrimonial Causes Act 1973	O	FPR 1991, r 2.28(1)
(1) Divorce	C	See Note 6
(2) Children (s 41)	C	
(3) Ancillary relief (except s 37(2)(a))	P	
(4) Restraint of disposal (s 37(2)(a))		
Matrimonial and Family Proceedings Act 1984, Pt III	C	
Protection from Harassment Act 1997	O	C: If welfare of children involved (CPR 1998, r 39.2(3)(d))
Supreme Court Act 1981, s 37 (inherent jurisdiction)		See Note 6
(1) Shipman order	P	
(2) Freezing (and CPA 1997, s 7(1)(a))	P	See Note 6

Type of proceedings	Court	References
Trustees of Land and Appointment of Trustees Act 1996, s 14	O	C: If involving personal financial matters or the welfare of children (e g alongside CA 1989, s 15) (CPR 1998, r 39.2(3), (d))
Wardship and inherent jurisdiction	C	

NOTE 4

As proceedings relating to a child, these may be confidential; but since they are essentially inter partes, they may be conducted in private.

NOTE 5

Save where children are involved, when they will normally be confidential. See *Clibbery v Allan* at para **A2.01** below.

NOTE 6

Though listed as private, these proceedings may attract the same restrictions as to openness of court as the proceedings to which they are interlocutory.

NOTE 7

To understand the principles underpinning this table, please see dicta from *Clibbery v Allan* set out in **Appendix 2** below and also para **1.05** above.

2

WHAT HAS NOT CHANGED?

WHAT HEARINGS ARE STILL BARRED TO THE MEDIA?

2.01 Media representatives do not have access to the following hearings (see PDs of the 20 April 2009, para 2.1, at paras **A1.13–A1.14** in Appendix 1):

(a) Hearings which are conducted for the purpose of judicially assisted conciliation or negotiation (which may include, subject to judicial direction, an IRH or CMC under the Public Law Outline (PLO). An IRH or a CMC will not be regarded as a conciliation opportunity unless a judge rules to the contrary).

(b) The bar set out in (a) above is lifted if:
   (i) the judge plays no part in the conciliation process; or
   (ii) where the conciliation element of a hearing is complete and the judge is adjudicating upon the issues between the parties.

(c) Hearings covered by the PDs of the 20 April 2009, para 2.1 are:
   (i) Financial Dispute Resolution hearings, which come within the exception at (a) above (as contrasted with ancillary relief hearings).
   (ii) First Hearing Dispute Resolution appointments in private law CA 1989 cases to the extent that the judge plays an active part in the conciliation process.
   (iii) Conciliation meetings or negotiations conducted between the parties with the assistance of an officer of the service or a Welsh Family Proceedings Officer and without the presence of the judge are not 'hearings' within the meaning of this rule and media representatives have no right to attend such appointments.

WHAT HEARINGS ARE OPEN TO THE MEDIA OUTSIDE THE PROVISION OF THE NEW RULES?

2.02 Media representatives continue to have the right to be present where that has hitherto been the position, namely where hearings are held in open court where the general public (including media representatives) may attend as of right, such as committal hearings or the hearing of matrimonial or civil partnership causes (see PDs of the 20 April 2009, para 1, footnotes 2 and 6 at paras **A1.13–A1.14** in Appendix 1).

3

SOURCES

CHANGES

3.01 The changes flow from the following source material.

(a) Statutory Instruments:
  (i) The Family Proceedings (Amendment) (No 2) Rules 2009 (SI 2009/857) and Explanatory Note.
  (ii) The Family Proceedings Courts (Miscellaneous Amendments) Rules 2009 (SI 2009/858).

(b) Practice Directions:
  (i) Attendance of Media Representatives at Hearings in Family Proceedings – High Court and county courts (PD of 20 April 2009).
  (ii) Attendance of Media Representatives at Hearings in Family Proceedings – Family Proceedings Court (PD of 20 April 2009).

(c) Guidance:
  (i) President's Guidance Note in relation to Care Proceedings involving Placement Order Applications – Attendance of the Media (PG of the 30 April 2009).
  (ii) President's Guidance in relation to Applicants Consequent Upon the attendance of the Media in Family Proceedings (PG of the 22 April 2009).

NOTE 1

The Explanatory Note to the Family Proceedings (Amendment) (No 2) Rules provides:

> 'Rule 4 inserts into the 1991 Rules a new rule 10.28, which makes provision governing who may be present during a hearing in proceedings which are held in private ("in private" meaning when the general public have no right to be present). This in particular allows for duly accredited media representatives to be present, subject to a power for the court to direct their exclusion for all or a part of the proceedings for one of the reasons specified in paragraph (4) of the new rule.'

NOTE 2

These provisions do *not* affect proceedings under the Adoption and Children Act 2002, which are governed by the Family Procedure (Adoption) Rules 2005. The Rules of 2005 have not been amended in parallel with the FPR 1991 to cater for the attendance of media representatives in relation to placement order applications in care proceedings (see PG of the 30 April 2009, para 4). For further commentary, see below at para **A1.15**.

INTERPRETATION/DEFINITION

3.02   Several terms in FPR 1991, r 10.28 are not provided with a definition. The following may be of assistance as a guide.

- 'Legal representative' is likely to carry the same definition as in FPR 1991, r 11.9.

- 'Children's guardian' presumably has the same definition as in FPR 1991, r 4.1 (although that rule is designed only for Part IV).

- 'Litigation friend' is not defined and, although CPR 1998 does not apply to family proceedings and to these rules, perhaps it may be assumed that the CPR 1998, Part 21 definition is intended.

- 'Officer of the court' is not defined, but see FPR 1991, r 1.2; 'Proper officer' means:
  (a)   in relation to the principal registry, the family proceedings department manager; and
  (b)   in relation to any other court or registry, the court manager, or other officer of the court or registry acting on his behalf in accordance with directions given by the Lord Chancellor.

- 'General public ... no right to be present': Whilst the general public may not attend 'in private' hearings, certain individuals, as listed in FPR 1991, r 10.28(3), are entitled to be in court, including '(h) duly accredited' members of the press and '(g) any other person whom the court permits to be present.' Thus a hearing at which accredited representatives of the media are permitted to be present remains 'a hearing held in private'. Relatives and other members of the public are not entitled to be present unless specifically permitted under the rules or by the court.

4

POLICY BACKGROUND TO THE NEW RULES

THE AIM

4.01 The aim is to improve scrutiny of, and public confidence in, the family court system (a recent case in this context is *S v Rochdale MBC;*[1] see para **A5.01** below).

THE POLICY ISSUE TO BE ADDRESSED

4.02 There is a public perception of a secret justice system, the secrecy of which permits sometimes extravagant and fundamentally misconceived criticisms of the workings of the family courts. By permitting media access, the framework of child care law and the reasoning of the judiciary become transparent to the public.

HOW DID THE SECRETARY OF STATE EXPRESS IT?

4.03 The Ministry of Justice's conclusions (*Family Justice in View*[2]) in December 2008 were foreworded by the Secretary of State inter alia in the following terms:

> 'The challenge we face is to raise public understanding of how decisions are made, and awareness of the daily duties of those working within the family courts to deliver the best solution to difficult problems. At the same time, we must protect the privacy of children and families involved in family court cases so they are not identified or stigmatised by their community or friends.'

---

[1] [2009] 1 FLR 1090.

[2] *'Family Justice in View'* can be accessed at: www.justice.gov.uk/news/announcement161208a. htm.

THE APPROACH OF THE CHANGES TO THE RULES AND THE SITUATIONS ENVISAGED BY THE MOJ

4.04   At page 31 of *Family Justice in View* (see footnote 2 above), the Secretary of State said (the subtitles are the author's and not from the Secretary of State):

(a)   Right of access limited to restricted information coming *out* of court rather than a free right of the access to the public *into* court:

> 'We have therefore come to the conclusion that we must increase the volume of information available about the family courts and open up the courts; but a right of access to proceedings cannot mean an untrammelled right to report anything and in any manner regardless of its impact on the children involved.'

(b)   The tension between the conflicting priorities of *openness* (Article 10) and *privacy* (Article 8):

> 'We propose to change the law to allow access to the court so that family justice can be seen. The family justice system is not secret, it has nothing to hide, but it does need to be private to safeguard and protect children and their families.'

NOTE 1

There is a contrast between *'private'* and *'secret'*. The new rules are aimed at avoiding *secrecy* while respecting *privacy;* see also *Re Child X (Residence and Contact – Rights of Media Attendance)*[3] at paras [32]–[34].

THE ROLE OF THE MEDIA

4.05   The role of the media is underpinned by responsible and honest reporting:

> 'The media have a role to play. Their reporting must be responsible and honest, providing information about the system without endangering the identities or welfare of children. We believe that they could be a positive influence in increasing understanding of the work of the courts.'

THE FOCUS

4.06   The focus is on 'system' rather than 'human interest':

> 'We can understand that journalists want to run human-interest stories where the parties and children are identified. Journalists have said they want to write the full detailed 'human' story with photos, but the rules limiting reporting are there for

---

[3]   [2009] EWHC 1728 (Fam).

the good of children experiencing very difficult situations. While the media will *not* be able to identify parties or the child subject to proceedings, they will certainly be able to discuss in a more informed way how the system works.'

Also see *Re Child X (Residence and Contact – Rights of Media Attendance)*[4] at paras [39] and [58].

THE TENSION

4.07 With regards to the tension between reporting fairly and openly, without risking disclosure of identities:

'Journalists who have attended family proceedings courts have been able to report sufficient outlines of several cases that allow the reader to understand the gist of proceedings, but without identifying those involved. The challenge for the media is to report fairly, openly and without any risk to the identities and welfare of those involved.'

COURT POWER TO EXCLUDE

4.08 The power of the court to exclude the media:

'That said, there is also strong support for the court to be able to exclude any member of the media or anybody else in attendance when they see fit, depending on the case.'

RAISING THE ISSUE OF EXCLUSION

4.09 Circumstances envisaged by the Secretary of State as raising the issue of exclusion are:

(a) *Child wishing to attend*:

'In children cases, there may be occasions where the child may wish to attend but will not do so if a representative of the media is present ...'

(b) *Indecent nature*:

'... or where the evidence being given is of an indecent nature, making a stressful experience all the more so if it has to be undergone in front of reporters.'

(c) *Non-children proceedings*:

---

[4]   [2009] EWHC 1728 (Fam).

'… In non-children proceedings, such as domestic violence or forced marriage cases, parties could be at risk if there are identified in court …'

(d) *Vulnerable adults*:

'… Some other cases may involve people who lack a full understanding of the significance of the media such as those with learning disabilities …'

(e) *Policy approach*:

'Therefore, in the interests of consistency, a limited discretion to exclude in the interests of children, or for the safety and protection of parties and witnesses, including those with learning disabilities, will be provided across all tiers of court. The parties and their legal representatives will, of course, be able to make representations to the court if the media are present and there are reasons why they should be excluded.'

ISSUES ARISING WITHIN THE FRAMEWORK PROVIDED BY THE AMENDED RULES

PROBLEM AREAS

5.01 The following issues may be expected.

(a) There will be a substantial administrative burden on the judiciary to produce anonymised judgments.

(b) Given a consent order, there will need to be a suitable accompanying document.

(c) What of the position of the journalist to whom a parent complains (rule 11(4)(1)(d)) after the end of care proceedings? Save perhaps for seeing an anonymised judgment, the journalist will be in no better position to assess/audit what happened in court.

(d) What of the journalist who is present during the care proceedings, who in the subsequent Crown Court case witnesses the same framework of issues being litigated – but with no reference to some of the evidence called/admitted in the family court proceedings? (Such a journalist would not in the family court have been privy to the case management record, evidence-in-chief and the contents of expert evidence unless cross-examined.)

6

'SPECIFIED GROUNDS' AND THE MAKING OF REPRESENTATIONS AS TO MEDIA ACCESS

WHAT ARE THE 'SPECIFIED GROUNDS' TO EXCLUDE THE MEDIA?

6.01   Rule 10.28 provides that at any stage of the proceedings the court may direct that accredited media representatives shall not attend the proceedings or any part of them, where satisfied that:

- It is necessary:
  - (a)   in the interests of any child concerned in, or connected with, the proceedings;
  - (b)   for the safety or protection of a party, a witness in the proceedings, or a person connected with such a party or witness; or
  - (c)   for the orderly conduct of the proceedings (see below at para **6.02** for meaning); or

- justice will otherwise be impeded or prejudiced (see below at para **6.03** for meaning), and also see *Re Child X (Residence and Contact– Rights of the Media Attendance)*,[1] (FPR 1991, r 10.28(4)); a case involving a child of a celebrity.

NOTE 1

This discretion to *exclude* is limited to specific and effectively narrow exceptions.

NOTE 2

The criterion is firmly expressed; *'necessary'*. Desirability is not a factor. See *Re Child X*[2] at paras [48], [53]–[54], [56] and [89].

NOTE 3

It is to be inferred from the wording of the rule that the burden of proof must be upon the one seeking to exclude the media; that burden must be in relation to at least one of the statutory factors.

---

[1]   [2009] EWHC 1728 (Fam), see para [45].
[2]   [2009] EWHC 1728 (Fam), see para [45].

WHAT IS THE RATIONALE FOR THE PHRASE 'THE ORDERLY CONDUCT OF PROCEEDINGS'?

6.02

- This enables the court to address practical problems presented by media attendance.

- In particular, it may be difficult or even impossible physically to accommodate all (or indeed any) media representatives who wish to attend a particular hearing on the grounds of the restricted size or layout of the court room in which it is being heard.

- Court staff will use their best efforts to identify more suitable accommodation in advance of any hearing which appears likely to attract particular media attention, and to move hearings to larger court rooms where possible.

- However the court should not be required to adjourn a hearing in order for larger accommodation to be sought where this will involve significant disruption or delay in the proceedings (see PDs of 20 April 2009, para 5.3 at paras **A1.13–A1.14** in Appendix 1).

WHAT IS THE RATIONALE FOR THE PHRASE 'JUSTICE WILL OTHERWISE BE IMPEDED OR PREJUDICED'?

6.03 Reasons of administrative inconvenience are not sufficient. Examples of circumstances where the impact on justice of continued attendance might be sufficient to necessitate exclusion may include:

- Parties finances: a hearing relating to the parties' finances where the information being considered includes price sensitive information (such as confidential information which could affect the share price of a publicly quoted company); or

- Credible reasons: any hearing at which a witness (other than a party) states for credible reasons that he or she will not give evidence in front of media representatives; or

- Full and frank: where there appears to the court to be a significant risk that a witness will not give full or frank evidence in the presence of media representatives.

See PDs of the 20 April 2009, para 5.4 (at paras **A1.13–A1.14** in Appendix 1); and also see *Re Child X*[3] at paras [45] and [52], vis à vis allegations of an outrageous intimate nature.

HOW IS THE COURT TO RULE IN RELATION TO THOSE GROUNDS?

6.04   When considering the question of exclusion on any of the grounds set out in para (4) of the Rule the court should approach the issue as follows:

- Exclusion for whole or only part? Specifically identify whether the risk to which such ground is directed arises from the mere fact of media presence at the particular hearing or hearings the subject of the application or whether the risk identified can be adequately addressed by exclusion of media representatives from a part only of such hearing or hearings;

- Are the court's powers sufficient, without exclusion? Consider whether the reporting or disclosure restrictions which apply by operation of law, or which the court otherwise has power to order will provide sufficient protection to the party on whose behalf the application is made or any of the persons referred to in para (4)(a) of the Rule;

- Safety of parties: Consider the safety of the parties in cases in which the court considers there are particular physical or health risks against which reporting restrictions may be inadequate to afford protection;

- Vulnerable adult/unrepresented child: in the case of any vulnerable adult or child who is unrepresented before the court, consider the extent to which the court should of its own motion take steps to protect the welfare of that child or adult.

See PDs of the 20 April 2009, para 5.2 (at paras **A1.13–A1.14** in Appendix 1); and also see *Re Child X*.[4]

REASONED DECISION

6.05   In the event of a decision to exclude media representatives, the court should state **brief** reasons for the decision. See PDs of the 20 April 2009, para 5.5 (at paras **A1.13–A1.14** in Appendix 1).

---

[3]   [2009] EWHC 1728 (Fam), see para [45].
[4]   [2009] EWHC 1728 (Fam), see para [45].

WHO HAS JURISDICTION TO MOVE THE JURISDICTION OF THE COURT?

6.06 Subject to giving to any accredited media representative who is in attendance an opportunity to make representations:

- The court may exercise this power of *its own motion*, or

- Pursuant to representations made by any of the following persons:
  (a) A party to the proceedings;
  (b) Any witness in the proceedings;
  (c) Where appointed, any children's guardian;
  (d) Where appointed, a CAFCASS officer of the Service or Welsh family proceedings officer, on behalf of the child the subject of the proceedings.
  (e) The child, if of sufficient age and understanding.

See PDs of the 20 April, para 6 at paras **A1.13–A1.14** in Appendix 1.

WHO CAN MAKE REPRESENTATIONS ON BEHALF OF THE MEDIA?

6.07 Where exclusion is proposed, any media representatives who are present are entitled to make representations about that proposal.

ADJOURN FOR MEDIA REPRESENTATIVES TO BE PRESENT?

6.08 There is no requirement to adjourn proceedings to enable media representatives who are not present to attend in order to make such representations. In such a case, the court should not adjourn unless satisfied of the necessity to do so having regard to the additional cost and delay which would thereby be caused. See PDs of the 20 April 2009, para 6.1 (at paras **A1.13–A1.14** in Appendix 1); but now see *Re Child X.*[5]

HOW AND WHEN ARE REPRESENTATIONS TO BE MADE?

6.09 Applications to exclude media representatives should normally be dealt with as they arise and by way of oral representations, unless the court directs otherwise. See PDs of the 20 April 2009, para 6.2 (at paras **A1.13–A1.14** in Appendix 1).

---

[5] [2009] EWHC 1728 (Fam), see para [45].

SHOULD A PARTY GIVE NOTICE TO MEDIA REPRESENTATIVES OF AN APPLICATION TO EXCLUDE?

6.10 When media representatives are expected to attend a particular hearing (for example, where a party is encouraging media interest and attendance) and a party intends to apply to the court for the exclusion of the media, that party should, if practicable, give advance notice to the court; to the other parties; and (where appointed) any children's guardian, officer of the service or Welsh Family Proceedings officer, NYAS or other representative of the child of any intention to seek the exclusion of media representatives from all or part of the proceedings. See PDs of the 20 April 2009, para 6.3 (at paras **A1.13–A1.14** in Appendix 1); and now also see *Re Child X*[6] and note the relevance of the CopyDirect Service of the Press Association.

DUTY ON LEGAL REPRESENTATIVES TO ALERT/INFORM WITNESSES

6.11 Legal representatives and parties should ensure that witnesses are aware of the right of media representatives to attend and should notify the court at an early stage of the intention of any witness to request the exclusion of media representatives. See PDs of the 20 April 2009, para 6.3 (at paras **A1.13–A1.14** in Appendix 1).

TO WHAT EXTENT – IF AT ALL – DOES THE COURT HAVE TO PUT THE MEDIA ON NOTICE?

6.12 Prior notification by the court of a pending application for exclusion will *not* be given to media interests *unless the court so directs*. However, where such an application has been made, the applicant must where possible, notify the relevant media organisations. See PDs of the 20 April 2009, para 6.4 (at paras **A1.13–A1.14** in Appendix 1). The position was further clarified by Sir Mark Potter P in *Re Child X* at para [87].

> '[87] In the light of the media interest to be anticipated in cases involving the children of "celebrities", whether national or local, I do not consider the provisions of para 6.4 to be adequate provision to protect the interests of the press and I am of the view that it requires to be reconsidered. Meanwhile, although the Practice Direction does not expressly so provide, I consider that it is incumbent upon an applicant who wishes to exclude the media from a substantive hearing *ab initio* to raise the matters with the Court prior to the hearing for consideration of the need to notify the media in advance of the proposed application and that, if this is done the Court should require the applicant to notify the media via the CopyDirect service in accordance with

---

6   [2009] EWHC 1728 (Fam), see paras [83] and [87].

the procedures provided for in the CAFCASS Practice Note. The Court should at the same time make directions for the hearing of the application whether by way of special appointment of consideration at the outset of the next substantive hearing. It is of course not necessary for the matter to be dealt with by a High Court Judge and it should, wherever possible, be dealt with by the trial judge. In the light of the view I have expressed, I consider that para 6.4 pf the Practice Direction of 20 April 2009 should be read as if there were added at the end of the final sentence in that paragraph the words: "and should do so by means of the Press Association CopyDirect service, following the procedures set out in the Official Solicitor/CAFCASS Practice Note dated 18 March 2005".'

7

CHECKLIST FOR AUTHENTICITY OF MEDIA REPRESENTATIVES?

WHAT DOES 'DULY ACCREDITED' MEAN?

7.01 This is defined in FPR 1991, r 10.28(8) in the following terms:

'... accreditation in accordance with any administrative scheme for the time being prepared for the purposes of this rule by the Lord Chancellor.'

7.02 Media representatives will be expected to carry with them identification sufficient to enable court staff, or if necessary the court itself, to verify that they are 'accredited' representatives of news gathering or reporting organisations within the meaning of the Rule, See PDs of the 20 April 2009, para 4.1 (at paras **A1.13–A1.14** in Appendix 1).

WHAT IDENTIFICATION IS SUFFICIENT?

7.03 The Lord Chancellor has decided that the scheme operated by the UK Press Car Authority provides sufficient accreditation. A card issued under that scheme will be the expected form of identification, and production of the card will be both necessary and sufficient to demonstrate accreditation. See PDs of the 20 April 2009, para 4.2 (at paras **A1.13–A1.14** in Appendix 1).

CHECKLIST FOR ACCREDITATION

7.04

- UK Press Card Scheme.

- Representatives must show and wear such a card.

- Cards are valid for two years.

- The core information on such cards is:
  (a) name of issuing organisation;
  (b) applicant's full name;
  (c) personal ID Number; and

(d) nature of employment (eg reporter, cameraman, sound engineer, journalist).

- Cards issued from January 2009 include enhanced security by incorporating a hologram.

- Each card has a unique number and an associated PIN number.

- Verification hotline: 0870 837 6477.

WHAT IF THE MEDIA REPRESENTATIVE DOES NOT HAVE PROOF OF ACCREDITATION?

7.05 A media representative unable to demonstrate accreditation in accordance with the UK Press Card Authority scheme, so as to be able to attend by virtue of para (3)(f) of the Rule, may nevertheless be permitted to attend at the court's discretion under para 3(g). See PDs of the 20 April 2009 (at paras **A1.13–A1.14** in Appendix 1).

THE POSITION OF OVERSEAS JOURNALISTS

7.06 Overseas journalists can secure a UK press card. If such a journalist is permitted access to family proceedings, he may be able to publish in his own jurisdiction, in the absence of a *contra mundum* injunction. Thus, the court may (in an appropriate case) have to enquire whether there is present a member of the press working in any way outside the jurisdiction of the court. If there is a possibility of overseas reporting, an injunction is capable of being granted on ordinary principles binding that other jurisdiction. For the purposes of service, enquiry would have to be made of the identity of the journalist and the identity and address of his/her publishing house, to protect against any risk of publication overseas. In this context, Sir Mark Potter said in *Re Child X*:[1]

'[66] Finally, this case is one in which there is a very high degree of interest on the part of the English media and an even greater interest in the media of a particular country who have already been active in approaching parties for comment on the proceedings, on one occasion by the press, and on another by the presences of a foreign television crew outside the Court. The reason for the Judge's granting of the *contra mundum* order was the presence of the press photographers outside the Court throughout the hearing. Shortly after the grant of the injunction, a foreign magazine published an article identifying the parents and speculating upon the outcome of the proceedings. Upon the day the matter was transferred to me by the Judge, a member of the press of that country was taking photographs in the Court corridors and of the door of the Court. Upon appearing before the Judge,

---

[1]   [2009] EWHC 1728 (Fam), see paras [83] and [87].

she said that she was intending to publish the pictures to illustrate a report of the proceedings in a foreign magazine.

[67] In these circumstances, and with this level of curiosity, as it seems to me, if the press are admitted to the proceedings at this stage at least, there is inevitably a danger of the details of the case as explored and discussed in Court leading to a wider audience and, in the case of the foreign media, being published in a country beyond the reach of this Court so far as proceedings for the contempt of court are concerned. If this happens, there is an obvious danger that the contents of the article may come to the attention of X via her own access to the internet or via her friends.'

8

WHAT IS THE POSITION VIS À VIS ADOPTION AND PLACEMENT HEARINGS?

POSITION IN THE HIGH COURT AND COUNTY COURTS

For hearings in adoption or placement proceedings held in private in the High Court and county courts

8.01 Representatives of the media are not entitled as of right to attend hearings in adoption or placement proceedings held in private. Nonetheless, in the High Court and county courts, the court has a discretion to allow them to be present (see PG of the 30 April 2009, para 5, at para **A1.15** in Appendix 1).

Distinguishing between applications for a placement order in care proceedings and adoption hearings

Placement

8.02 Where an application for a placement order is heard together with care proceedings, the court should, when considering whether to admit media representatives, take into account their general right to attend hearings in care proceedings. In such a case, it would normally be appropriate for the court to allow representatives of the media to be present, unless a direction under FPR 1991, r 10.28(4) is necessary in relation to the care proceedings or there is some feature of the placement application which means that media representatives should not be present (for example, where there is a need to preserve the confidentiality of a proposed placement or where the interest of a prospective adopter or other person who is not before the court may be adversely affected by the attendance of the media). The existence of a placement application should not, by itself, be treated as a reason for making a direction under FPR 1991, r 10.28(4) excluding the attendance of media representatives in respect of the care proceedings (see PG of the 30 April 2009, para 7, at para **A1.15** in Appendix 1).

Adoption

8.03 The personal and confidential nature of proceedings for an adoption order means that it would not generally be appropriate for the court to permit media representatives to be present at an adoption hearing (see PG of the 30 April 2009, para 6, at para **A1.15** in Appendix 1).

POSITION IN THE MAGISTRATES' COURT

8.04   The effect of the Magistrates' Court Act 1980, s 69(2) and (3) (as amended by the Adoption and Children Act 2002, Schedule 3) is that media representatives are not permitted to be present at hearings in proceedings under the 2002 Act.

9

THE OVERRIDING STATUTORY REGIME AS TO REPORTING CASES IN THE FAMILY COURTS

HAS THE OVERALL STATUTORY REGIME CHANGED?

9.01 No, there is no change to the statutory regime which underpins the rules limiting reporting. The following statutory provisions remain in force, and are set out in Appendix 1 below.

The Children Act 1989, s 97

9.02 Identification of a child as being involved in a children's case is criminally unlawful.

NOTE 1

(i) The prohibition in the CA 1989, s 97 does not apply after the end of the case; see *Clayton v Clayton*.[1]

(ii) The permissive power in the CA 1989, s 97(4) might be used by the court where, for example, a child is missing and press publicity may help in tracing him. It would appear that an order may be made of the court's own motion or on application. If an application is to be made, it may be appropriate to use the directions procedure under Family Proceedings Courts (Children Act 1989) Rules 1991, r 14. In a series of cases the court has moved towards the lifting of reporting restrictions in certain circumstances: In *Re Webster, Norfolk County Council v Webster and Ors*,[2] Munby J analysed publicity issues both in principle and in relation to detailed statutory provisions and rights under the ECHR 1950; see below at para **A3.05** et seq.

The Administration of Justice Act 1960, s 12

9.03 The AJA 1960, s 12(1); s 12(1)(a) substituted by the CA 1989, s 108(5)(6), Sch 13, para 14 (see amending SI 1991/828, Art 3(2)).

NOTE 2

Leading cases on AJA 1960, s 12 in this context are *Clayton v Clayton* supra; and *Re B (A Child) (Disclosure)*.[3] As to the meaning of the word 'publication' see Munby J in *Kent County Council v B and Others*[4] at paras [62]–[82], which also covers what documents are covered by 'contempt' (see

---

[1] [2006] EWCA Civ 878, [2007] 1 FLR 11.
[2] [2006] EWHC 2733 (Fam), [2007] 1 FLR 1146.
[3] [2004] EWHC 411 (Fam), [2004] 2 FLR 142.
[4] [2004] EWHC 411 (Fam), [2004] 2 FLR 142.

para **A3.02** et seq). Also see the CYPA 1933, s 39. If an order is sought which goes beyond the scope of s 12(1) of the AJA 1960 and s 97(2) of the CA 1989; such as application must be founded on Convention rights. This being so it is subject for the provisions of s 12(2) of the Human Rights Act 1998 with its very robust provision as to notification and service; see *Re Child X (Residence and Contact – Rights of Media Attendance)*[5] at paras [11] and [12].

---

[5]   [2009] EWHC 1728 (Fam).

10

HOW ARE THE CHILD'S INTERESTS PROTECTED AFTER THE END OF A HEARING?

PROTECTING A CHILD'S INTERESTS AFTER A HEARING

10.01   The AJA 1960, s 12 prohibits the following.

(a)   Publication or reporting of the substance of, or the evidence or issues in, the proceedings (save as may be permitted by the court) by rendering such publication a contempt of court.

(b)   Publication of:
    (i)   an account of what has gone on in front of the judge sitting in private; or
    (ii)   of any of the court documents (other than the order) or extracts from, or a summary of, those documents; and
    (iii) the Case Management Record, position statements, witness statements, reports of experts and CAFCASS, etc and any reference to any other documents.

NOTE 1

In other words, AJA 1960, s 12 prevents parties and journalists from publishing what went on during the court process itself.

NOTE 2

As to the respective arguments vis à vis access to court documents, see the PG of the 22 April 2009, paras 15 and 16 at para **A1.16** below).

10.02   The AJA Act 1960, s 12 does not of itself prohibit:

(a)   Identification of a child as being involved in a children's case (but see the CA 1989, s 97 and the broader protection of the CYPA 1933).

(b)   Reporting the fact that a particular person was a witness in relevant proceedings.

(c)   The 'nature of the dispute'.

(d)   Date, time and place of a past or future hearing.

(e)   Text or summary of the whole or part of any order made.

(f)   The identity of witnesses.

(g)   The identity of the parties.

See further Appendix 3 at para **A3.02** below.

POST-HEARING RESTRICTIONS ON IDENTIFICATION

10.03   The statutory prohibition preventing the identification of a child as being involved in a children case does not apply after the end of the case; *Clayton v Clayton.*[1] Thus, post-hearing restrictions on identification must be dealt with on a case-by-case basis. As McFarlane J said in a speech to Resolution's annual conference in March 2009:

> 'The Ministry has stated its intention to reverse the effect of *Clayton v Clayton* so that "the identity of children will be automatically protected beyond the conclusion of a case, unless the court otherwise directs." For the present, however, the current law as described in *Clayton* remains, with the result that publication may be made (subject to contrary judicial ruling) "of the fact that a particular child, or parent, has been involved in children proceedings albeit that the substance of what was put before the court may not".'

10.04   For the full text of the speech, go to the Resolution website.[2]

WHAT IF THE COURT DOES NOT MAKE A DIRECTION?

10.05   The effect of *Clayton* (see above) is that publication is permitted of the fact that a particular child, or parent, has been involved in children proceedings, albeit that the substance of what was put before the court may not.

CHILDREN AND YOUNG PERSONS ACT 1933

10.06   Within the CYPA 1933, s 39 as amended, the Court retains broad general powers:

> 'In relation to any proceedings in any court ... the court may direct that:
>
> (a)   no newspaper report of the proceedings shall reveal the name, address, or school, or include any particulars calculated to lead to the identification, of

---

[1]   [2006] EWCA Civ 878, [2007] 1 FLR 11.
[2]   Website can be accessed at: www.resolution.org.uk.

any child or young person concerned in the proceedings, either, as being the person by, or against, or in respect of whom the proceedings are taken, or as being a witness therein;

(b)   no picture shall be published in any newspaper as being or including a picture except in so far (if at all) as may be permitted by the court.'

NOTE 3

The media in family proceedings continue to be prevented from seeing any document.

THE LAW RELATING TO DISCLOSURE AND GUIDANCE FROM THE PRESIDENT OF THE FAMILY DIVISION

INTRODUCTION

11.01 Part XI of the new Rules (FPR 1991, r 11) replaces FPR 1991, r 10.20A for the High Court and county court; and for the family proceedings courts, a new Part IIC is inserted into the Family Proceedings Courts (Children Act 1989) Rules 1991. The effect of these provisions is considerably to widen the circumstances in which information relating to children in court proceedings can be communicated to third parties.

WHAT IS THE POSITION VIS À VIS REPRESENTATIVES OF THE MEDIA?

11.02 Representatives of the media are not entitled to receive information without the permission of the court or as provided by the Rules.

COMMUNICATION OF INFORMATION FOR PURPOSES CONNECTED WITH THE PROCEEDINGS

11.03 Within FPR 1991, the new rule 11.4 inter alia provides:

(1) A party or the legal representative of a party, on behalf of and upon the instructions of that party, may communicate information relating to the proceedings to any person where necessary to enable that party:
  (a) by confidential discussion, to obtain support, advice or assistance in the conduct of the proceedings;
  (b) to engage in mediation or other forms of alternative dispute resolution;
  (c) to make and pursue a complaint regarding the law, policy or procedure relating to a category of proceedings to which this Part applies.

(2)   Where information is communicated to any person in accordance with para (1)(a) of this rule, no further communication by that person is permitted.

(3)   *****

NOTE 1

There is now *no express limitation* on the categories of people to whom a party to proceedings may communicate information relating to the proceedings for the purposes of:

(i)   obtaining support, advice or assistance in the conduct of the proceedings (but no further communication by that person is permitted; unlike with (ii) to (iv) immediately below – see the full terms of the rule. By implication, this provision would appear to include Members of Parliament and local councillors).

(ii)   to engage in mediation or other forms of alternative dispute resolution;

(iii)   to make or pursue a complaint against a person or body concerned in the proceedings; or

(iv)   to make or pursue a complaint regarding to the law, policy or procedure relating to family proceedings.

NOTE 2

There is no express provision that permits a party to disclose information to an *outside expert* without the court's permission.

NOTE 3

As yet, it is not clear whether a journalist will be a person to whom a parent may disclose information within the meaning of para (i) above for the purpose of obtaining support, advice and assistance with the conduct of the case. And even if a journalist is entitled to receipt of such information, any further communication beyond that is unlawful: see Rule 11.4(2).

THE LAW AS TO DISCLOSURE

11.04   The law as to disclosure has also not changed; see PDs of the 20 April 2009, para 2.2 at paras **A1.13–A1.14** in Appendix 1.

•   A media representative is not entitled to receive or peruse court documents referred to in the course of evidence, submissions or judgment without the permission of the court or otherwise in accordance with the new Part XI of the FPR 1991 (rules relating to disclosure to third parties).

•   This is in contrast to the position in civil proceedings, where the court sits in public and where members of the public are entitled to seek copies of certain documents (*GIO Services v Liverpool and London Ltd*[1]); see PDs of the 20 April 2009, para 2.3 at paras **A1.13–A1.14** in Appendix 1.

•   As to the words above 'without the permission of the court' the discretion falls to be exercised by the judge trying the individual case. Authoritative

---

[1]   [1999] 1 WLR 984.

guidance from the higher courts is required on this issue to avoid significantly different approaches arising around the country.

- The question of attendance of media representatives at hearings in family proceedings to which FPR 1991, r 10.28 and the PD of the 20 April 2009 apply must be distinguished from statutory restrictions on publication and disclosure of information relating to proceedings, which continue to apply and are unaffected by the rule and this guidance. See PDs of the 20 April 2009, para 2.4 at paras **A1.13–A1.14** in Appendix 1.

WHAT IS THE PRESENT STATE OF THE LAW AS TO IDENTIFYING A CHILD IN THE PROCEEDINGS, AFTER JUDGMENT?

11.05 See PDs of the 20 April 2009, para 2.5 at paras **A1.13–A1.14** in Appendix 1.

- The prohibition in the CA 1989, s 97(2) on publishing material intended to, or likely to, identify a child as being involved in proceedings or the address or school of any such child (generating a criminal offence), is limited to the duration of the proceedings: *Clayton v Clayton.*[2] (Contrast the position under the Administration of Justice Act 1960, s 12.)

- Further in proceedings to which the CA 1989, s 97(2) applies, the court should continue to consider at the conclusion of the proceedings whether there are any outstanding welfare issues which require a continuation of the protection afforded during the course of the proceedings by the provision.

- However, the limitations imposed by the AJA 1960, s 12 on publication of information relating to certain proceedings in private apply during and after the proceedings. In particular proceedings which:
  - (a) relate to the exercise of the inherent jurisdiction of the High Court with respect to minors;
  - (b) are brought under the CA 1989; or
  - (c) otherwise relate wholly or mainly to the maintenance or upbringing of a minor.

---

[2]   [2006] EWCA Civ 878, [2007] 1 FLR 11.

Appendix 1

SOURCE MATERIAL

A1.01

CHILDREN AND YOUNG PERSONS ACT 1933

Chapter 12

****

39 Power to prohibit publication of certain matter in newspapers

(1) In relation to any proceedings in any court the court may direct that –

   (a) no newspaper report of the proceedings shall reveal the name, address, or school, or include any particulars calculated to lead to the identification, of any child or young person concerned in the proceedings, either as being the person by or against or in respect of whom the proceedings are taken, or as being a witness therein;

   (b) no picture shall be published in any newspaper as being or including a picture of any child or young person so concerned in the proceedings as aforesaid;

except in so far (if at all) as may be permitted by the direction of the court.

(2) Any person who publishes any matter in contravention of any such direction shall on summary conviction be liable in respect of each offence to a fine not exceeding level 5 on the standard scale.

[*(3) In this section 'proceedings' means proceedings other than criminal proceedings.*]

Amendments—Words repealed and substituted Children and Young Persons Act 1963, ss 57(1), 64(3), Sch 5; Youth Justice and Criminal Evidence Act 1999, s 48, Sch 2, paras 1, 2.

Prospective Amendments—Sub-s (3): inserted by the Youth Justice and Criminal Evidence Act 1999, s 48, Sch 2, paras 1, 2 with effect from a date to be appointed.

****

A1.02

ADMINISTRATION OF JUSTICE ACT 1960

Chapter 65

****

12 Publication of information relating to proceedings in private

(1) The publication of information relating to proceedings before any court sitting in private shall not of itself be contempt of court except in the following cases, that is to say –

- (a) where the proceedings –
  - (i) relate to the exercise of the inherent jurisdiction of the High Court with respect to minors;
  - (ii) are brought under the Children Act 1989 or the Adoption and Children Act 2002; or
  - (iii) otherwise relate wholly or mainly to the maintenance or upbringing of a minor;
- (b) where the proceedings are brought under the Mental Capacity Act 2005, or under any provision of the Mental Health Act 1983 authorising an application or reference to be made to the First-tier Tribunal, the Mental Health Review Tribunal for Wales or a county court;
- (c) where the court sits in private for reasons of national security during that part of the proceedings about which the information in question is published;
- (d) where the information relates to a secret process, discovery or invention which is in issue in the proceedings;
- (e) where the court (having power to do so) expressly prohibits the publication of all information relating to the proceedings or of information of the description which is published.

(2) Without prejudice to the foregoing subsection, the publication of the text or a summary of the whole or part of an order made by a court sitting in private shall not of itself be contempt of court except where the court (having power to do so) expressly prohibits the publication.

(3) In this section references to a court include references to a judge and to a tribunal and to any person exercising the functions of a court, a judge or a tribunal; and references to a court sitting in private include references to a court sitting in camera or in chambers.

(4) Nothing in this section shall be construed as implying that any publication is punishable as contempt of court which would not be so punishable apart from this section (and in particular where the publication is not so punishable by reason of being authorised by rules of court).

Amendments—Children Act 1989, s 108(5), Sch 13, para 14; Adoption and Children Act 2002, s 101(2); Children Act 2004, s 62(2); Mental Capacity Act 2005, s 67(1), Sch 6, para 10; SI 2008/2833.

****

A1.03

CONTEMPT OF COURT ACT 1981

****

Strict liability

1 The strict liability rule

In this Act "the strict liability rule" means the rule of law whereby conduct may be treated as a contempt of court as tending to interfere with the course of justice in particular legal proceedings regardless of intent to do so.

2 Limitation of scope of strict liability

(1) The strict liability rule applies only in relation to publications, and for this purpose 'publication' includes any speech, writing, programme included in a programme service or other communication in whatever form, which is addressed to the public at large or any section of the public.

(2) The strict liability rule applies only to a publication which creates a substantial risk that the course of justice in the proceedings in question will be seriously impeded or prejudiced.

(3) The strict liability rule applies to a publication only if the proceedings in question are active within the meaning of this section at the time of the publication.

(4) Schedule 1 applies for determining the times at which proceedings are to be treated as active within the meaning of this section.

(5) In this section 'programme service' has the same meaning as in the Broadcasting Act 1990.

Amendment—Broadcasting Act 1990, s 203(1), Sch 20, para 31(1). Sub-s (5).

3 Defence of innocent publication or distribution

(1) A person is not guilty of contempt of court under the strict liability rule as the publisher of any matter to which that rule applies if at the time of publication (having taken all reasonable care) he does not know and has no reason to suspect that relevant proceedings are active.

(2) A person is not guilty of contempt of court under the strict liability rule as the distributor of a publication containing any such matter if at the time of distribution (having taken all reasonable care) he does not know that it contains such matter and has no reason to suspect that it is likely to do so.

(3) The burden of proof of any fact tending to establish a defence afforded by this section to any person lies upon that person.

(4) …

Amendment—Statute Law (Repeals) Act 2004.

4 Contemporary reports of proceedings

(1) Subject to this section a person is not guilty of contempt of court under the strict liability rule in respect of a fair and accurate report of legal proceedings held in public, published contemporaneously and in good faith.

(2) In any such proceedings the court may, where it appears to be necessary for avoiding a substantial risk of prejudice to the administration of justice in those proceedings, or in any other proceedings pending or imminent, order that the publication of any report of the proceedings, or any part of the proceedings, be postponed for such period as the court thinks necessary for that purpose.

(2A) Where in proceedings for any offence which is an administration of justice offence for the purposes of section 54 of the Criminal Procedure and Investigations Act 1996 (acquittal tainted by an administration of justice offence) it appears to the court that there is a possibility that (by virtue of that section) proceedings may be taken against a person for an offence of which he has been acquitted, subsection (2) of this section shall apply as if those proceedings were pending or imminent.

(3) For the purposes of subsection (1) of this section a report of proceedings shall be treated as published contemporaneously

- (a) in the case of a report of which publication is postponed pursuant to an order under subsection (2) of this section, if published as soon as practicable after that order expires;
- (b) in the case of a report of committal proceedings of which publication is permitted by virtue only of subsection (3) of section 8 of the Magistrates' Courts Act 1980, if published as soon as practicable after publication is so permitted;
- [(b) in the case of a report of allocation or sending proceedings of which publication is permitted by virtue only of subsection (6) of section 52A of the Crime and Disorder Act 1998 ('the 1998 Act'), if published as soon as practicable after publication is so permitted;
- (c) in the case of a report of an application of which publication is permitted by virtue only of sub-paragraph (5) or (7) of paragraph 3 of Schedule 3 to the 1998 Act, if published as soon as practicable after publication is so permitted].

(4) ...

Amendment—Criminal Procedure and Investigations Act 1996; Defamation Act 1996, s 16, Sch 2; Sub-s (4); Statute Law (Repeals) Act 2004.

Prospective Amendments—Sub-s (3): para (b) substituted, by subsequent paras (b), (c), by the Criminal Justice Act 2003, s 41, Sch 3, Pt 2, para 53 with effect from a date to be appointed.

5 Discussion of public affairs

A publication made as or as part of a discussion in good faith of public affairs or other matters of general public interest is not to be treated as a contempt of court under the strict liability rule if the risk of impediment or prejudice to particular legal proceedings is merely incidental to the discussion.

6 Savings

Nothing in the foregoing provisions of this Act

    (a)   prejudices any defence available at common law to a charge of contempt of court under the strict liability rule;

    (b)   implies that any publication is punishable as contempt of court under that rule which would not be so punishable apart from those provisions;

    (c)   restricts liability for contempt of court in respect of conduct intended to impede or prejudice the administration of justice.

7 Consent required for institution of proceedings

Proceedings for a contempt of court under the strict liability rule (other than Scottish proceedings) shall not be instituted except by or with the consent of the Attorney General or on the motion of a court having jurisdiction to deal with it.

11 Publication of matters exempted from disclosure in court

In any case where a court (having power to do so) allows a name or other matter to be withheld from the public in proceedings before the court, the court may give such directions prohibiting the publication of that name or matter in connection with the proceedings as appear to the court to be necessary for the purpose for which it was so withheld.

****

A1.04

CHILDREN ACT 1989

Chapter 41

****

97 Privacy for children involved in certain proceedings

(1) Rules made under section 144 of the Magistrates' Courts Act 1980 may make provision for a magistrates' court to sit in private in proceedings in which any powers under this Act or the Adoption and Children Act 2002 may be exercised by the court with respect to any child.

(2) No person shall publish to the public at large or any section of the public any material which is intended, or likely, to identify –

(a)   any child as being involved in any proceedings before the High Court, a county court or a magistrates' court in which any power under this Act or the Adoption and Children Act 2002 may be exercised by the court with respect to that or any other child; or

(b)   an address or school as being that of a child involved in any such proceedings.

(3) In any proceedings for an offence under this section it shall be a defence for the accused to prove that he did not know, and had no reason to suspect, that the published material was intended, or likely, to identify the child.

(4) The court or the Lord Chancellor may, if satisfied that the welfare of the child requires it and, in the case of the Lord Chancellor, if the Lord Chief Justice agrees, by order dispense with the requirements of subsection (2) to such extent as may be specified in the order.

(5) For the purposes of this section –

'publish' includes –
(a)   include in a programme service (within the meaning of the Broadcasting Act 1990); or
(b)   cause to be published; and

'material' includes any picture or representation.

(6) Any person who contravenes this section shall be guilty of an offence and liable, on summary conviction, to a fine not exceeding level 4 on the standard scale.

(7) Subsection (1) is without prejudice to –

(a)   the generality of the rule making power in section 144 of the Act of 1980; or

(b)   any other power of a magistrates' court to sit in private.

(8) Sections 69 (sittings of magistrates' courts for family proceedings) and 71 (newspaper reports of certain proceedings) of the Act of 1980 shall apply in

relation to any proceedings (before a magistrates' court) to which this section applies subject to the provisions of this section.

(9) The Lord Chief Justice may nominate a judicial office holder (as defined in section 109(4) of the Constitutional Reform Act 2005) to exercise his functions under subsection (4).

Amendments—Broadcasting Act 1990, s 203(1), Sch 20, para 53; Courts and Legal Services Act 1990, s 116, Sch 16, para 24; SI 1992/709; Access to Justice Act 1999, s 72; Adoption and Children Act 2002, s 101(3); Children Act 2004, s 62(1); Constitutional Reform Act 2005, s 15(1), Sch 4, Pt 1, paras 203, 208(1)–(3).

****

A1.05

HUMAN RIGHTS ACT 1998

Chapter 42

****

12   Freedom of expression

(1)   This section applies if a court is considering whether to grant any relief which, if granted, might affect the exercise of the Convention right to freedom of expression.

(2)   If the person against whom the application for relief is made ('the respondent') is neither present nor represented, no such relief is to be granted unless the court is satisfied –

(a)   that the applicant has taken all practicable steps to notify the respondent; or
(b)   that there are compelling reasons why the respondent should not be notified.

(3)   No such relief is to be granted so as to restrain publication before trial unless the court is satisfied that the applicant is likely to establish that publication should not be allowed.

(4)   The court must have particular regard to the importance of the Convention right to freedom of expression and, where the proceedings relate to material which the respondent claims, or which appears to the court, to be journalistic, literary or artistic material (or to conduct connected with such material), to –

(a)   the extent to which –
　(i)   the material has, or is about to, become available to the public; or
　(ii)   it is, or would be, in the public interest for the material to be published;
(b)   any relevant privacy code.

(5)   In this section –

'court' includes a tribunal; and
'relief' includes any remedy or order (other than in criminal proceedings).

****

A1.06

EUROPEAN CONVENTION ON HUMAN RIGHTS

****

Article 6
Right to a fair trial

1

In the determination of his civil rights and obligations or of any criminal charge against him, everyone is entitled to a fair and public hearing within a reasonable time by an independent and impartial tribunal established by law. Judgment shall be pronounced publicly but the press and public may be excluded from all or part of the trial in the interest of morals, public order or national security in a democratic society, where the interests of juveniles or the protection of the private life of the parties so require, or to the extent strictly necessary in the opinion of the court in special circumstances where publicity would prejudice the interests of justice.

2

Everyone charged with a criminal offence shall be presumed innocent until proved guilty according to law.

3

Everyone charged with a criminal offence has the following minimum rights –

    (a)   to be informed promptly, in a language which he understands and in detail, of the nature and cause of the accusation against him;
    (b)   to have adequate time and facilities for the preparation of his defence;
    (c)   to defend himself in person or through legal assistance of his own choosing or, if he has not sufficient means to pay for legal assistance, to be given it free when the interests of justice so require;
    (d)   to examine or have examined witnesses against him and to obtain the attendance and examination of witnesses on his behalf under the same conditions as witnesses against him;
    (e)   to have the free assistance of an interpreter if he cannot understand or speak the language used in court.

****

Article 8
Right to respect for private and family life

1

Everyone has the right to respect for his private and family life, his home and his correspondence.

2

There shall be no interference by a public authority with the exercise of this right except such as is in accordance with the law and is necessary in a democratic society in the interests of national security, public safety or the economic well-being of the country, for the prevention of disorder or crime, for the protection of health or morals, or for the protection of the rights and freedoms of others.

****

Article 10
Freedom of expression

1

Everyone has the right to freedom of expression. This right shall include freedom to hold opinions and to receive and impart information and ideas without interference by public authority and regardless of frontiers. This Article shall not prevent States from requiring the licensing of broadcasting, television or cinema enterprises.

2

The exercise of these freedoms, since it carries with it duties and responsibilities, may be subject to such formalities, conditions, restrictions or penalties as are prescribed by law and are necessary in a democratic society, in the interests of national security, territorial integrity or public safety, for the prevention of disorder or crime, for the protection of health or morals, for the protection of the reputation or rights of others, for preventing the disclosure of information received in confidence, or for maintaining the authority and impartiality of the judiciary.

****

A1.07

FAMILY PROCEEDINGS RULES 1991

SI 1991/1247

****

2.66 Arrangements for hearing of application etc by judge

(1) Where an application for ancillary relief or any question arising thereon has been referred or adjourned to a judge, the proper officer shall fix a date, time and place for the hearing of the application or the consideration of the question and give notice thereof to all parties.

(2) The hearing or consideration shall, unless the court otherwise directs, take place in chambers.

(3) In a matrimonial cause, where the application is proceeding in a divorce county court which is not a court of trial or is pending in the High Court and proceedings in a district registry which is not in a divorce town, the hearing or consideration shall take place at such court of trial or divorce town as in the opinion of the district judge is the nearest or most convenient.

 For the purposes of this paragraph the Royal Courts of Justice shall be treated as a divorce town.

(3A) In a civil partnership cause, where an application is proceeding in a civil partnership proceedings county court which is not a court of trial or pending in the High Court and proceeding in a district registry which is not in a dissolution town, the hearing or consideration shall take place at such court of trial or dissolution town as in the opinion of the district judge is the nearest or most convenient.

For the purposes of this paragraph the Royal Courts of Justice shall be treated as a dissolution town.

(4) In respect of any application referred to him under this rule, a judge shall have the same powers to make directions as a district judge has under these rules.

Amendments—SI 1999/3491; SI 2005/2922.

****

PART IV
PROCEEDINGS UNDER THE CHILDREN ACT 1989[, ETC]

4.16 Attendance at directions appointment and hearing

(1) Subject to paragraph (2), a party shall attend a directions appointment of which he has been given notice in accordance with rule 4.14(5) unless the court otherwise directs.

(1A) Paragraphs (2) to (4) do not apply where –

    (a)   the hearing relates to –

        (i)   a decision about whether to make a contact activity direction or to attach a contact activity condition to a contact order; or

        (ii)   an application for a fi2861cial compensation order, an enforcement order or an order under paragraph 9(2) of Schedule A1; and

    (b)   the court has yet to obtain sufficient evidence from, or in relation to, the person who may be the subject of the direction, condition or order to enable it to determine the matter.

(2) Proceedings or any part of them shall take place in the absence of any party, including the child, if –

    (a)   the court considers it in the interests of the child, having regard to the matters to be discussed or the evidence likely to be given, and

    (b)   the party is represented by a children's guardian or solicitor;

and when considering the interests of the child under sub-paragraph (a) the court shall give the children's guardian, the solicitor for the child and, if he is of sufficient understanding, the child an opportunity to make representations.

(3) Subject to paragraph (4), where at the time and place appointed for a hearing or directions appointment the applicant appears but one or more of the respondents do not, the court may proceed with the hearing or appointment.

(4) The court shall not begin to hear an application in the absence of a respondent unless –

    (a)   it is proved to the satisfaction of the court that he received reasonable notice of the date of the hearing; or

    (b)   the court is satisfied that the circumstances of the case justify proceeding with the hearing.

(5) Where, at the time and place appointed for a hearing or directions appointment one or more of the respondents appear but the applicant does not, the court may refuse the application or, if sufficient evidence has previously been received, proceed in the absence of the applicant.

(6) Where at the time and place appointed for a hearing or directions appointment neither the applicant nor any respondent appears, the court may refuse the application.

(7) Unless the court otherwise directs, a hearing of, or directions appointment in, proceedings to which this Part applies shall be in chambers.

Amendment—SI 2008/2861; SI 2001/821.

****

10.20 Inspection etc of documents retained in court

(1) Subject to rule 10.21, a party to any family proceedings or his solicitor or the Queen's Proctor or a person appointed under rule 2.57 or 9.5 or under paragraph 2 of Appendix 4 to be the guardian ad litem of a child in any family proceedings may have a search made for, and may inspect and bespeak a copy of, any document filed or lodged in the court office in those proceedings.

(2) Any person not entitled to a copy of a document under paragraph (1) above who intends to make an application under the Hague Convention (as defined in section 1(1) of the Child Abduction and Custody Act 1985) in a Contracting State (as defined in section 2 of that Act) other than the United Kingdom shall, if he satisfies the court that he intends to make such an application, be entitled to obtain a copy bearing the seal of the court of any order relating to the custody of the child in respect of whom the application is to be made.

(3) Except as provided by rules 2.36(4) and (5), 3.16(10) and Part XI and paragraphs (1) and (2) of this rule, no document filed or lodged in the court office other than a decree, civil partnership order or other order made in open court shall be open to inspection by any person without the leave of the district judge, and no copy of any such document, or of an extract from any such document, shall be taken by, or issued to, any person without such leave.

Amendments—SI 1992/2067; SI 2005/2922; SI 2005/1976; SI 2009/857.

****

A1.08

THE FAMILY PROCEEDINGS (AMENDMENT) (NO 2) RULES 2009

SI 2009/857

1 Citation and commencement

These rules may be cited as the Family Proceedings (Amendment) (No. 2) Rules 2009 and come into force on 27th April 2009.

2 Amendments to the Family Proceedings Rules 1991

The Family Proceedings Rules 1991(b) are amended in accordance with rules 3 to 5 of these rules.

3

In the Arrangement of Rules –

    (a)   after the entry for rule 10.20, omit the entry '10.20A Communication of information relating to proceedings'; and

    (b)   after the entry for rule 10.27, insert –

      '**10.28 Attendance at private hearings**

PART XI
COMMUNICATION OF INFORMATION: PROCEEDINGS RELATING TO

CHILDREN

    11.1 Application

    11.2 Communication of information: general

    11.3 Instruction of experts

    11.4 Communication of information for purposes connected with the proceedings

    11.5 Communication of information by a party etc. for other purposes

    11.6 Communication for the effective functioning of Cafcass and CAFCASS CYMRU

    11.7 Communication to and by Ministers of the Crown and Welsh Ministers

    11.8 Communication by persons lawfully in receipt of information

    11.9 Interpretation'.

4 In Part 10 –

    (a)   in rule 10.20(3), after '3.16(10) and', for '10.20A' substitute 'Part XI';

(b)   omit rule 10.20A;

(c)   in rule 10.21A(1), after 'nothing in rules 10.20 (inspection etc of documents in court)', for '10.20A (communication of information relating to proceedings)', substitute 'Part XI (communication of information: proceedings relating to children)'; and

(d)   after rule 10.27, insert –

'Attendance at private hearings

10.28

(1) This rule applies when proceedings are held in private, except in relation to hearings conducted for the purpose of judicially assisted conciliation or negotiation.

(2) For the purposes of these Rules, a reference to proceedings held 'in private' means proceedings at which the general public have no right to be present.

(3) When this rule applies no person shall be present during any hearing other than –

(a)   an officer of the court;

(b)   a party to the proceedings;

(c)   a litigation friend for any party, or legal representative instructed to act on that party's behalf;

(d)   an officer of the service or Welsh family proceedings officer;

(e)   a witness;

(f)   duly accredited representatives of news gathering and reporting organisations; and

(g)   any other person whom the court permits to be present.

(4) At any stage of the proceedings the court may direct that persons within paragraph (3)(f) shall not attend the proceedings or any part of them, where satisfied that –

(a)   this is necessary –

    (i)   in the interests of any child concerned in, or connected with, the proceedings;

    (ii)   for the safety or protection of a party, a witness in the proceedings, or a person connected with such a party or witness; or

    (iii) for the orderly conduct of the proceedings; or

(b)   justice will otherwise be impeded or prejudiced.

(5) The court may exercise the power in paragraph (4) of its own motion or pursuant to representations made by any of the persons listed in paragraph (6), and in either case having given to any person within paragraph (3)(f) who is in attendance an opportunity to make representations.

(6) At any stage of the proceedings, the following persons may make representations to the court regarding restricting the attendance of persons within paragraph (3)(f) in accordance with paragraph (4) –

(a)   a party to the proceedings;

(b)   any witness in the proceedings;

(c)   where appointed, any children's guardian;

(d)   where appointed, an officer of the service or Welsh family proceedings officer, on behalf of the child the subject of the proceedings;

(e)   the child, if of sufficient age and understanding.

(7) This rule does not affect any power of the court to direct that witnesses shall be excluded until they are called for examination.

(8) In this rule 'duly accredited' refers to accreditation in accordance with any administrative scheme for the time being approved for the purposes of this rule by the Lord Chancellor.'.

5 After Part X, insert –

'PART XI
COMMUNICATION OF INFORMATION: PROCEEDINGS RELATING TO CHILDREN

11.1 Application

The provisions of this Part apply to family proceedings which –

(a)   relate to the exercise of the inherent jurisdiction of the High Court with respect to minors;

(b)   are brought under the Act of 1989; or

(c)   otherwise relate wholly or mainly to the maintenance or upbringing of a minor. Communication of information: general.

11.2 Communication of information: general

(1) For the purposes of the law relating to contempt of court, information relating to proceedings held in private (whether or not contained in a document filed with the court) may be communicated –

(a)   where the communication is to –
   (i)   a party;
   (ii)   the legal representative of a party;
   (iii)   a professional legal adviser;
   (iv)   an officer of the service or a Welsh family proceedings officer;
   (v)   the welfare officer;
   (vi)   the Legal Services Commission;
   (vii)   an expert whose instruction by a party has been authorised by the court for the purposes of the proceedings;
   (viii) a professional acting in furtherance of the protection of children; or
   (ix)   an independent reviewing officer appointed in respect of a child who is, or has been, subject to proceedings to which this rule applies;

(b)   where the court gives permission; or

(c)   subject to any direction of the court, in accordance with rules 11.4 to 11.8.

(2) Nothing in this Part permits the communication to the public at large, or any section of the public, of any information relating to the proceedings.

(3) Nothing in rules 11.4 to 11.8 permits the disclosure of an unapproved draft judgment handed down by any court.

11.3 Instruction of experts

(1) No party may instruct an expert for any purpose relating to proceedings, including to give evidence in those proceedings, without the leave of the court.

(2) Where the leave of the court has not been given under paragraph (1), no evidence arising out of an unauthorised instruction may be introduced without leave of the court.

11.4 Communication of information for purposes connected with the proceedings

(1) A party or the legal representative of a party, on behalf of and upon the instructions of that party, may communicate information relating to the proceedings to any person where necessary to enable that party –

(a) by confidential discussion, to obtain support, advice or assistance in the conduct of the proceedings;

(b) to engage in mediation or other forms of alternative dispute resolution;

(c) to make and pursue a complaint against a person or body concerned in the proceedings; or

(d) to make and pursue a complaint regarding the law, policy or procedure relating to a category of proceedings to which this Part applies.

(2) Where information is communicated to any person in accordance with paragraph (1)(a) of this rule, no further communication by that person is permitted.

(3) When information relating to the proceedings is communicated to any person in accordance with paragraphs (1)(b),(c) or (d) of this rule –

(a) the recipient may communicate that information to a further recipient, provided that –

(i) the party who initially communicated the information consents to that further communication; and

(ii) the further communication is made only for the purpose or purposes for which the party made the initial communication; and

(b) the information may be successively communicated to and by further recipients on as many occasions as may be necessary to fulfil the purpose for which the information was initially communicated, provided that on each such occasion the conditions in sub-paragraph (a) are met.

11.5 Communication of information by a party etc. for other purposes

A person specified in the first column of the following table may communicate to a person listed in the second column such information as is specified in the third column for the purpose or purposes specified in the fourth column –

A party	A lay adviser, a McKenzie Friend, or a person arranging or providing pro bono legal services		To enable the party to obtain advice or assistance in relation to the proceedings
A party	A health care professional or a person or body providing counselling services for children or families		To enable the party or any child of the party to obtain health care or counselling
A party	The Secretary of State, a McKenzie Friend, a lay adviser or the First-tier Tribunal dealing with an appeal made under section 20 of the Child Support Act 1991		For the purposes of making or responding to an appeal under section 20 of the Child Support Act 1991 or the determination of such an appeal
A party	An adoption panel		To enable the adoption panel to discharge its functions as appropriate
A party	The European Court of Human Rights		For the purpose of making an application to the European Court of Human Rights

A party or any person lawfully in receipt of information	The Children's Commissioner or the Children's Commissioner for Wales		To refer an issue affecting the interests of children to the Children's Commissioner or the Children's Commissioner for Wales
A party, any person lawfully in receipt of information or a proper officer	A person or body conducting an approved research project		For the purpose of an approved research project
A legal representative or a professional legal adviser	A person or body responsible for investigating or determining complaints in relation to legal representatives or professional legal advisers		For the purposes of the investigation or determination of a complaint in relation to a legal representative or a professional legal adviser
A legal representative or a professional legal adviser	A person or body assessing quality assurance systems		To enable the legal representative or professional legal adviser to obtain a quality assurance assessment
A legal representative or a professional legal adviser	An accreditation body	Any information relating to the proceedings providing that it does not, or is not likely to, identify any person involved in the proceedings	To enable the legal representative or professional legal adviser to obtain accreditation

A party	A police officer	The text or summary of the whole or part of a judgment given in the proceedings	For the purpose of a criminal investigation
A party or any person lawfully in receipt of information	A member of the Crown Prosecution Service		To enable the Crown Prosecution Service to discharge its functions under any enactment

11.6 Communication for the effective functioning of Cafcass and CAFCASS CYMRU

An officer of the service or a Welsh family proceedings officer, as appropriate, may communicate to a person listed in the second column such information as is specified in the third column for the purpose or purposes specified in the fourth column –

A Welsh family proceedings officer	A person or body exercising statutory functions relating to inspection of CAFCASS CYMRU	Any information relating to the proceedings which is required by the person or body responsible for the inspection	For the purpose of an inspection of CAFCASS CYMRU by a body or person appointed by the Welsh Ministers

An officer of the service or a Welsh family proceedings officer	The General Social Care Council or the Care Council for Wales	Any information relating to the proceedings providing that it does not, or is not likely to, identify any person involved in the proceedings	For the purpose of initial and continuing accreditation as a social worker of a person providing services to Cafcass or CAFCASS CYMRU in accordance with s.13(2) of the Criminal Justice and Courts Services Act 2000(a) or s.36 of the Children Act 2004(b) as the case may be
An officer of the service or a Welsh family proceedings officer	A person or body providing services relating to professional development or training to Cafcass or CAFCASS CYMRU	Any information relating to the proceedings providing that it does not, or is not likely to, identify any person involved in the proceedings without that person's consent	To enable the person or body to provide the services, where the services cannot be effectively provided without such disclosure

| An officer of the service or a Welsh family proceedings officer | A person employed by or contracted to Cafcass or CAFCASS CYMRU for the purposes of carrying out the functions referred to in column 4 of this row | Any information relating to the proceedings | Engagement in processes internal to Cafcass or CAFCASS CYMRU which relate to the maintenance of necessary records concerning the proceedings, or to ensuring that Cafcass or CAFCASS CYMRU functions are carried out to a satisfactory standard |

11.7 Communication to and by Ministers of the Crown and Welsh Ministers

A person specified in the first column of the following table may communicate to a person listed in the second column such information as is specified in the third column for the purpose or purposes specified in the fourth column –

A party or any person lawfully in receipt of information relating to the proceedings	A Minister of the Crown with responsibility for a government department engaged, or potentially engaged, in an application before the European Court of Human Rights relating to the proceedings	Any information relating to the proceedings of which he or she is in lawful possession	To provide the department with information relevant, or potentially relevant, to the proceedings before the European Court of Human Rights
A Minister of the Crown	The European Court of Human Rights		For the purpose of engagement in an application before the European Court of Human Rights relating to the proceedings
A Minister of the Crown	Lawyers advising or representing the United Kingdom in an application before the European Court of Human Rights relating to the proceedings		For the purpose of receiving advice or for effective representation in relation to the application before the European Court of Human Rights.

A Minister of the crown or a Welsh Minister	Another Minister, or Ministers, of the Crown or a Welsh Minister		For the purpose of notification, discussion and the giving or receiving of advice regarding issues raised by the information in which the relevant departments have, or may have, an interest

11.8 Communication by persons lawfully in receipt of information

(1) This rule applies to communications made in accordance with rules 11.5, 11.6 and 11.7 and the reference in this rule to 'the table' means the table in the relevant rule.

(2) A person in the second column of the table may only communicate information relating to the proceedings received from a person in the first column for the purpose or purposes –

(a) for which he received that information; or
(b) of professional development or training, providing that any communication does not, or is not likely to, identify any person involved in the proceedings without that person's consent.

11.9 Interpretation

In this Part –

'accreditation body' means –

(a) The Law Society,
(b) Resolution, or
(c) The Legal Services Commission;

'adoption panel' means a panel established in accordance with regulation 3 of the Adoption Agencies Regulations 2005(a) or regulation 3 of the Adoption Agencies (Wales) Regulations 2005(b);
'alternative dispute resolution' means methods of resolving a dispute, including mediation, other than through the normal court process;
'approved research project' means a project of research –

(a) approved in writing by a Secretary of State after consultation with the President of the Family Division,
(b) approved in writing by the President of the Family Division, or
(c) conducted under section 83 of the Act of 1989(c) or section 13 of the Criminal Justice and Court Services Act 2000;

'body assessing quality assurance systems' includes –

(a)   The Law Society,
(b)   The Legal Services Commission, or
(c)   The General Council of the Bar;

'body or person responsible for investigating or determining complaints in relation to legal representatives or professional legal advisers' means –

(a)   The Law Society,
(b)   The General Council of the Bar,
(c)   The Institute of Legal Executives, or
(d)   The Legal Services Ombudsman;

'Cafcass' has the meaning assigned to it by section 11 of the Criminal Justice and Courts Services Act 2000;
'CAFCASS CYMRU' means the part of the Welsh Assembly Government exercising the functions of Welsh Ministers under Part 4 of the Children Act 2004(a);
'criminal investigation' means an investigation conducted by police officers with a view to it being ascertained –

(a)   whether a person should be charged with an offence, or
(b)   whether a person charged with an offence is guilty of it;

'health care professional' means –

(a)   a registered medical practitioner,
(b)   a registered nurse or midwife,
(c)   a clinical psychologist, or
(d)   a child psychotherapist;

'independent reviewing officer' means a person appointed in respect of a child in accordance with regulation 2A of the Review of Children's Cases Regulations 1991(b), or regulation 3 of the Review of Children's Cases (Wales) Regulations 2007(c);
'lay adviser' means a non-professional person who gives lay advice on behalf of an organisation in the lay advice sector;
'legal representative' means a barrister or a solicitor, solicitor's employee or other authorised litigator (as defined in the Courts and Legal Services Act 1990) who has been instructed to act for a party in relation to the proceedings;
'McKenzie Friend' means any person permitted by the court to sit beside an unrepresented litigant in court to assist that litigant by prompting, taking notes and giving him advice;
'professional acting in furtherance of the protection of children' includes –

(a)   an officer of a local authority exercising child protection functions,
(b)   a police officer who is –
        (i)   exercising powers under section 46 of the Act of 1989, or
        (ii)   serving in a child protection unit or a paedophile unit of a police force,
(c)   any professional person attending a child protection conference or review in relation to a child who is the subject of the proceedings to which the information relates, or
(d)   an officer of the National Society for the Prevention of Cruelty to Children;

(a) Section 38 was repealed by sections 156 and 184 of and Schedule 18 to the Education and Inspections Act 2006

'professional legal adviser' means a barrister or a solicitor, solicitor's employee or other authorised litigator (as defined in the Courts and Legal Services Act 1990) who is providing advice to a party but is not instructed to represent that party in the proceedings;
'social worker' has the meaning assigned to it by section 55 of the Care Standards Act 2000;
'welfare officer' means a person who has been asked to prepare a report under section 7(1)(b) of the Act of 1989.'

Explanatory Note

(This note is not part of the Rules)

These rules amend the Family Proceedings Rules 1991 ('the 1991 Rules') in relation to the attendance of persons, in particular representatives of the media, during family proceedings heard in private and the communication of information regarding proceedings relating to children, giving effect, for family proceedings in the High Court and county courts, to policy changes arising out of the Ministry of Justice consultation Confidence and confidentiality: openness in family courts – a new approach (Cm 7131) and outlined in the response to consultation Family Justice in View (Cm 7502).

Rule 4 inserts into the 1991 Rules a new rule 10.28, which makes provision governing who may be present during a hearing in proceedings which are held in private ('in private' meaning when the general public have no right to be present). This in particular allows for duly accredited media representatives to be present, subject to a power for the court to direct their exclusion for all or a part of the proceedings for one of the reasons specified in paragraph (4) of the new rule.

Rule 5 inserts into the 1991 Rules a new Part XI, which replaces rule 10.20A, dealing with the communication of information relating to proceedings relating to children. New rule 11.1 defines the proceedings in relation to which the new rules apply, new rule 11.9 provides for interpretation of terms used in the new rules, and new rules 11.2 to 11.8 provide for communication of information. New rule 11.2 lists when it is permissible for the purposes of the law relating to contempt of court to communicate information: communication is allowed as a general rule to parties and their legal representatives and certain associated officers and professionals; or in more specific instances where the court gives permission, or (subject to any direction of the court) in accordance with rules 11.4 to 11.8. Paragraph (2) establishes that general publication, to the public at large or any section of the public, is not permitted by these rules; and paragraph (3) that where an unapproved draft judgment is handed down by a court, rules 11.4 to 11.8 do not allow for its disclosure. New rule 11.3 prohibits use of the rules so as to instruct an expert without the leave of the court and bars use without such leave of any evidence arising out of unauthorised instruction.

A1.09

THE FAMILY PROCEEDINGS COURTS (MISCELLANEOUS AMENDMENTS) RULES 2009

SI 2009/858

****

5

16A Restrictions on presence of persons at directions appointment and hearing

(1) No person shall be present at any directions appointment or hearing in relevant proceedings other than –

(a)   an officer of the court;

(b)   a party to the proceedings;

(c)   a litigation friend for any party, or legal representative instructed to act on that party's behalf;

(d)   an officer of the service or Welsh family proceedings officer;

(e)   a witness;

(f)   duly accredited representatives of news gathering and reporting organisations; and

(g)   any other person whom the court permits to be present.

(2) Paragraph (1) does not entitle persons within paragraph (1)(*f*) to be present at any hearing conducted for the purpose of judicially assisted conciliation or negotiation.

(3) At any stage of the proceedings the court may direct that persons within paragraph (1)(*f*) shall not attend the proceedings or any part of them, where satisfied that –

(a)   this is necessary –

(i)   in the interests of any child concerned in or connected with the proceedings;

(ii)   for the safety or protection of a party, a witness in the proceedings, or a person connected with such a party or witness; or

(iii)   for the orderly conduct of the proceedings; or

(b)   justice will otherwise be impeded or prejudiced.

(4) The court may exercise the power in paragraph (3) of its own motion or pursuant to representations made by any of the persons listed in paragraph (5), and in either case having given to any person within paragraph (1)(*f*) who is in attendance an opportunity to make representations.

(5) At any stage of the proceedings, the following persons may make representations to the court regarding restricting the attendance of persons within paragraph (1)(*f*) in accordance with paragraph (3) –

(a)   a party to the proceedings;

    (b)   any witness in the proceedings;

    (c)   where appointed, any children's guardian;

    (d)   where appointed, an officer of the service or Welsh family proceedings officer, on behalf of the child the subject of proceedings;

    (e)   the child, if of sufficient age and understanding.

(6) This rule does not affect any power of the court to direct that witnesses shall be excluded until they are called for examination.

(7) In this rule, 'duly accredited' refers to accreditation in accordance with any administrative scheme for the time being approved for the purposes of this rule by the Lord Chancellor.'

Amendments—Inserted by SI 2009/858.

****

Explanatory Note

(This note is not part of the Rules)

These rules amend the Family Proceedings Courts (Children Act 1989) Rules 1991 ('the 1991 Rules') and the Family Proceedings Courts (Child Support Act 1991) Rules 1993 ('the 1993 Rules'). The amendments to the 1991 Rules concern the attendance of persons, in particular representatives of the media, during proceedings relating to children, and the communication of information relating to such proceedings. The amendment to the 1993 Rules is consequential on those made to the 1991 Rules.

These rules give effect, for family proceedings in the magistrates' courts, to policy changes arising out of the Ministry of Justice consultation Confidence and confidentiality: openness in family courts a new approach (Cm 7131) and outlined in the response to consultation Family Justice in View (Cm 7502).

Amendment of the 1991 Rules

Rule 5 inserts into the 1991 Rules a new rule 16A, which provides for who may be present during a hearing in 'relevant proceedings' (which has the same meaning as in section 93(3) of the Children Act 1989). This in particular allows for duly accredited media representatives to be present, subject to a power for the court to direct their exclusion for all or a part of the proceedings for one of the reasons specified in paragraph (3) of the new rule.

Rule 6 inserts into the 1991 Rules a new Part IIC, which replaces rule 23A, dealing with the communication of information relating to proceedings relating to children. New rule 21Q defines the proceedings in relation to which the new rules apply, new rule 21Y provides for interpretation of terms used in the new rules, and new rules 21R to 21X provide for communication of information. New rule 21R lists when it is permissible for the purposes of the law relating to contempt of court to communicate information: communication is allowed as a general rule to parties and their legal representatives and certain associated officers and professionals; or in more specific instances where the court gives permission, or (subject to any direction of the court) in accordance with rules 21T to 21X. Paragraph (2) establishes that general publication, to the public at large or any section of the public, is not permitted by these rules. New rule 21S prohibits use of the rules so as to instruct an expert without the leave of the court and bars use without such leave of any evidence arising out of unauthorised instruction.

Amendment of the 1993 Rules

Rule 9 makes a consequential amendment to a cross-reference in the 1993 Rules, reflecting the replacement in the 1991 Rules of rule 23A by the new Part IIC.

A1.10

CIVIL PROCEDURE RULES

SI 1998/3132

****

Rule 39.2 General rule – hearing to be in public

(1) The general rule is that a hearing is to be in public.

(2) The requirement for a hearing to be in public does not require the court to make special arrangements for accommodating members of the public.

(3) A hearing, or any part of it, may be in private if –

(a) publicity would defeat the object of the hearing;
(b) it involves matters relating to national security;
(c) it involves confidential information (including information relating to personal financial matters) and publicity would damage that confidentiality;
(d) a private hearing is necessary to protect the interests of any child or [protected party];
(e) it is a hearing of an application made without notice and it would be unjust to any respondent for there to be a public hearing;
(f) it involves uncontentious matters arising in the administration of trusts or in the administration of a deceased person's estate; or
(g) the court considers this to be necessary, in the interests of justice.

(4) The court may order that the identity of any party or witness must not be disclosed if it considers non-disclosure necessary in order to protect the interests of that party or witness.

****

A1.11

PRESIDENT'S PRACTICE DIRECTION APPLICATIONS FOR REPORTING RESTRICTION ORDERS

(18 MARCH 2005)

Citations: [2005] Fam Law 398

This direction is issued by and reproduced with the kind permission of the President of the Family Division.

1

This direction applies to any application in the Family Division founded on Convention rights for an order restricting publication of information about children or incapacitated adults.

2 Applications to be heard in the High Court

Orders can only be made in the High Court and are normally dealt with by a Judge of the Family Division. If the need for an order arises in existing proceedings in the county court, judges should either transfer the application to the High Court or consult their Family Division Liaison Judge. Where the matter is urgent, it can be heard by the Urgent Applications Judge of the Family Division (out of hours contact number 020 7947 6000).

3 Service of Application on the National News Media

Section 12(2) of the Human Rights Act 1998 means that an injunction restricting the exercise of the right to freedom of expression must not be granted where the person against whom the application is made is neither present nor represented unless the court is satisfied (a) that the applicant has taken all practicable steps to notify the respondent, or (b) that there are compelling reasons why the respondent should not be notified.

Service of applications for reporting restriction orders on the national media can now be effected via the Press Association's CopyDirect service, to which national newspapers and broadcasters subscribe as a means of receiving notice of such applications.

The court will bear in mind that legal advisers to the media (i) are used to participating in hearings at very short notice where necessary; and (ii) are able to differentiate between information provided for legal purposes and information for editorial use. Service of applications via the CopyDirect service should henceforth be the norm.

The court retains the power to make without notice orders, but such cases will be exceptional, and an order will always give persons affected liberty to apply to vary or discharge it at short notice.

4 Further Guidance

The Practice Note Applications for Reporting Restriction Orders dated 18 March 2005 and issued jointly by the Official Solicitor and the Deputy Director of Legal Services, provides valuable guidance and should be followed.

5 Issued with the concurrence and approval of the Lord Chancellor.

Dame Elizabeth Butler-Sloss

President

A1.12

PRACTICE NOTE (OFFICIAL SOLICITOR: DEPUTY DIRECTOR LEGAL SERVICES: CAFCASS; APPLICATION FOR REPORTING RESTRICTION ORDERS)

(18 MARCH 2005)

Citations: [2005] Fam Law 398

This Note is issued by and reproduced with the kind permission of CAFCASS.

1 Introduction

This Note sets out recommended practice in relation to any application in the Family Division founded on Convention rights for an order which restricts freedom of expression. It is issued in conjunction with the President's Practice Direction Applications For Reporting Restriction Orders dated 18 March 2005 and is subject to decisions of the courts. It applies directly to any proceedings in which CAFCASS or the Official Solicitor represent a child or incapacitated adult, and follows discussions between the Official Solicitor, the Deputy Director of Legal Services CAFCASS, and representatives of media interests.

2 Statutory provisions

An application founded on Convention rights need only be made where statutory provisions cannot provide adequate protection. Relevant provisions are Administration of Justice Act 1960, s 12(1); Children and Young Persons Act 1933, s 39; Contempt of Court Act 1981, s 11; Children Act 1989, s 8 (prohibited steps order preventing disclosure of information by parental figure) and s 97(2). While the President's Practice Direction is not aimed at applications under these provisions, s 12(2) of the Human Rights Act 1998 applies to any application for relief which might affect the exercise of the Convention right to freedom of expression and the procedures set out in this Note, including the arrangements for advance notification, can be used to secure compliance with this section in relation to any such application under these provisions.

An order founded on Convention rights may be required, for example, because:

- the need for protection is not linked to particular court proceedings;
- the statutory provisions do not prevent publication of all kinds of information;
- an injunction is needed to prevent approaches to family, doctors or carers.

3 Application and evidence

The application may be a freestanding claim brought under the Part 8 procedure in the Civil Procedure Rules 1998 or it may be made within existing proceedings to which either the CPR or Family Proceedings Rules 1991 apply. It may be appropriate to seek a direction under CPR 39.2(4), where it applies, that the identity of a party or witness should not be disclosed, and for documents to be drafted identifying individuals by initials.

The applicant should prepare (a) the application/claim form (b) a witness statement justifying the need for an order (c) any legal submissions (d) a draft order and (e) an explanatory note.

Model Forms of Order and an example of an explanatory note are attached to this Practice Note and can be downloaded from the websites of either the Official Solicitor (www.offsol.demon.co.uk) or CAFCASS (www.cafcass.gov.uk).

In the rare event that it is not possible to draft such documentation in the time available before the hearing, the court is likely to require the applicant to file a statement at the earliest opportunity, setting out the information placed orally before the Court.

Subject to any contrary direction of the court, this material should be made available on request to any person who is affected by the order. See *W v H* (Family Division: Without Notice Orders) [2001] 2 WLR 253; [2001] 2 FLR 927.

4 Service of application

As required by the Practice Direction, advance notice should normally be given to the national media via the Press Association's CopyDirect service. Applicants should first telephone CopyDirect (tel 0870 837 6429). Documentation should be sent either by fax (fax 0870 830 6949) or to the e-mail address provided by CopyDirect. CopyDirect will be responsible for notifying the individual media organisations. In the case of an application against the world at large this is sufficient service for the purposes of advance notice. The website: http://www.medialawyer.press.net/courtapplications gives details of the organisations represented and instructions for service of the application. Unless there is a particular reason not to do so, copies of all the documents referred to above should be served. If there is a reason for not serving some or all of the documents (or parts of them), the applicant should ensure sufficient detail is given to enable the media to make an informed decision as to whether it wishes to attend or be legally represented.

The CopyDirect service does not extend to local or regional media or magazines. If service of the application on any specific organisation or person not covered is required it should be effected directly. The Official Solicitor and CAFCASS Legal hold lists of contact details for many national and some regional news organisations, and these are posted on their websites.

5 The hearing

Any application invoking Convention rights will involve a balancing of rights under Article 8 (right to respect for private and family life) and Article 10 (freedom of expression). There is no automatic precedence as between these Articles, and both are subject to qualification where (among other considerations) the rights of others are engaged. Section 12(4) of the Act requires the court to have particular regard to the importance of freedom of expression. It must also have regard to the extent to which material has or is about to become available to the public, the extent of the public interest in such material being published and the terms of any relevant privacy code (such as those of the Press Complaints Commission).

The court's approach is laid down in *Re S (A Child) (Identification: Restriction on Publication)* [2004] EWCA Civ 963, [2004] Fam 43(CA) and [2004] UKHL 47, 3 FCR 407(HL) *and Campbell v Mirror Group Newspapers Ltd* [2004] UKHL 22. *Guidance on the application of s 12(3) is now also provided in Cream Holdings Ltd v Bannerjee* [2004] UKHL 44.

6 Scope of order

Persons protected

The aim should be to protect the child or incapacitated adult, rather than to confer anonymity on other individuals or organisations. However, the order may include restrictions on identifying or approaching specified family members, carers, doctors or organisations in cases where the absence of such restriction is likely to prejudice their ability to care for the child or patient, or where identification of such persons might lead to identification of the child or patient and defeat the purpose of the order. In cases where the court receives expert evidence the identity of the experts (as opposed to treating clinicians) is not normally subject to restriction.

Identifying persons protected

Once an order has been made, the details of those protected by the order should normally be contained in the Schedule. In exceptional cases (for example *Leeds NHS Trust v A & B* [2003] 1 FLR 1091) where it is not appropriate for details to be given, a description by reference to the facts of the case should be contained in the Schedule to enable those reading the order to identify whether a person is likely to be the subject of the order.

Information already in the public domain

Orders will not usually prohibit publication of material which is already in the public domain, other than in exceptional cases such as *Venables and Thompson v News Group Newspapers Ltd* [2001] Fam 430.

Duration of Order

Orders should last for no longer than is necessary to achieve the purpose for which they are made. The maximum extent of an order in a child case will usually be the child's 18th birthday. In the case of an incapacitated adult the order will normally end on death. In some cases a later date may be necessary, to protect safety or welfare, or the anonymity of other children who are named in the order and who are still under age, or to maintain the anonymity of doctors or carers after the death of a patient. See for example:

Re C (Adult Patient: Publicity) [1996] 2 FLR 251; *Venables and Thompson v News Group Newspapers Ltd* [2001] Fam 430; X *(formerly known as Mary Bell) v Y and others* [2003] EWHC QB 1101.

7 Service of orders

Service of orders should be effected in the usual way, i.e. by fax or by post. Contact details for the national press and broadcasters can be found at http://www.medialawyer.press.net/courtapplications.

8 Undertakings in damages

The court will consider whether it is appropriate to require an applicant to give such an undertaking in an individual case, particularly when an order is made without notice, and will bear in mind the applicant's capacity to fulfil any such undertaking.

9 Explanatory notes

It is helpful if applications and orders are accompanied by an explanatory note, from which persons served can readily understand the nature of the case. In any case where notice of an application has not been given, the explanatory note should explain why.

10 Advice and assistance

Applicants or respondents are welcome to consult:

Deputy Director

CAFCASS Legal Services and Special Casework

8th floor, Wyndham House,

South Quay Plaza, London E14 9SH

DX: 42691 Isle of Dogs

Telephone: 020 7510 7080

Fax: 020 7510 7104

Email: legal@cafcass.gov.uk

Website: www.cafcass.gov.uk

Official Solicitor

81 Chancery Lane

London WC2A 1D

Telephone: 020 7911 7127

Fax: 020 7911 7105

Email: enquiries@offsol.gsi.gov.uk

Website: www.offsol.demon.co.uk

Mike Hinchliffe

Deputy Director of Legal Services, CAFCASS

Laurence Oates

Official Solicitor

A1.13

ATTENDANCE OF MEDIA REPRESENTATIVES AT HEARINGS IN FAMILY PROCEEDINGS – FAMILY PROCEEDINGS COURT

20 APRIL 2009

This Practice Direction below is made by the President of the Family Division under the powers delegated to him by the Lord Chief Justice under Schedule 2, Part 1, paragraph 2(2) of the Constitutional Reform Act 2005, and is approved by Bridget Prentice, Parliamentary Under Secretary of State, by the authority of the Lord Chancellor.

1 Introduction

1.1 This Practice Direction supplements rule 16A of the Family Proceedings Courts (Children Act 1989) Rules 1991 ("the Rules") and deals with the right of representatives of news gathering and reporting organisations ("media representatives") to attend at hearings of relevant proceedings[1] subject to the discretion of the court to exclude such representatives from the whole or part of any hearing on specified grounds[2] It takes effect on 27th April 2009. References to a "hearing" within this Practice Direction include reference to a directions appointment, whether conducted by the justices, a district judge or a justices' clerk.

2 Matters unchanged by the rule

2.1 Rule 16A(2) contains an express exception in respect of hearings which are conducted for the purpose of judicially assisted conciliation or negotiation and media representatives do not have a right to attend these hearings. First Hearing Dispute Resolution appointments in private law Children Act cases will come within this exception to the extent that the justices, a district judge or a justices' clerk play an active part in the conciliation process. Where the justices, a district judge or a justices' clerk play no part in the conciliation process or where the conciliation element of a hearing is complete and the court is adjudicating upon the issues between the parties, media representatives should be permitted to attend subject to the discretion of the court to exclude them on the specified grounds. Conciliation meetings or negotiation conducted between the parties with the assistance of an officer of the service or a Welsh Family Proceedings officer, and without the presence of the justices, a district

---

[1]   "Relevant proceedings" are defined in rule 1 of the Rules by reference to section 93(3) of the Children Act 1989.
[2]   It does not, accordingly, apply where hearings are held in open court where the general public including media representatives attend as of right.

judge or a justices' clerk, are not "hearings" within the meaning of this rule and media representatives have no right to attend such appointments.

The exception in rule 16A(2) does not operate to exclude media representatives from:

- Hearings to consider applications brought under Parts IV and V of the Children Act 1989, including Case Management Conferences and Issues Resolution Hearings
- Hearings relating to findings of fact
- Interim hearings
- Final hearings.

The rights of media representatives to attend such hearings are limited only by the powers of the court to exclude such attendance on the limited grounds and subject to the procedures set out in paragraphs (3) to (5) of rule 16A.

2.2 During any hearing, the court should consider whether the exception in rule 16A(2) becomes applicable so that media representatives should be directed to withdraw.

2.3 The provisions of the rules permitting the attendance of media representatives and the disclosure to third parties of information relating to the proceedings do not entitle a media representative to receive or peruse court documents referred to in the course of evidence, submissions or decisions of the court (in particular, written reasons) without the permission of the court or otherwise in accordance with Part IIC (rules relating to disclosure to third parties).

2.4 The question of attendance of media representatives at hearings in family proceedings to which rule 16A and this guidance apply must be distinguished from statutory restrictions on publication and disclosure of information relating to proceedings, which continue to apply and are unaffected by the rule and this guidance.

2.5 The prohibition in section 97(2) of the Children Act 1989, on publishing material intended to or likely to identify a child as being involved in proceedings or the address or school of any such child, is limited to the duration of the proceedings[3]. However, the limitations imposed by section 12 of the Administration of Justice Act 1960 on publication of information relating to certain proceedings in private[4] apply during and after the proceedings. In addition, in the course of proceedings to which s.97(2) of the Children Act 1989 applies the court should consider whether at the conclusion of the proceedings there may be outstanding welfare issues which may require a continuation of the protection afforded during the course of the proceedings by s. 97 (2) of the Children Act 1989 and which are not fully met by a direction

---

[3]   See *Clayton v Clayton* [2006] EWCA Civ 878.
[4]   In particular proceedings which (a) relate to the exercise of the inherent jurisdiction of the High Court with respect to minors; (b) are brought under the Children Act 1989; or (c) otherwise relate wholly or mainly to the maintenance or upbringing of a minor.

under section 39 Children and Young Persons Act 1933,[5] so that any party seeking such protection has an opportunity to apply to the county court or High Court for the appropriate order before the proceedings are finally concluded.

3 Aims of the guidance

3.1 This Practice Direction is intended to provide guidance regarding: the handling of applications to exclude media representatives from the whole or part of a hearing: and the exercise of the court's discretion to exclude media representatives whether upon the court's own motion or any such application.

3.2 While the guidance does not aim to cover all possible eventualities, it should be complied with so far as consistent in all the circumstances with the just determination of the proceedings.

4 Identification of media representatives as "accredited"

4.1 Media representatives will be expected to carry with them identification sufficient to enable court staff, or if necessary the court itself, to verify that they are "accredited" representatives of news gathering or reporting organisations within the meaning of the rule.

4.2 By virtue of paragraph (7) of the rule, it is for the Lord Chancellor to approve a scheme which will provide for accreditation. The Lord Chancellor has decided that the scheme operated by the UK Press Card Authority provides sufficient accreditation: a card issued under that scheme will be the expected form of identification, and production of the Card will be both necessary and sufficient to demonstrate accreditation.

4.3 A media representative unable to demonstrate accreditation in accordance with the UK Press Card Authority scheme so as to be able to attend by virtue of paragraph (1)(f) of the rule may nevertheless be permitted to attend at the court's discretion under paragraph (1)(g).

5 Exercise of the discretion to exclude media representatives from all or part of the proceedings.

5.1 The rule anticipates and should be applied on the basis that media representatives have a right to attend family proceedings throughout save and to the extent that the court exercises its discretion to exclude them from the whole or part of any proceedings on one or more of the grounds set out in paragraph (3) of the rule.

5.2 When considering the question of exclusion on any of the grounds set out in paragraph (3) of the rule the court should specifically identify whether the risk to which such ground is directed arises from the mere fact of media presence at the particular hearing or hearings the subject of the application or whether the risk identified can be adequately addressed by exclusion of media representatives from a part only of such hearing or hearings; consider whether

---

[5]   Power of court to prohibit publication of certain matters in newspapers.

the reporting or disclosure restrictions which apply by operation of law, or which the court otherwise has power to order will provide sufficient protection to the party on whose behalf the application is made or any of the persons referred to in paragraph (3)(a) of the rule; consider the safety of the parties in cases in which the court considers there are particular physical or health risks against which reporting restrictions may be inadequate to afford protection; in the case of any vulnerable adult or child who is unrepresented before the court, consider the extent to which the court should of its own motion take steps to protect the welfare of that adult or child.

5.3 Paragraph (3)(a)(iii) of the rule permits exclusion where necessary "for the orderly conduct of proceedings". This enables the court to address practical problems presented by media attendance. In particular, it may be difficult or even impossible physically to accommodate all (or indeed any) media representatives who wish to attend a particular hearing on the grounds of the restricted size or layout of the court room in which it is being heard. Court staff will use their best efforts to identify more suitable accommodation in advance of any hearing which appears likely to attract particular media attention, and to move hearings to larger court rooms where possible.

However, the court should not be required to adjourn a hearing in order for larger accommodation to be sought where this will involve significant disruption or delay in the proceedings.

5.4 Paragraph (3)(b) of the rule permits exclusion where, unless the media are excluded, justice will be impeded or prejudiced for some reason other than those set out in sub-paragraph (a). Reasons of administrative inconvenience are not sufficient. An example of circumstances where the impact on justice of continued attendance might be sufficient to necessitate exclusion would be any hearing at which a witness (other than a party) states for credible reasons that he or she will not give evidence in front of media representatives, or where there appears to the court to be a significant risk that a witness will not give full or frank evidence in the presence of media representatives.

5.5 In the event of a decision to exclude media representatives, the court should state brief reasons for the decision.

6 Applications to exclude media representatives from all or part of proceedings.

6.1 The court may exclude media representatives on the permitted grounds of its own motion or after hearing representations from the interested persons listed at paragraph (5) of the rule. Where exclusion is proposed, any media representatives who are present are entitled to make representations about that proposal. There is, however, no requirement to adjourn proceedings to enable media representatives who are not present to attend in order to make such representations, and in such a case the court should not adjourn unless satisfied of the necessity to do so having regard to the additional cost and delay which would thereby be caused.

6.2 Applications to exclude media representatives should normally be dealt with as they arise and by way of oral representations, unless the court directs otherwise.

6.3 When media representatives are expected to attend a particular hearing (for example, where a party is encouraging media interest and attendance) and a party intends to apply to the court for the exclusion of the media, such party should, if practicable, give advance notice to the court, to the other parties and (where appointed) any children's guardian, officer of the service or Welsh Family Proceedings officer, NYAS or other representative of the child of any intention to seek the exclusion of media representatives from all or part of the proceedings. Equally, legal representatives and parties should ensure that witnesses are aware of the right of media representatives to attend and should notify the court at an early stage of the intention of any witness to request the exclusion of media representatives

6.4 Prior notification by the court of a pending application for exclusion will not be given to media interests unless the court so directs. However, where such an application has been made, the applicant must where possible, notify the relevant media organisations.

Sir Mark Potter

President of the family Division

A1.14

ATTENDANCE OF MEDIA REPRESENTATIVES AT HEARINGS IN FAMILY PROCEEDINGS – HIGH COURT AND COUNTY COURTS

20 APRIL 2009

This Practice Direction below is made by the President of the Family Division under the powers delegated to him by the Lord Chief Justice under Schedule 2, Part 1, paragraph 2(2) of the Constitutional Reform Act 2005, and is approved by Bridget Prentice, Parliamentary Under Secretary of State, by the authority of the Lord Chancellor.

1 Introduction

1.1 This Practice Direction supplements rule 10.28 of the Family Proceedings Rules 1991("FPR 1991") and deals with the right of representatives of news gathering and reporting organisations ("media representatives") to attend at hearings of family proceedings which take place in private subject to the discretion of the court to exclude such representatives from the whole or part of any hearing on specified grounds.[6] It takes effect on 27 April 2009.

2 Matters unchanged by the rule

2.1 Rule 10.28(1) contains an express exception in respect of hearings which are conducted for the purpose of judicially assisted conciliation or negotiation and media representatives do not have a right to attend these hearings. Financial Dispute Resolution hearings will come within this exception. First Hearing Dispute Resolution appointments in private law Children Act cases will also come within this exception to the extent that the judge plays an active part in the conciliation process. Where the judge plays no part in the conciliation process or where the conciliation element of a hearing is complete and the judge is adjudicating upon the issues between the parties, media representatives should be permitted to attend, subject to the discretion of the court to exclude them on the specified grounds. Conciliation meetings or negotiation conducted between the parties with the assistance of an officer of the service or a Welsh Family Proceedings officer, and without the presence of the judge, are not "hearings" within the meaning of this rule and media representatives have no right to attend such appointments.

The exception in rule 10.28(1) does not operate to exclude media representatives from:

---

[6] It does not, accordingly, apply where hearings are held in open court where the general public including media representatives may attend as of right, such as committal hearings or the hearing of matrimonial or civil partnership causes.

- Hearings to consider applications brought under Parts IV and V of the Children Act 1989, including Case Management Conferences and Issues Resolution Hearings
- Hearings relating to findings of fact
- Interim hearings
- Final hearings.

The rights of media representatives to attend such hearings are limited only by the powers of the court to exclude such attendance on the limited grounds and subject to the procedures set out in paragraphs (4)–(6) of rule 10.28.

2.2 During any hearing, courts should consider whether the exception in rule 10.28(1) becomes applicable so that media representatives should be directed to withdraw.

2.3 The provisions of the rules permitting the attendance of media representatives and the disclosure to third parties of information relating to the proceedings do not entitle a media representative to receive or peruse court documents referred to in the course of evidence, submissions or judgment without the permission of the court or otherwise in accordance with Part 11 of the FPR 1991 (rules relating to disclosure to third parties). (This is in contrast to the position in civil proceedings, where the court sits in public and where members of the public are entitled to seek copies of certain documents.[7])

2.4 The question of attendance of media representatives at hearings in family proceedings to which rule 10.28 and this guidance apply must be distinguished from statutory restrictions on publication and disclosure of information relating to proceedings, which continue to apply and are unaffected by the rule and this guidance.

2.5 The prohibition in section 97(2) of the Children Act 1989, on publishing material intended to or likely to identify a child as being involved in proceedings or the address or school of any such child, is limited to the duration of the proceedings.[8] However, the limitations imposed by section 12 of the Administration of Justice Act 1960 on publication of information relating to certain proceedings in private[9] apply during and after the proceedings. In addition, in proceedings to which s.97(2) of the Children Act 1989 applies the court should continue to consider at the conclusion of the proceedings whether there are any outstanding welfare issues which require a continuation of the protection afforded during the course of the proceedings by that provision.

3 Aims of the guidance

3.1 This Practice Direction is intended to provide guidance regarding:

---

[7]   See *GIO Services Ltd v Liverpool and London Ltd* [1999] 1 WLR 984.

[8]   See *Clayton v Clayton* [2006] EWCA Civ 878.

[9]   In particular proceedings which: (a) relate to the exercise of the inherent jurisdiction of the High Court with respect to minors; (b) are brought under the Children Act 1989; or (c) otherwise relate wholly or mainly to the maintenance or upbringing of a minor.

- the handling of applications to exclude media representatives from the whole or part of a hearing: and
- the exercise of the court's discretion to exclude media representatives whether upon the court's own motion or any such application

3.2 While the guidance does not aim to cover all possible eventualities, it should be complied with so far as consistent in all the circumstances with the just determination of the proceedings.

4 Identification of media representatives as "accredited"

4.1 Media representatives will be expected to carry with them identification sufficient to enable court staff, or if necessary the court itself, to verify that they are "accredited" representatives of news gathering or reporting organisations within the meaning of the rule.

4.2 By virtue of paragraph (8) of the rule, it is for the Lord Chancellor to approve a scheme which will provide for accreditation. The Lord Chancellor has decided that the scheme operated by the UK Press Card Authority provides sufficient accreditation; a card issued under that scheme will be the expected form of identification, and production of the Card will be both necessary and sufficient to demonstrate accreditation.

4.3 A media representative unable to demonstrate accreditation in accordance with the UK Press Card Authority scheme, so as to be able to attend by virtue of paragraph (3)(f) of the rule, may nevertheless be permitted to attend at the court's discretion under paragraph (3)(g).

5 Exercise of the discretion to exclude media representatives from all or part of the proceedings.

5.1 The rule anticipates and should be applied on the basis that media representatives have a right to attend family proceedings throughout save and to the extent that the court exercises its discretion to exclude them from the whole or part of any proceedings on one or more of the grounds set out in paragraph (4) of the rule.

5.2 When considering the question of exclusion on any of the grounds set out in paragraph (4) of the rule the court should –

- specifically identify whether the risk to which such ground is directed arises from the mere fact of media presence at the particular hearing or hearings the subject of the application or whether the risk identified can be adequately addressed by exclusion of media representatives from a part only of such hearing or hearings;
- consider whether the reporting or disclosure restrictions which apply by operation of law, or which the court otherwise has power to order will provide sufficient protection to the party on whose behalf the application is made or any of the persons referred to in paragraph (4)(a) of the rule;

- consider the safety of the parties in cases in which the court considers there are particular physical or health risks against which reporting restrictions may be inadequate to afford protection;
- in the case of any vulnerable adult or child who is unrepresented before the court, consider the extent to which the court should of its own motion take steps to protect the welfare of that adult or child.

5.3 Paragraph (4)(a)(iii) of the rule permits exclusion where necessary "for the orderly conduct of proceedings". This enables the court to address practical problems presented by media attendance. In particular, it may be difficult or even impossible physically to accommodate all (or indeed any) media representatives who wish to attend a particular hearing on the grounds of the restricted size or layout of the court room in which it is being heard. Court staff will use their best efforts to identify more suitable accommodation in advance of any hearing which appears likely to attract particular media attention, and to move hearings to larger court rooms where possible. However, the court should not be required to adjourn a hearing in order for larger accommodation to be sought where this will involve significant disruption or delay in the proceedings.

5.4 Paragraph (4)(b) of the rule permits exclusion where, unless the media are excluded, justice will be impeded or prejudiced for some reason other than those set out in sub-paragraph (a). Reasons of administrative inconvenience are not sufficient. Examples of circumstances where the impact on justice of continued attendance might be sufficient to necessitate exclusion may include:

- a hearing relating to the parties' finances where the information being considered includes price sensitive information (such as confidential information which could affect the share price of a publicly quoted company); or
- any hearing at which a witness (other than a party) states for credible reasons that he or she will not give evidence in front of media representatives, or where there appears to the court to be a significant risk that a witness will not give full or frank evidence in the presence of media representatives.

5.5 In the event of a decision to exclude media representatives, the court should state brief reasons for the decision.

6 Applications to exclude media representatives from all or part of proceedings

6.1 The court may exclude media representatives on the permitted grounds of its own motion or after hearing representations from the interested persons listed at paragraph (6) of the rule. Where exclusion is proposed, any media representatives who are present are entitled to make representations about that proposal. There is, however, no requirement to adjourn proceedings to enable media representatives who are not present to attend in order to make such representations, and in such a case the court should not adjourn unless satisfied of the necessity to do so having regard to the additional cost and delay which would thereby be caused.

6.2 Applications to exclude media representatives should normally be dealt with as they arise and by way of oral representations, unless the court directs otherwise.

6.3 When media representatives are expected to attend a particular hearing (for example, where a party is encouraging media interest and attendance) and a party intends to apply to the court for the exclusion of the media, that party should, if practicable, give advance notice to the court, to the other parties and (where appointed) any children's guardian, officer of the service or Welsh Family Proceedings officer, NYAS or other representative of the child of any intention to seek the exclusion of media representatives from all or part of the proceedings. Equally, legal representatives and parties should ensure that witnesses are aware of the right of media representatives to attend and should notify the court at an early stage of the intention of any witness to request the exclusion of media representatives

6.4 Prior notification by the court of a pending application for exclusion will not be given to media interests unless the court so directs. However, where such an application has been made, the applicant must where possible, notify the relevant media organisations.

Sir Mark Potter

President of the Family Division

A1.15

PRESIDENT'S GUIDANCE NOTE: CARE PROCEEDINGS INVOLVING PLACEMENT ORDER APPLICATIONS – ATTENDANCE OF THE MEDIA

1

One of the principal drivers behind the recent change in government policy in relation to the attendance of the media in family proceedings was the concern widely expressed that Public Law Care Proceedings in particular should be more open to scrutiny. It is, of course, the case that many such proceedings also involve the consideration of a placement order application by the local authority which is dealt with as part of the care proceedings.

2

It was also the position that, in response to successive government consultations, the vast majority of consultees objected to the attendance of the press at "adoption proceedings" strictly so called, and it was accepted by the government that further consideration was required in respect of such proceedings before any changes in the rules or practice were made.

3

Following circulation of ministry guidance within HMCS, a question has arisen about the extent to which media representatives are entitled to attend care proceedings when heard together with an application for a placement order and whether the existence of a concurrent placement application should, by itself, be treated as a reason to exclude representatives of the media from hearings in the linked care proceedings, where a direction for non-attendance would not otherwise be justified on the limited grounds set out in rule 10.28(4) of the Family Proceedings Rules 1991 ("FPR 1991").

4

The changes introduced by FPR 1991, r 10.28 (and in the magistrates' court by the Family Proceedings Courts (Children Act 1989) Rules 1991, r 16A) do not affect proceedings under the Adoption and Children Act 2002, which are governed by the Family Procedure (Adoption) Rules 2005. These have not been amended in parallel with the Family Proceedings Rules to cater for the attendance of media representatives in relation to placement order applications in care proceedings.

5

Thus, representatives of the media are not entitled as of right to attend hearings in adoption or placement proceedings held in private. Nonetheless, in the High Court and county courts, the court has a discretion to allow them to be present.

6

The personal and confidential nature of proceedings for an adoption order means that it would not generally be appropriate for the court to permit media representatives to be present at an adoption hearing. However, the same considerations do not usually apply in proceedings for a placement order and, in such proceedings in the High Court or a county court, the court may consider it appropriate to allow media representatives to be present.

7

In particular, where an application for a placement order is heard together with care proceedings, the court should, when considering whether to admit media representatives, take into account their general right to attend hearings in care proceedings. In such a case, it would normally be appropriate for the court to allow representatives of the media to be present, unless a direction under FPR 1991, r 10.28(4) is necessary in relation to the care proceedings or there is some feature of the placement application which means that media representatives should not be present (for example, where there is a need to preserve the confidentiality of a proposed placement or where the interests of a prospective adopter or other person who is not before the court may be adversely affected by the attendance of the media). The existence of a placement application should not, by itself, be treated as a reason for making a direction under FPR 1991, r 10.28(4) excluding the attendance of media representatives in respect of the care proceedings.

8

It should be noted that the position is different in the magistrates' court (Family Proceedings Court), where the effect of section 69(2) and (3) of the Magistrates' Courts Act 1980 (as amended by the Adoption and Children Act 2002, Schedule 3) is that media representatives are not permitted to be present at hearings in proceedings under the 2002 Act.

Sir Mark Potter

President of Family Division

30th April 2009

A1.16

PRESIDENT'S GUIDANCE IN RELATION TO APPLICATIONS CONSEQUENT UPON THE ATTENDANCE OF THE MEDIA IN FAMILY PROCEEDINGS

1

The Government's announcement about the attendance of the media at hearings in family proceedings (see Family Justice in View Cm 7502, December 2008) has been implemented by a change to the Family Proceedings Rules made by The Family Proceedings (Amendment) (No 2) Rules 2009 SI 2009 No 857 (county court and High Court) and The Family Proceedings Courts (Miscellaneous Amendments) Rules 2009 SI 2009 No 858 (magistrates' courts) and two Practice Directions Attendance of Media Representatives at Hearings in Family Proceedings dated 20th April 2009 made by the President to support the rule changes in the respective courts.

2

In the county court and High Court media attendance is implemented by the change to FPR Rule 10.28. (to which the Practice Direction applies). Change regarding media attendance in the family proceedings courts is introduced through amendment to the Family Proceedings Courts (Children Act 1989) Rules 1991, with the insertion of rule 16A.

3

In broad terms the changes for the county court and the High Court relating to media attendance permit duly accredited representatives of news gathering and reporting organisations, and any other unaccredited person whom the court permits, to be present at hearings of all family proceedings (defined by s. 32 Matrimonial and Family Proceedings Act 1984) except hearings conducted for the purposes of judicially assisted conciliation or negotiation. They also provide that the court can exclude media representatives.

4

For the county court and the High Court, the change relates to most of the proceedings which are for the time being heard in private. It therefore covers a wide range of proceedings including for example public and private law proceedings under the Children Act 1989 and claims for ancillary relief under the Matrimonial Causes Act 1973.

5

Representatives of newspapers or news agencies are admitted to the family proceedings courts under section 69 (2) Magistrates' Courts Act 1980. Media attendance will now be regulated by the insertion of rule "16A Restrictions on presence of persons at directions appointment and hearing". Duly accredited representatives of news gathering and reporting organisations are not entitled to be present at hearings conducted for the purposes of judicially assisted conciliation or negotiation. They may also be excluded for reasons set out in rule 16A(3).

6

In respect of the county court and the High Court the new Part 11 of the FPR, and in respect of the family proceedings court the new Part 11C of the Family Proceedings Courts (Children Act 1989) Rules 1991 as amended, regarding communication of information only apply to proceedings concerning children. In particular, they do not apply to proceedings for ancillary relief. Nor do they expressly cover communication of information to representatives of the media.

7

As appears from the Practice Direction governing the county court and High Court, it is a premise of the change for these courts that the proceedings remain proceedings held in private and that therefore the existing position relating to the publication of matters relating to proceedings which are so heard continues to apply, both whilst the proceedings continue and when they have ended (see the Practice Direction paras 2.4 and 2.5).

8

Useful summaries of the position relating to the publication of matters relating to proceedings heard in private can be found in: *Clayton v Clayton* [2006] EWCA Civ 878 [2007] 1 FLR 11 (in particular at paragraphs 23 to 60, 82 to 85, 92 to 104 and 118 to 136 and *Re B (A Child) (Disclosure)* [2004] EWHC 411 (Fam), [2004] 2 FLR 142 (in particular at paragraphs 62 to 82 (on s. 12 AJA 1960) and 83 to 107 (on the jurisdiction to relax or increase the statutory restrictions on publication). Other useful cases are listed in the footnote to this paragraph.[10]

9

It is to be noted that the above decisions all concern the interests and welfare of children and that the approach in ancillary relief proceedings (which are also likely to be productive of media applications) has not been the subject of similar judicial consideration and guidance.

---

[10]   *Re S (A Child) (Identification: Restrictions on Publication)* [2004] UKHL 47, [2005] 1 AC 593 *Pelling v Bruce-Williams (Secretary of State for Constitutional Affairs Intervening)* [2004] EWCA Civ 845, [2004] Fam 155, [2004] 2 FLR 823; *Re Webster; Norfolk County Council v Webster and Others (No 1)* [2006] EWHC 2733 (Fam), [2007] 1 FLR 1146; *Re Webster; Norfolk County Council v Webster and Others (No 2)* [2006] EWHC 2898 (Fam), [2007] 2 FLR 415; *Re B; X Council v B* [2007] EWHC 1622 (Fam), [2008] 1 FLR 482; *Re B; X Council v B (No 2)* [2008] EWHC 270 (Fam), [2008] 1 FLR 1460; *BBC v Cafcass* [2007] EWHC 616 (Fam), [2007] 2 FLR 765 *Oldham Metropolitan Borough Council v GW & PW* [2007] EWHC 136 (Fam), [2007] 2 FLR 597.

10

The new Rules and the Practice Directions include provisions relating to the exclusion of media representatives but are silent on the approach to be taken by the courts to the exercise of their discretion in respect of other issues which may well arise as a consequence of the attendance of media representatives at hearings in family proceedings. In this respect the Government declined to adopt the recommendation of the High Court judges to address the detail of such issues when introducing the change. It is therefore left to the courts to determine how such issues are to be approached and decided. It is clear that a principled approach to such issues should be applied by the courts and that this can only properly be developed by the courts with the benefit of full argument from the interested parties.

11

The change to admit media representatives to hearings in family proceedings in county courts and the High Court is likely to give rise to a number of issues relating to the exercise of discretion by all levels of court. In particular it is likely that courts will quickly be faced with applications for the provision of documents to media representatives present in court to enable them the better to follow the substance of the proceedings. If minded to grant such application, the court will need to consider the terms of any restriction relating to the use (and in particular the publication) of information contained in any such documents provided to media representatives as a condition of their being so provided.

12

In cases involving children, applications, whether by the media or the parties, are also likely to raise issues as to
  (i)   The proper application of the existing statutory provisions restricting the publication of the identity of children and information relating to proceedings heard in private;
  (ii) the adequacy of the protection afforded in children cases by Section 12 of the Administration of Justice Act 1960 ('AJA 1960') which, inter alia, does not extend to the identity of the parties or witnesses;
  (iii) the effect of the publication of any anonymised judgment; and whether or not injunctive relief may be required upon a wider basis.

13

In relation to the need for injunctive relief in cases affecting children, particularly in local courts, it may be necessary to consider how far it is appropriate to protect from identification not only the children and the parties, but also witnesses and others whose identities will be known locally as associated with the child or his family.

14

Finally, there will be issues over the need on child welfare grounds for protection to extend beyond the end of the hearing (see paragraph 2.5 of the respective Practice Directions).

15

No doubt the basic opposing arguments in relation to the question of access to documents will be, on the one hand, that the Government has sought to retain the basic structure and rationale of the long standing policy of privacy in relation to children proceedings, while at the same time admitting the press, to avoid charges of "secret justice" and to promote better understanding of the working of the family courts. For these purposes, however, access to court documents is not generally necessary or desirable having regard to their confidential nature.

16

On the other hand, the media may argue that, particularly in those cases where there is not a formal oral opening, they should be enabled to see statements and documents filed in order fully to understand the nature and progress of the proceedings, and so as to be able to publish articles, within appropriate reporting constraints, about the cases which they attend. In this connection, it is likely, if not inevitable, that in individual cases of high interest to the media, courts at all levels and all over the country will be faced with detailed legal argument relating to rival Convention Rights, public and private interests, the welfare of children, and the construction and application of the primary and secondary legislation.

17

Inconsistency of approach in children cases as to the principles to be applied to the determination of such issues on the part of the courts, parties, witnesses, other persons involved in the relevant events (e.g. social workers and doctors) and the media could well give rise to justified criticism on grounds of uncertainty. It would not promote the public interest in the proper administration of justice and could be damaging to children.

18

So far as ancillary relief proceedings are concerned, policy, privacy and Convention issues may also arise for decision, albeit the interests of children may not be engaged.

19

The purpose of this guidance is therefore to try to avoid, or at least to minimise, inconsistency by providing that decisions are made by the High Court (and the Appellate Courts) as soon as possible as to the principled approach to be taken. Its purpose is also to provide that, until that is done, delay in decision making in individual cases, (particularly those concerning children) should be avoided. It is to be hoped that the media will co-operate in these aims.

20

Pending the availability of formal judicial guidance from the High Court or Court of Appeal as to the principled approach to be adopted, all County Courts and Magistrates' Courts hearing family proceedings should carefully consider adopting the following course:

(i) The court should deal in accordance with the Rules and Practice Directions with any application made for exclusion of the media from the proceedings or any part of them on any of the grounds set out in the Practice Directions.

(ii) Where a representative of the media in attendance at the proceedings applies to be shown court documents, the court should seek the consent of the parties to such representative being permitted (subject to appropriate conditions as to anonymity and restrictions upon onward disclosure) to see such summaries, position statements and other documents as appear reasonably necessary to a broad understanding of the issues in the case.

(iii) If the objection of any of the parties is maintained, then in any case where the objecting party demonstrates reasonably arguable grounds for resisting disclosure of the document or documents sought, no order for disclosure should be made, but the following course of action should be considered.

(iv) If considered necessary or appropriate the court should transfer (or, in the case of a family proceedings court, take the first step to bring about an urgent transfer of) the proceedings to the High Court for the determination of any disclosure and/or reporting issues.

(v) Alternatively, in order to avoid delay in decision making on the substantive issues in the case, the court should adjourn determination of any disclosure and/or reporting issues pending a decision by the High Court (or the Appellate Courts) on the principled approach to be taken to them and should make any necessary interim orders in accordance with the argument mentioned in paragraph 15 above in order to secure the position meanwhile.

(vi) Similarly, if a representative of the media applies for reporting restrictions to be lifted during the currency of a case, in the absence of agreement between the parties the court should consider following one or the other of the alternative steps set out in sub-paragraphs iv) –v) above.

(vii) If injunctive relief is sought restraining publication based on Convention rights rather than statutory provisions, the matter should in any event be transferred to the High Court to be dealt with under the President's Practice Direction (Applications for

Reporting Restriction Orders) 18 March 2005 and the Practice Note (Official Solicitor: Deputy Director of Legal Services CAFCASS: Applications for Reporting Restriction Orders [2005] 2 FLR 111 and, if interim injunctive relief appears necessary under threat of publication before such application can be dealt with by a High Court judge, the county court should comply with s.12(2) of Human Rights Act 1998.

21

The underlying aim of this guidance is to seek to ensure that the principled approach to be taken is determined by the High Court (and the Appellate Courts) as soon as possible and that in the interim changes of practice do not take place which may not accord with that principled approach. Though this may result in delayed rulings on some early contested applications involving arguments such as those mentioned in paragraphs 15 and 16 above, it may be considered desirable, in the absence of legislative guidance, that such rulings should only be made on the basis of authoritative judicial guidance following proper determination, with the benefit of full argument, of the relevant principled approach for the longer term.

22

To assist in the early determination of the principled approach:
- (i) Arrangements will be made in the High Court to identify appropriate test cases and for their early determination, and
- (ii) Arrangements will be made to seek to ensure that directions are given as soon as is practicable in any proceedings that are transferred to the High Court because they raise substantial issues arising from the attendance of media representatives,
- (iii) Proceedings which are transferred to the High Court other than in the PRFD should be put before a family High Court Judge on circuit or, failing the presence on circuit of a High Court Judge, before the Family Division Liaison Judge as an urgent application for directions.

Sir Mark Potter

President of the Family Division

22nd April 2009

Appendix 2

FOUNDATION DICTA FLOWING FROM *CLIBBERY V ALLAN*[1]

(Note that font emphasis is that of the author's)

A2.01

'[1] This is an appeal by Ivan Allan, (the appellant), from the refusal of Munby J on 14 June 2001 to continue injunctions granted ex parte by Connell J on 3 May 2001 restraining Glory Anne Clibbery, (the respondent), from disclosing information about the appellant. The appeal raises fundamental issues over the procedures for hearing family cases in the High Court and in county courts round the country. **The specific question raised on this appeal is whether the practice of hearing the majority of family cases in chambers has the consequence that information about those proceedings may not be reported.**

[20] I would therefore suggest that there are three categories of case, those heard in open court, those heard in private and those heard in secret where the information disclosed to the court and the proceedings remain confidential.

[47] Part IV of the 1991 Rules deals with children applications under the Children Act 1989. **There is no disagreement that children applications fall to be determined in private.** Confidentiality in wardship cases was specifically recognised in *Scott (Otherwise Morgan) and Another v Scott*[2] and s 12(1)(a) of the Administration of Justice Act 1960, treated children cases as an exception to the general rule of publication of court proceedings, see below. **The procedure in children cases is set out in careful detail in the 1991 Rules and the confidentiality of all aspects of the proceedings, the evidence of the parties, the reports filed, and the documents disclosed is specifically provided for in r 4.23, headed 'Confidentiality of documents'. Rule 4.16 deals with the hearing:**

"Unless the court otherwise directs, a hearing of, or '(7) directions appointment in, proceedings to which this Part applies shall be in chambers".

[50] Parliament has provided for rules to be made to regulate the statutory framework of the family justice system. The 1991 Rules are properly based upon the 1984 Act. In those rules the court has the power to exclude the public in family proceedings. **For my part, I can see no problem in the application of this procedure under the 1991 Rules, designed as it is to provide a measure of privacy, not necessarily confidentiality, to family proceedings. The CPR give a similar degree of privacy to groups of civil cases. There remains also the power to allow the public in if the judge or district judge**

---

[1] [2002] EWCA Civ 45, [2002] 1 FLR 565.
[2] [1913] AC 417.

directs. **This discretion is similar to that set out by Buxton LJ in The Queen on the application of** *Pelling v Bow County Court,*[3] see above. In the 1984 Act, the authority to make the 1991 Rules was provided by s 40. There is no statutory prohibition against providing for hearings in chambers in the family cases; on the contrary, there is a statutory basis for the rules. The Administration of Justice Act 1960, s 12 (see below) does not concern itself with the legitimacy of hearings in private but with the publication of information from those proceedings. In my judgment, Munby J's judgment was expressed in too broad terms in stating that family proceedings could not, with the exception of children cases, be heard in private. The 1991 Rules are not ultra vires any Act of Parliament and there is no objection to family courts hearing cases in private and excluding the public where the 1991 Rules permit them to do so.'

PUBLICATION OF INFORMATION RELATING TO B PROCEEDINGS

A2.02

'[51] As I have already said above, the hearing of a case in private does not, of itself, prohibit the publication of information about the proceedings or given in the proceedings. The general rule is that it is not a contempt of court to report what has happened at a hearing in chambers, see Lord Loreburn in *Scott (Otherwise Morgan) and Another v Scott,*[4] at p 444 and Lord Shaw at p 484. The principle of open justice is to be derogated from only to the extent that it is strictly necessary to do so and applies equally to publication of information. In *Attorney-General v Leveller Magazine and Others; Attorney-General v National Union of Journalists; Attorney-General v Peace News Ltd and Others,*[5] Lord Edmund-Davies said at p 465:

"And what appears certain is that at common law the fact that a court sat wholly or partly in camera (and even where in such circumstances the court gave a direction prohibiting publication of information relating to what had been said or done behind closed doors) did not of itself and in every case necessarily mean that publication thereafter constituted contempt of court. ... **For that to arise something more than disobedience of the court's direction needs to be established. That something more is that the publication must be of such a nature as to threaten the administration of justice either in the particular case in relation to which the prohibition was pronounced or in relation to cases which may be brought in the future.**"

[71] **In each of the above cases, the obligation on the parties to make full and frank disclosure in their financial disputes was of such importance that it was in the public interest to preserve confidentiality of that information by means of the implied undertaking.** In order to achieve compliance with disclosure by the party under the obligation to do so, the party seeking the disclosure is

---

[3]   [2001] UKHRR 165.
[4]   [1913] AC 417.
[5]   [1979] AC 440.

required by the court only to use that information for the purposes of the proceedings. It is the protection provided by the court in cases of compulsion. Ancillary relief applications are appropriately heard in private in accordance with the 1991 Rules, see above. **The public may not, without leave of the court, hear the evidence given in these applications. It would make a nonsense of the use of an implied undertaking if information about the means of a party, in some cases sensitive information, could be made public as soon as the substantive hearing commenced. Information disclosed under the compulsion of ancillary relief proceedings is, in my judgment, protected by the implied undertaking, before, during and after the proceedings are completed.** Munby J, in his judgment, did not suggest to the contrary. He also pointed out that the 1926 Act (as amended in 1968) protects ancillary relief proceedings from press publication. This may be the case but we heard no argument on it.

[77] Parliament in the Contempt of Court Act 1981 has provided by s 11 exemption from disclosure in court:

"In any case where a court (having **power to do so**) allows a name or other matter to be withheld from the public in proceedings before the court, the court may give such directions prohibiting the publication of that name or matter in connection with the proceedings as appear to the court to be necessary for the purpose for which it was so withheld."

[78] **This section gives statutory protection for non-disclosure of information which should remain secret, where, and only where, a court has the power to do so. This requirement takes the court back to the general principles and the recognised exceptions to them. It has not been the practice of the family courts in the past to apply this section, but there may be cases, as possibly the present appeal might have been, for the court hearing the case in private to decide whether any or even all the information should not be disclosed.** It cannot properly be a blanket protection of non-publication in all cases heard in private in chambers under the 1991 Rules. It can, however, apply not only to the actual case before the court but also to groups of cases arising out of the same type of circumstances: see Lord Edmund-Davies in *Attorney-General v Leveller Magazine and Others; Attorney-General v National Union of Journalists; Attorney-General v Peace News Ltd and Others*.[6] The 1991 Rules, r 3.9 has no requirement to file evidence, unless the court requires it and makes an order. I would suggest, however, that in applications for occupation orders where there are children, the welfare of those children is likely to be a major issue or often the major issue. Consequently the s 12 exemption would be likely to apply. **If the financial affairs of any of the parties have to be investigated, and bearing in mind the requirement that the court shall have regard to all the circumstances, that information, if required or likely to be required by the court, would probably be protected.** The general principles of discovery would apply. It will, however, require the parties and the court to consider in each case whether the proper working of the administration of justice requires there to be continuing confidentiality after the end of the proceedings. That is, in my view, no bad thing.

---

6   [1979] AC 440.

[79] Before the speeches in *Scott (Otherwise Morgan) and Another v Scott*[7] set out in ringing tones the crucial importance of open justice it had already been a corner stone of the common law. The statutory framework, providing the procedures in civil and family cases, recognises the necessity to hold some proceedings in private and that there should be protection against publication of some of those proceedings. **Such protection must be proportionate to the requirements of the administration of justice.** It might be thought to be inconvenient and time-consuming to have to look at this problem in individual cases heard in private. There are groups of cases in which the answer is obvious and, in my view, there will only be a small number of cases, in particular under Part IV, where the advocates and the court may have to consider the point.

[92] It therefore seems to me that Parliament has been sparse in its contribution to unravelling the question of what, if anything, may be extracted from family proceedings in private for subsequent publication. That may be because there seemed to be little need for Parliament to legislate. In the family justice system the designation "in chambers" has always been accepted to mean strictly private. Judges, practitioners and court staff are vigilant to ensure that no one crosses the threshold of the court who has not got a direct involvement in the business of the day. One of the parties may have formed a new relationship. But if the new partner has not party status in the litigation application must be made to the judge despite the obvious and direct involvement in the life of the family. This strict boundary has always been scrupulously observed by the press. **Of course the judge always retains a residual discretion and, accordingly, a hearing in chambers may culminate in a judgment in open court. Alternatively the judge may make an abbreviated statement in order that the public interest in the proceedings may be at least partially satisfied.**

[105] **Accordingly I have no difficulty in concluding that in the important area of ancillary relief, where the table confirms that the volume of business is large all the evidence (whether written, oral or disclosed documents) and all the pronouncements of the court are prohibited from reporting and from ulterior use unless derived from any part of the proceedings conducted in open court or otherwise released by the judge.'**

NOTE 1

There have been editorially emphasised above the words *'power to do so'*. In other words, if a court makes an order which it does not have power to make, then s 11 of the Contempt of Court Act 1981 cannot bite.

NOTE 2

These dicta should be seen in the context of the wording of the new FPR 1991, rr 10.28 and 11.

---

[7]   [1913] AC 417.

Appendix 3

FAMILY COURTS – REPORTING RESTRICTIONS

(Note that font emphasis is that of the author's)

PART A

Statutory provisions

A3.01

- During the court process: s 97(2) bites, subject to s 97(4); but, ceases to bite after the proceedings are ended: See *Clayton v Clayton.*[1]

- Under s 97(4) the court has a discretion to dispense with the s 97(2) restriction '*if … the welfare of the child requires it*' – eg to advertise for adoptive parents or to publicise the disappearance of an identified child who is the subject of the relevant proceedings.

- Of general application: Administration of Justice Act 1960, s 12 subject to any application for disclosure, which will attract the balancing exercise between Articles 8 and 10.

Relevant dicta

Kent County Council v B and Others

A3.02 Per Munby J in *Kent County Council v B and Others,*[2] paras [81]–[82]; (emphasis added):

> '[81] Since it is apparent that there is still widespread misunderstanding as to the precise ambit of section 12 it may be helpful if I attempt to summarise the learning. In doing so I wish to emphasise that **what follows is not to be treated as if it were a statutory formulation – it is not – nor as a substitute for applying the words of section 12 itself.** Moreover, any attempt to summarise an extensive and subtle jurisprudence will inevitably suffer from the inherent difficulties and defects of the exercise. **There is no substitute for a careful study of the reported cases.** That said, I hope that what follows may provide some practical assistance to those, unfamiliar with all the nuances of the jurisprudence, who may lack the time or opportunity to study the case law.

---

[1]   [2007] 1 FLR 11.
[2]   [2004] EWHC [Fam] 411, [2004] 2 FLR 142.

[82] **For present purposes the relevant principles can, I think, be summarised as follows**:

(i) Section 12(1)(a) of the Administration of Justice Act 1960 has the effect of prohibiting the **publication** of:

"**information relating to proceedings** before any court sitting in private ... where the proceedings (i) relate to the exercise of the inherent jurisdiction of the High Court with respect to minors; (ii) are brought under the Children Act 1989; or (iii) otherwise relate wholly or mainly to the ... upbringing of a minor."

(ii) Subject only to **proof of knowledge** that the proceedings in question are of the type referred to in section 12(1)(a), the publication of such information is a contempt of court.

(iii) There is a **"publication" for** this purpose whenever the law of defamation would treat there as being a publication. **This means that most forms of dissemination, whether oral or written, will constitute a publication. The only exception is where there is a communication of information by someone to a professional, each acting in furtherance of the protection of children**.

(iv) Specifically, there is a **"publication" for** this purpose whether the dissemination of information or documents is to a **journalist** or to a **Member of Parliament, a Minister of the Crown, a Law Officer, the Director of Public Prosecutions**, the **Crown Prosecution Service**, the **police** (except when exercising child protection functions), the **General Medical Council**, or **any other public body or public official**. The Minister of State for Children is not a child protection professional. Disclosure to the Minister of State cannot therefore be justified on the footing of the exception to the general principle.

(v) Section 12 does **not of itself** prohibit the publication of:
   (a) the fact, if it be the case, that a **child is a ward of court** and is the subject of wardship proceedings or that a **child is the subject of residence or other proceedings under the Children Act 1989 or of proceedings relating wholly or mainly to his maintenance or upbringing**;
   (b) the **name, address** or **photograph** of such a child;
   (c) the **name, address** or **photograph** of the parties (or, if the child is a party, the other parties) to such proceedings;
   (d) the **date, time** or **place** of a past or future hearing of such proceedings;
   (e) **the nature of the dispute** in such proceedings;
   (f) anything which has been seen or heard by a person conducting himself lawfully **in the public corridor** or **other public precincts outside the court** in which the hearing in private is taking place;
   (g) the **name, address** or **photograph** of the **witnesses** who have given evidence in such proceedings;
   (h) **the party on whose behalf such a witness has given evidence**; and
   (i) **the text or summary of the whole or part of any order made in such proceedings**.

(vi) **Section 12 prohibits** the publication of:
   (a) **accounts of what has gone on in front of the judge sitting in private**;

(b) **documents such as affidavits, witness statements, reports, position statements, skeleton arguments or other documents filed in the proceedings, transcripts or notes of the evidence or submissions, and transcripts or notes of the judgment** (*this list is not necessarily exhaustive*);

(c) **extracts or quotations from such documents**;

(d) **summaries of such documents**.

These prohibitions apply whether or not the information or the document being published has been anonymised.

(vii) (By way of example of how the principles in (v) and (vi) inter-relate) **in a case such as the present case section 12 does not of itself prohibit the publication of**:

(a) the issues in the case as being whether the mother suffered from Munchausen's Syndrome by Proxy and whether she had killed (or attempted to kill) her child(ren) by, for instance, smothering or poisoning;

(b) the identity of the various medical experts who have given evidence in relation to those issues; and

(c) which of the parties each expert has given evidence for or against.

(viii) Irrespective of the ambit of section 12 **of the 1960 Act, section 97(2) of the 1989 Act makes it a criminal offence to**:

"publish any material which is intended, or likely, to identify ... any child as being involved in any proceedings before [a family court] in which any power under [the 1989] Act may be exercised by the court with respect to that or any other child."

(ix) **This is all subject to any specific injunction or other order that a court of competent jurisdiction may have made in any particular case.**'

Re Webster; Norfolk County Council v Webster and Others[3]

A3.03 Authoritative and comprehensive dicta of Munby J in relation to the following issues:

(a) Open justice: paras [17]–[25].

(b) Freedom of speech: paras [26]–[28].

(c) The role of the media: paras [29]–[36].

(d) Family courts – confidentiality in children proceedings: paras [42]-[46].

(e) The balancing exercise between Articles 8 and 10: paras [53]–[64] and [97]–[121].

'[48] **Section 12 of the Administration of Justice Act 1960**, as amended, provides, so far as material for present purposes:

---

[3]   [2004] EWHC [Fam] 411, [2004] 2 FLR 142.

"(1) The publication of information relating to proceedings (1) before any court sitting in private shall not of itself be contempt of court except in the following cases, that is to say – (a) where the proceedings – (i) relate to the exercise of the inherent jurisdiction of the High Court with respect to minors; (ii) are brought under the Children Act 1989; or (iii) otherwise relate wholly or mainly to the maintenance or upbringing of a minor …

(2) Without prejudice to the foregoing subsection, the (2) publication of the text or a summary of the whole or part of an order made by a court sitting in private shall not of itself be contempt of court except where the court (having power to do so) expressly prohibits the publication.

(4) Nothing in this section shall be construed as implying (4) that any publication is punishable as contempt of court which would not be so punishable apart from the section (and in particular where the publication is not so punishable by reason of being authorised by rules of court."

[49] There is no need on this occasion for any detailed exegesis of s 12. **It suffices for present purposes to note that the effect of s 12 is to prohibit the publication of accounts of what has gone on in front of the judge sitting in private, as also the publication of documents (or extracts or quotations from documents) such as affidavits, witness statements, reports, position statements, skeleton arguments or other documents filed in the proceedings, transcripts or notes of the evidence or submissions, and transcripts or notes of the judgment. On the other hand, s 12 does not of itself prohibit publication of the fact that a child is the subject of proceedings under the Children Act 1989; of the dates, times and places of past or future hearings; of the nature of the dispute in the proceedings; of anything which has been seen or heard by a person conducting himself lawfully in the public corridor or other public precincts outside the court in which the hearing in private is taking place; or of the text or summary of any order made in such proceedings. Importantly, it is also to be noted that s 12 does not (Judge's emphasis) prohibit the identification or publication of photographs of the child, the other parties or the witnesses, nor the identification of the party on whose behalf a witness is giving or has given evidence.**

[50] Section 12 also has to be read in conjunction with r 10.20A of the Family Proceedings Rules 1991, but as nothing turns for present purposes on its specific provisions I need say no more about it.

[51] **Section 97 of the Children Act 1989**, as amended, **provides in material part as follows**:

    (2)   No person shall publish to the public at large or any (2) section of the public any material which is intended, or likely, to identify:

        (a)   any child as being involved in any proceedings before the High Court, a county court or a magistrates' court in which any power under this Act or the Adoption and Children Act 2002 may be exercised by the court with respect to that or any other child; or

        (b)   an address or school as being that of a child being involved in any such proceedings.

        …

    The court or the Lord Chancellor may, if satisfied that (4) the welfare of the child requires it, and in the case of the Lord Chancellor, if the

Lord Chief Justice agrees, by order dispense with the requirements of subsection (2) to such extent as may be specified in the order.

[52] The meaning and effect of s 97 has recently been considered by the Court of Appeal in *Clayton v Clayton*,[4] where it was held that **the prohibition in s 97(2) comes to an end when the proceedings are concluded**. The common belief (which I confess I shared) that the statutory prohibition outlasted the existence of the proceedings has now been exploded for what it always was – yet another of the many fallacies and misunderstandings which have tended to bedevil this particular area of the law. On the other hand, and as Sir Mark Potter P was at pains to point out (at para [53]), the fact that, **following an end to the proceedings, the prohibition on identification under s 97 will cease to have effect does not of course mean that the provisions of s 12 of the Administration of Justice Act 1960 are diluted or otherwise affected**. The limitation upon reporting information relating to the proceedings themselves **under s 12 of that Act will remain**.

[53] So much for the automatic restraints which apply in cases of this kind. But it is clear that the court has power both to relax and to increase these restrictions. **A judge can authorise disclosure of what would otherwise be prohibited. And a judge can impose additional restrictions.** This involves the exercise of discretion – the carrying out of a balancing exercise – where a number of often conflicting rights and interests have to be balanced. How is this exercise to be performed?

[54] The answer is provided by the speech of Lord Steyn in *Re S (Identification: Restrictions on Publication)*,[5] at para [17]:

"The interplay between articles 8 and 10 has been illuminated by the opinions in the House of Lords in *Campbell v MGN Ltd*.[6] For present purposes the decision of the House on the facts of Campbell and the differences between the majority and the minority are not material. What does, however, emerge clearly from the opinions are four propositions. First, neither article has as such precedence over the other. Secondly, where the values under the two articles are in conflict, an intense focus on the comparative importance of the specific rights being claimed in the individual case is necessary. Thirdly, the justifications for interfering with or restricting each right must be taken into account. Finally, the proportionality test must be applied to each. For convenience I will call this the ultimate balancing test."

[55] In *A Local Authority v W, L, W, T and R (by the Children's Guardian)*,[7] at para [53], Sir Mark Potter P summarised the effects of the judgment in *Re S* in this way:

"There is express approval of the methodology in *Campbell v MGN Ltd*[8] in which it was made clear that each article propounds a fundamental right which there is a pressing social need to protect. Equally, each article qualifies the right it propounds so far as it may be lawful, necessary and proportionate to do so in order to accommodate the other. The exercise to

---

4   [2006] EWCA Civ 878, [2007] 1 FLR 11.
5   [2005] 1 FLR 591.
6   [2004] 2 AC 457.
7   [2005] EWHC 1564 (Fam), [2006] 1 FLR 1.
8   [2005] EWHC 1564 (Fam), [2006] 1 FLR 1.

be performed is one of parallel analysis in which the starting point is presumptive parity, in that neither article has precedence over or "trumps" the other. The exercise of parallel analysis requires the court to examine the justification for interfering with each right and the issue of proportionality is to be considered in respect of each. It is not a mechanical exercise to be decided upon the basis of rival generalities. An intense focus on the comparative importance of the specific rights being claimed in the individual cases is necessary before the ultimate balancing test in the terms of proportionality is carried out."

[56]   It is clear from In *Re S and A Local Authority v W* that in this context at least the interests of the child are *not* paramount. Nor is there anything novel in this. As I said in *Re X (Disclosure of Information)*,[9] at para [23], summarising the relevant pre-Convention case law:

"The interests of the child (which … typically point against disclosure) are a "major factor" and "very important" … But … it is clear that the child's interests are not paramount".'

PART B

Issues arising out of s 12 taken together with the dicta of Munby J in '*Kent CC*' and '*Webster*'

As to whether a publication is caught vis à vis matters relating to a child

A3.04   Hale J (as she then was) held that proceedings under the Child Support Act 1991 were not on their facts caught by s 12: *M v BBC*.[10] The applicant father had objected to the part of the programme which revealed his infertility. His former wife had given the information during an interview due to be televised. The applicant did not object to the identification of the children. Hale J inter alia held that the jurisdiction under s 12 could only be invoked to restrain publication of matters relating to *children* over whose welfare publicity might threaten the effective working of the court's jurisdiction. Therefore, notwithstanding that the proceedings were brought under the Child Support Act 1991, an adult involved in those proceedings could not claim protection from publication of information given in court. Consequently, in the circumstances of the present case the public interest in freedom of speech should prevail.

What is a 'publication'?

A3.05

(a)   Communication to the world at large in a newspaper.

---

9   [2001] 2 FLR 440.
10   [1997] 1 FLR 51.

(b)   Communication to any third party; see Munby J in *Kent*.[11]

What is the position vis à vis communication to a journalist?

A3.06

(a)   Such communication is caught by s 12.

(b)   There is no express provision in the new rules sanctioning communication to a journalist.

(c)   A party may be able to justify communication to a journalist within the new **FPR 1991, r 11.2(1)(a)** – but the burden will be on the party to prove that communication of *'information relating to the proceedings'* was *'necessary'* to enable that party *'by confidential discussion, to obtain support, advice or assistance in the conduct of the proceedings'*.

(d)   And even if **FPR 1991, r 11.2(2)(a)** legitimates communication to a journalist, **s 12 of the AJA 1960 bites** on any communication by such journalist to a third party, be it editor or legal advisor.

(e)   Thus, a journalist in court is bound by the AJA 1960, s 12 and cannot discuss a case with his editor or legal advisors without the permission of the court.

What is the meaning of the statutory phrase, 'the nature of the dispute' and how is it to be defined?

A3.07   This phrase has been considered in *X v Dempster*[12] *by* Wilson J and in *Kent County Council v B*,[13] by Munby J, who in that case inter alia said:

> 'I turn finally to the question of the extent to which section 12 prohibits discussion of the details of a case. Now as Wilson J accepted in *X v Dempster*, and with respect I entirely agree, **whilst section 12 does not prohibit publication of "the nature of the dispute", it does prohibit publication of even summaries of the evidence**. Where is the line to be drawn? In *Kelly*, as we have seen, I said that section 12 does not prevent "public identification and at least some discussion of the issues in the ... proceedings". That is not very helpful. More helpful is the light thrown on the matter by Wilson J's analysis in *X v Dempster*. There the question (see at p 896) was whether there was a breach of section 12 by publishing the words:
>
>> Says a friend of [the mother]: "She has been portrayed as a bad mother who is unfit to look after her children. Nothing could be further from the truth. She is wonderful to [them] and they love her. She wants custody of [them] and we will see what happens in court".'

---

[11]   [1997] 1 FLR 51.
[12]   [1999] 1 FLR 894.
[13]   [1999] 1 FLR 894.

Immediately preceded by the statement that the mother was said to be distraught that four people, who were named, had provided affidavits – they were in fact signed witness statements – in support of the father's case.'

Wilson J said this at p 901:

'I turn to the third alleged feature, namely that in the piece Mr Dempster recounts an allegation to the effect that the mother has been portrayed in the proceedings as a bad mother who is unfit to look after the children.'

He continued at p 903:

'I am satisfied that the reference to the portrayal of the mother in the proceedings as a bad mother went far beyond a description of the nature of the dispute and reached deeply into the substance of the matters which the court has closed its doors to consider. If the reference could successfully be finessed as a legitimate identification of the nature of the dispute, the privacy of the proceedings in the interests of the child would be not just appropriately circumscribed but gravely invaded.'

I agree with Wilson J's analysis and, if I may respectfully say so, with the particular conclusion to which he came in that case.

'[79] **Every case will, in the final analysis, turn on its own particular facts. The circumstances of the human condition, and thus of litigation, being infinitely various, it is quite impossible to define in abstract or purely formal terms where precisely the line is to be drawn. Wilson J's discussion in *X v Dempster*, if I may respectfully say so, comes as close as anyone is likely to be able to illuminating the essential distinction between publication of "the nature of the dispute", which is permissible, and publication of even summaries of the evidence, which is not.**

[80] Reverting to the circumstances of the present case, it seems to me that the material published in the two paragraphs of *The Daily Mail* to which the local authority has taken objection, whilst fairly close to the line, was almost certainly on the wrong side of the line. Beyond that provisional view it would not be proper to go in the absence of any representations from the editor and publisher of the *Daily Mail*. **On the other hand, it would not seem to me to be a breach of s 12, for example, to identify the issues in a case as being whether the mother suffered from Munchausen's Syndrome by Proxy and whether she had killed (or attempted to kill) her child(ren) by, for instance, smothering or poisoning, and to identify the various medical experts who have given evidence in relation to those issues, and to state which of the parties each expert has given evidence for or against. To go beyond that might well, however, involve a breach of s 12.'**

The paragraphs in *The Daily Mail* to which Munby J referred at para [24]:

'A paediatrician called as an expert witness at an initial family court hearing suggested, out of the blue, that Sheila might have deliberately injected her child with the water from a flower bowl or a lavatory. It was a claim considered ludicrous by one of the country's leading forensic toxicologists, who provided evidence for the police in Harold Shipman's case.

He told the court it was a medical impossibility for Sheila to have done such a thing. But for the family courts – which do not require the standard of proof of a criminal court – this was not enough to save her. Sheila has had her daughter forcibly removed with little hope of appeal.'

Appendix 4

EASY ACCESS GUIDE TO CASES SET OUT IN APPENDIX 5

(Note that font emphasis is that of the author's)

2009

S (A CHILD ACTING BY THE OFFICIAL SOLICITOR) V ROCHDALE METROPOLITAN BOROUGH COUNCIL AND THE INDEPENDENT REVIEWING OFFICER[1]

A4.01   The court approved a confidentiality clause reached by agreement between the child and the authority as part of a compromise approved by the court. However, nothing in the confidentiality clause prevented public dissemination of the court order, which was a public document, or of the particulars of the claim, which had been in the public domain when the order was made. Furthermore, the authority was to be named publicly; identifying the authority was not likely to lead to the identification of the child, and no good reason had been shown to justify maintaining the authority's anonymity.

2008

RE N (MCKENZIE FRIEND: RIGHTS OF AUDIENCE)[2]

A4.02   Public discussion of the issues was not going to be significantly inhibited by reason only of the fact that the parties' names would not be in the public domain, in contrast to the names of their lawyers and the name of the McKenzie friend.

Z County Council v TS, DES, ES and A[3]

A4.03   Where **most unusually**, the court had granted permission for care proceedings to be heard in public subject to a **schedule of anonymisations**, and

---

[1]   [2008] EWHC 3283 (Fam), [2009] 1 FLR 1090.
[2]   [2008] EWHC 2042, [2008] 2 FLR 1899.
[3]   [2008] EWHC 1773 (Fam), [2008] 2 FLR 1800.

the family had been the subject of a documentary, Hedley J refused the mother's later application to relax some of the anonymisation provisions, because to do so would have been highly likely to lead to the identification of the child who lived in a **rural community** and was therefore more likely to be identifiable than if he lived in a massive **conurbation**.

Medway Council v G and Others[4]

A4.04   In the course of care proceedings, the court gave permission for a newspaper to **interview the stepfather about related criminal proceedings** on the basis of an agreed statement of facts prepared by the parties, provided that the **child was not identified**. Further the President authorised the release of an agreed summary of the facts of the case to the media in the following circumstances: there was publicity involving the mother of the children who had been the subject of care proceedings, which gave an **inaccurate and/or misleading** account of those proceedings, and the reasons why the children were removed from the mother (including criticisms of the secrecy of the family courts).

Re H (Care Plan)[5]

A4.05   An order allowing a **short summary of the judicial criticism of the social workers involved** and of the local authority's response, with the former referred to by initial but the latter by name, to be published to local Family Court User Groups, to Cafcass offices in Essex, and to relevant judges.

Re B; X Council v B (No 2)[6]

A4.06   An order allowing the mother and two of her children to **waive their anonymity** should they so wish.

Re LM (Reporting Restrictions: Coroner's Inquest[7]

A4.07   The court was not satisfied that there would be lasting harm to a child arising from the reporting of a **coroner's inquest** relating to the **death of a sibling**. However, the court placed an embargo on publication of the name or existence of the surviving child or any information that was likely to lead to her identification.

Re R (Identification: Restriction on Publication)[8]

A4.08   The court made injunctions restraining the parents from seeking to identify the **prospective adopters** and stopping them from contacting the

---

4   [2008] EWHC 1681 (Fam), [2008] 2 FLR 1687.
5   [2008] EWHC 327 (Fam), [2008] 2 FLR 21.
6   [2008] EWHC 270 (Fam), [2008] 1 FLR 1460.
7   [2007] EWHC 1962 (Fam), [2008] 1 FLR 1360.
8   [2007] EWHC 2742 (Fam),[2008] 1 FLR 1252.

children, and restraining publication of any details identifying the children, since it was satisfied that the parents were not seeking publicity just for their cause but wanted **to interfere with the court process** by deterring prospective adopters.

Re X Children[9]

A4.09 Striking the balance between the confidentiality of material in the family proceedings and the public interest in such material being passed to the CPS following the conviction of a father for attempted murder of a social worker and there then emerging **in the family proceedings evidence of serious offences** committed by the father against one of the children.

Re B: X Council v B[10]

A4.10 An order enabling a local authority to be named.

Re F (Children) (DNA Evidence)[11]

A4.11 Naming of a company (DNA Diagnostics) because those potentially affected by the **breakdown in the administrative** *systems* of the company had a clear right to know both what had occurred and to take such steps as they considered right to reassure themselves.

2007

BBC v CAFCASS Legal & Ors[12]

A4.12 The court granted **anonymity** to both domestic and foreign **experts.**

Re R (Secure editing of documents)[13]

A4.13 In contact proceedings the court made an order permitting omission of the mother's address and contact details from any evidence and documents filed and served in the course of the proceedings in order to protect her and the children from the father. **Due to inadequate editing of the documents by the various solicitors involved, the father discovered the mother's new name and he contacted her.** The court held that this amounted to a gross breach of the mother's rights under ECHR 1950, Art 8. In order to avoid repetition of such instances, the court issued **detailed guidelines with the approval of the President of the Family Division** and these are set out in the judgment.

---

9   [2007] EWHC 1622 (Fam), [2008] 1 FLR 589.
10 [2007] EWHC 1622 (Fam), [2008] 1 FLR 482.
11 [2007] EWHC 3235 (Fam), [2008] 1 FLR 348.
12 [2007] EWHC 616 (Fam), [2007] 2 FLR 765.
13 [2007] 2 FLR 759.

Re K (Adoption: Permission to Advertise)[14]

A4.14 Publications that advertise children as available for adoption are unlikely to advertise a child unless the adoption agency is authorised to place for adoption or a court has given leave for such advertising.[15] **This case sets out the court's approach when asked to give leave to advertise**. It was not open to a local authority to place a full identifying advertisement for the adoption of a particular child **until they had obtained the necessary recommendation from the adoption panel** and had **decided that the child ought to be placed for adoption**. When such an application is made before a final care hearing and where the care plan for adoption has yet to be endorsed, **the court is unlikely to give permission** to advertise unless the adoption plan is unopposed or there is some exceptional feature to the case justifying advertising.

Norfolk County Council v Webster & Ors[16]

A4.15 Munby J analysed publicity issues both in principle and in relation to detailed statutory provisions and rights under the ECHR 1950. In exercising his discretion as he did in relation to matters to be considered when prohibiting the publication of information relating to proceedings in private, Munby J addressed four factors:

(i)   that the case was alleged to involve a **miscarriage of justice;**

(ii)   that the **parents** themselves **wished** for publicity;

(iii) that the case had already been **extensively publicised;** and

(iv)   that, very importantly, there was a need for the **full facts** to emerge in a way which would **command public confidence** in the judicial system.

A4.16 Munby J allowed **publication of counsel's position statement** in view of the current practice of significant advocacy **being in written form,** which is pre-read by the judge and not dealt with orally in court; **such written material should be disclosed to allow the media to report in a fully informed way**. However, Munby J declined to approve a draft press release prepared on behalf of the parents: it is not the function of a judge to give advice.

Leeds County Council & Ors v Channel 4 Television Corporation[17]

A4.17 Surreptitious filming of state school sector showing disruption and teacher demoralisation. Article 8 rights of children engaged. Article 10 rights of press and the wider public engaged. Balance came down firmly in favour of broadcasting.

---

[14]   [2007] EWHC 544 (Fam), [2007] 2 FLR 326.
[15]   See: www.everychildmatters.gov.uk.
[16]   [2006] EWHC 2733 (Fam), [2007] 1 FLR 1146.
[17]   [2007] 1 FLR 678.

BBC v Rochdale BC & X & Y[18]

A4.18 This case held that s 12 of the 1960 AJA does not prevent the identification of witnesses. Ryder J also conducted an extensive analysis of the relevant domestic and ECHR 1950 case law and an illustration of the balancing exercise required.

Clayton v Clayton[19]

A4.19 The prohibition is not an absolute prohibition against publishing material about a child. **The s 97(2) prohibition ends once the proceedings have been concluded;** but the provisions of **s 12 of the AJA 1960 remain**. Furthermore, in the course of the proceedings the judge may make an injunction or order prohibiting identification for a period beyond the proceedings in the **welfare interests** of the child, or in order to protect *privacy* under ECHR 1950, Art 8. However in deciding to make a long-term injunction aimed at restricting the reporting and publication of proceedings, *the court is obliged to conduct a balancing exercise* between the Art 8 rights of the child and the Art 10 (freedom of expression) rights of a parent asserting such a right.

2006

Re H (Freeing Orders: Publicity)[20]

A4.20 The CA stated that there was a strong argument for judges in controversial cases, or cases that attracted media attention, to **accompany delivery of their judgments with a short written summary of their conclusions and reasons**, which could be made publicly available.

Re Z (Shared Parenting Plan: Publicity)[21]

A4.21 Balance struck in favour of child (Art 8) against father's freedom of speech (Art 10) vis à vis publicity for a **shared parenting arrangement against a fraught historical backdrop.**

Her Majesty's A-G v Pelling[22]

A4.22 **Section 12 of the AJA 1960** has the effect of abrogating the strict liability rule of contempt of court, except in certain types of proceedings (ie those mentioned in s 12(1)(a) which relate to **most types of family proceedings in which children** are the focal point). **Section 12 is deigned to prevent publication of information in respect of child law cases which are heard in private.** It does not apply solely to **wardship** proceedings but includes

---

18   [2005] EWHC 2862, [2007] 1 FLR 101.
19   [2006] EWCA Civ 878, [2007] 1 FLR 11.
20   [2005] EWCA Civ 1325, [2006] 1 FLR 815.
21   [2006] 1 FLR 405.
22   [2005] EWHC 414 (Admin), [2006] 1 FLR 93.

proceedings under the CA 1989 and the Adoption and Children Act 2002. The publication of a judgment, which in the interests of the child the court had determined should be kept private, is an interference with the interests of justice and is punishable as a criminal contempt.

A Local Authority v W, L, W, T and R (by the Children's Guardian)[23]

A4.23 As to matters to be considered when prohibiting the publication of information relating to proceedings in private: **The proper approach is for the court to identify the various rights that are engaged and then to conduct the necessary balancing exercise between the competing rights,** considering the **proportionality** of the potential interference with each right considered **independently**; and also see *Re B (A child) (Disclosure)*.[24]

2005

Blunkett v Quinn[25]

A4.24 Having regard to the quantity of material concerning this case that was in the **public domain,** some of it, even in the most responsible commentaries, wholly inaccurate, and having regard to the private and family lives of all concerned, it was right to **hear the appeal in private**, but to give this judgment in public, albeit **excluding from the judgment unnecessary personal material**.

Re S (Identification: Restrictions on Publication)[26]

A4.25 The House of Lords was of the view that the foundation of the jurisdiction to restrain publicity was now derived from rights under ECHR 1950 and that since the Human Rights Act 1998 came into force, the earlier case law concerning the existence and scope of the inherent jurisdiction need not be considered. The court needs to balance the Art 8 rights of the child and the Art 10 rights of the proposed publisher and to consider the proportionality of the potential interference with each right.

A4.26 Where an **injunction** is sought to impose a restraint on the freedom of the press and the media generally, the case should be transferred to the High Court (see **Appendix 1**):

- Practice Note (Official Solicitor: Deputy Director of Leal Services: Cafcass; Applications for Reporting Restriction Orders);[27]

---

23   [2005] EWHC 1564 (Fam), [2006] 1 FLR 1.
24   [2004] EWHC 411 (Fam), [2004] 2 FLR 142.
25   [2004] EWHC 2816 (Fam), [2005] 1 FLR 648.
26   [2004] UKHL 47, [2005] 1 FLR 591.
27   [2005] 2 FLR 111.

- President's Practice Direction (Applications for Reporting Restriction Orders).[28]

2004

Re Roddy (A child) (Identification: Restriction on Publication)[29]

A4.27 A 12 year old child had a child by a father of similar age, having been given money by the **Roman Catholic Church** to dissuade her from having an abortion. Could the story be told at all, and if yes, with what restraints? Balancing of **Article 8 and 10 rights of the mother** (the mother wanted to tell her story); the Article 10 rights of the press and public interest, against the **Article 10 rights of the child** (since adopted) and the identity of the father.

Pelling v Bruce-Williams (Secretary of State for Constitutional Affairs Intervening)[30]

A4.28 Dame Butler-Sloss P stated that it may be worth giving consideration to increasing the frequency in which **anonymised family court judgments** in general are made public, not just in cases where there are principles of law involved.

Re B (A Child) (disclosure)[31]

A4.29

- Munby J reviewed many of the authorities and **gave a useful summary of the ambit of** s 12 at p 171 of his judgment.

- He held that, **subject to the exception** where here is communication of information by someone to a professional, each acting in furtherance of the protection of children, there is a **'publication' for the purposes of s 12 whenever the law of defamation** would treat such communication as amounting to publication.

- This must now be read in conjunction with CA 1989, s 97(2) which prevents publication at large or to any section of the public.

- In this context, **reference should now be made to the revised FPR 1991 Pt XI which permits parties and other specified people to disclose certain information from family proceedings heard in private involving children,** to other specified people for specific purposes without needing permission of the court and without being in contempt of court.

---

28 [2005] 2 FLR 120.
29 [2003] EWHC 2927 (Fam), [2004] 2 FLR 949.
30 [2004] EWCA Civ 485, [2004] 2 FLR 823.
31 [2004] EWHC 411 (Fam), [2004] 2 FLR 142.

- These rules are not applicable to **disclosure in adoption proceedings** where different rules apply.

2002

Re M (Disclosure: Children and Family Reporter)[32]

A4.30 The word 'publish' in s 97(2) of the CA 1989 should be given its ordinary meaning. It **does not extend** to a situation where a **CAFCASS Officer** communicates **concerns** to the relevant statutory authority charged with collection and investigation of material suggestive of child abuse. Where the CAFCASS officer in the course of his enquiries encounters suspicion of child abuse, he/she has **an unfettered independent discretion** as to whether to make an **immediate report to social services or the police**; he must, however, **inform the judge** of any such steps he has taken at the earliest convenient opportunity.

Clibbery v Allan[33]

A4.31 Ruling permitting publicity in relation to proceedings between a man and woman as to allegations of domestic violence (no children). **The chambers procedure under the 1991 Rules was designed to provide a measure of privacy, although not necessary confidentiality, in family proceedings.** (*Hodgson v Imperial Tobacco Ltd*:[34] Disclosure of what takes place in chambers is not a contempt if any comment made does not substantially prejudice the administration of justice, unless the case falls within s 12 of the AJA 1960.)

2001

Harris v Harris; Attorney-General v Harris[35]

A4.32 The High Court can use its inherent jurisdiction both to relax and increase the restrictions imposed by s 12 of the AJA 1960. However, the court should **only exercise its powers to restrain publicity under the inherent jurisdiction if the automatic restraints under s 12 of the 1960 Act, s 2 Contempt of Court Act 1981 and s 97(2) of the Children Act 1989 were inadequate to protect the child from harm** and if the interests of the child could not be adequately protected under **s 39 of the** CYPA 1933.

B v United Kingdom; P v United Kingdom[36]

A4.33 Hearings confirmed by Europe as being heard in private, inter alia on the basis that copies of the **full text and/or judgments in children cases were**

---

[32] [2002] EWCA Civ 1199, [2002] 2 FLR 893.
[33] [2002] EWCA Civ 45, [2002] 1 FLR 565.
[34] [1998] 1 WLR 1056.
[35] [2001] 2 FLR 895.
[36] [2001] 2 FLR 261.

available to anyone who could establish an interest; and given such a ruling under Art 6; it was not necessary to examine the complaints under Art 10.

Kelly v BBC[37]

A4.34 Assistance of media invoked by the court to find a 16 year old ward who had left home to join a religious group. Court refused to restrain **BBC** from a **telephone interview** with the boy because an interview by the media was not an 'important' or 'major' step in a child's life. **Since the boy's participation in the interview did not raise any question with respect of his upbringing, his welfare was not the paramount consideration.**

1999

Re G (Celebrities: Publicity)[38]

A4.35 The Court of Appeal indicated that it was hard to conceive of circumstances which would justify preventing the media from publishing the bare outcome of a hearing; **the court should issue a terse statement approved by the judge and agreed between the parties.**

1996

PB (Hearings in Open Court)[39]

A4.36 Failed pre-HRA application for a hearing of children case in public.

Re Z (A Minor) (Freedom of Publication)[40]

A4.37 Court ordered mother not to be involved in the making and publication of a film as to her daughter's special educational needs for such film would harm the welfare of the child and the child had the right of confidentiality in respect of her attendance at the unit. **Whilst the mother could waive the right to confidentiality in respect of her treatment, this was an exercise of parental responsibility which could be controlled under the CA by a prohibited steps order.**

---

[37]   [2001] 1 FLR 197.
[38]   [1999] 1 FLR 409.
[39]   [1996] 2 FLR 765.
[40]   [1996] 1 FLR 191.

1994

Mrs R v Central Independent Television Plc[41]

A4.38   Mother of father's child unsuccessfully sought to prevent broadcasting of TV report as to sexual indecency of father, to avoid any possibility of identification of the mother or child. **Since the programme was in no way concerned with the care or upbringing of children, the element of confidentiality belonged not to the child but to the court**; and there was no threat to the exercise of the court's jurisdiction by the proposed broadcast. **The court's jurisdiction can only be invoked where the child concerned is the subject of the proceedings before the court and the court is concerned with the care and upbringing of the child.**

1991

E (A Minor)(Child Abuse: Evidence)[42]

A4.39   Under s 12(1)(a)(i) of the AJA 1960 **the prohibition on publication is not limited in time**, and it thus remains a contempt of court to publish such information even if wardship proceedings are discharged. Presumably the same principle applies to prohibitions in s 12(1)(a)(ii) and (iii).

---

[41]   [1994] 2 FLR 151.
[42]   [1991] 1 FLR 420.

Appendix 5

CASES HAVING A BEARING ON WHAT IS AND IS NOT TO BE REPORTED

(Note that font emphasis is that of the author's)

S (A CHILD ACTING BY THE OFFICIAL SOLICITOR) V ROCHDALE METROPOLITAN BOROUGH COUNCIL AND THE INDEPENDENT REVIEWING OFFICER[1]

Family Division

Munby J

31 December 2008

Headnote

A5.01   The teenage child, who suffered from autism, early attachment disorder and learning difficulties, had had a difficult and damaged childhood. Her mother, who was the only person with parental responsibility, agreed to the child being accommodated by the local authority when the child was 13. Thereafter, the mother played no effective part in parenting the child, being unable to meet any of the child's needs, or to participate in working with the authority. **By the time the child was 15 she was frequently absconding from foster placements, had been involved in inappropriate and exploitative sexual relationships with a number of older men, and had attempted suicide on a number of occasions. Shortly after her 15th birthday, the child gave birth to a daughter. Care proceedings were issued in relation to the daughter**, and the Official Solicitor was appointed to act on behalf of the teenage child, who was not competent to give instructions. **The Official Solicitor took the view that the local authority should have issued care proceedings in respect of the teenage child, who was an extremely vulnerable young person, in respect of whom nobody had been exercising parental responsibility for some time, and who, in his view, was suffering significant harm**. The local authority declined to do so. **The Official Solicitor applied for judicial review of the authority's decision and brought a claim for relief under the Human Rights Act 1998.** Eventually, after the teenage child had been placed in secure accommodation to prevent further absconding, the authority did issue care proceedings, and the judicial review proceedings were withdrawn. **The teenage child, acting by the Official Solicitor, persisted with the human rights claim against the local authority and the independent review officer. Eventually the**

---

[1]   [2008] EWHC 3283 (Fam), [2009] 1 FLR 1090.

court approved a compromise between the parties, which included a confidentiality clause; the court reserved only the issue whether the local authority should be named. **At the hearing the issues that remained were the extent to which the confidentiality clause had been approved, whether the local authority was to be identified publicly, notwithstanding the confidentiality clause, and whether wider issues concerning the duties owed to looked-after children should be dealt with.**

Held

Having made an order in the terms of the compromise, and staying the action:

(1)   By approving the compromise, and making an order to the same effect, the court had satisfied itself both that the **confidentiality clause within it was lawful, and that it was in the child's best interests**. Public policy required that confidentiality negotiated between parties not be breached by the court. In any event having approved the compromise the court could not resile from its own order; a clause approved and made part of an order bound the court as much as it bound the parties (see paras [49], [51]).

(2)   In considering the compromise, the court's duty was to decide whether or not to approve it in the child's best interests. **The local authority's use of the confidentiality clause to immunise itself from public discussion and criticism was not a factor to which the court could properly have regard.** However, **the court should be very slow to approve a confidentiality clause of this kind on behalf of a child**; if it were to approve such a clause **it must be satisfied that what was being gained by the child under the compromise adequately reflected both the value of the claim being compromised, and the value of the human rights being surrendered.**

(3)   In assessing and evaluating those rights, and in striking the final balance, the court must have regard to any expressed wishes and feelings of the child. In this case the child's welfare, now and into adulthood, justified, indeed **demanded, approval of the compromise, including the confidentiality clause, not only because of the considerable value to the child of the arrangements under the compromise, but also because the child was unlikely to express any wish to 'go public'** (see paras [59], [66], [68], [69]).

(4)   However, nothing in the confidentiality clause as agreed prevented public dissemination of the court order, which was a public document, or of the particulars of claim, which had been in the public domain when the order was made. **The local authority was to be named publicly: identifying the authority was not likely to lead to the identification of the child and no good reason had been shown to justify maintaining the authority's anonymity** (see paras [53], [54], [90] and [93]).

NOTE

The court attached for public record concerns expressed by the Official Solicitor (see paras [78], [81], [94]–[101]).

RE N (MCKENZIE FRIEND: RIGHTS OF AUDIENCE)[2]

Family Division

Munby J

20 August 2008

Headnote

A5.02   The mother and father were involved in various lengthy disputes concerning the child. In Children Act 1989, Sch 1 proceedings the mother was at first represented by solicitors and counsel, while the father appeared in person with the assistance of **a McKenzie friend**. On occasion the judge permitted the father's McKenzie friend to address him and to make submissions on technical points of law and procedure. Later, in Children Act 1989, s 8 proceedings, the mother's solicitors came off the record, and she also appeared in person with the assistance of a McKenzie friend. A different judge permitted both McKenzie friends to address her. **However, by the time the s 8 proceedings came before the judge who had dealt with the Sch 1 proceedings, the father had obtained legal representation; his former McKenzie friend was now acting as his solicitors' clerk. The father's counsel objected to the mother's request that her McKenzie friend be allowed to speak on her behalf, examine and cross-examine witnesses and make submissions;** counsel argued that the mother had not made an application for rights of audience at the start of the hearing, and had not given any notice of such an application, and that in any event there were no exceptional circumstances to justify granting rights of audience to the mother's McKenzie friend. The mother, supported by the child's guardian, argued that she had run out of money and could no longer afford the costs of legal representation, that this was an exceptionally emotionally fraught case which she could not present properly without assistance, that the father's use of a McKenzie friend had never been challenged, and that if the mother's McKenzie friend were not able to act for her she would have to request an adjournment to enable her to instruct new solicitors. Ultimately the parties reached agreement in relation to the s 8 proceedings but the McKenzie friend dispute had, in the meantime, been raised in the Sch 1 proceedings. **It was agreed that although argument would be in chambers, to enable the father's solicitor's clerk to address the judge, judgment would be delivered in open court; however, the mother and guardian opposed lifting the reporting restrictions that still applied as a result of a review ordered in the s 8 proceedings.**

---

[2]   [2008] 2 FLR 1899.

Held

Granting the mother's McKenzie friend specific rights of audience:

(1)   A McKenzie friend did not have a right of audience. **The court's discretion to grant a McKenzie friend a right of audience under s 27(2)(c) of the Courts and Legal Services Act 1990 was to be granted 'only ... for good reason' and in the light of and bearing in mind the 'general objective' set out in s 17(1) and the 'general principle' set out in s 17(3).** Moreover, the court should be 'very slow' to grant a McKenzie friend a right of audience (see para [39]).

(2)   However, **that did not mean that, as a general principle, a right of audience could be granted only in 'exceptional circumstances'**; s 27(2)(c) conferred an unfettered discretion. The law was as set out in *Clarkson v Gilbert*[3], CA: all would depend on the circumstances, which might vary widely, and the overriding objective was that the courts should do justice. Also, the court had to bear in mind the reality that legal aid was not available as readily as it had been in the past. **There would be occasions when the grant of rights of audience to a McKenzie friend would be of advantage to the court in ensuring that the litigant in person received a fair hearing, and sometimes the grant of such rights would be essential if justice were to be done and, equally importantly, perceived by the litigant in person as having been done (see paras [38], [40]–[42]).**

(3)   The mother had been able to show good reason why her McKenzie friend should be granted a right of audience; had it been necessary to do so, she could have established exceptional circumstances, in particular the nature of the proceedings, the fact that she had, through no fault of her own, been **lulled into a false assumption that her McKenzie friend would be allowed to address the court,** and the likelihood that otherwise an adjournment, gravely **prejudicial to the child,** would have been necessary (see paras [43], [44]).

(4)   **The court would not exercise its powers under s 97(4) of the Children Act 1989 to lift the statutory anonymity that arose under s 97(2).** The detriment the child would suffer were his anonymity to be removed significantly outweighed any detriment either the father or the world at large would suffer by being denied the right to discuss matters by reference to the names of the parties. **Public discussion of the issues was not going to be significantly inhibited by reason only of the fact that the parties' names would not be in the public domain, in contrast to the names of their lawyers and the name of the McKenzie friend (see paras [55], [56]).** See also President's Guidance: McKenzie Friends, 14 October 2008.

---

[3]   [2000] 2 FLR 839.

Z COUNTY COUNCIL V TS, DES, ES AND A[4]

Family Division

Hedley J

25 July 2008

Headnote

A5.03 A, aged almost 11, **suffered from significant learning difficulties and would be dependent on adult care indefinitely into his majority**. His grandparents were his principal carers, with his mother assuming an increasing role. **Hedley J, who authorised the care proceedings to be heard in public, found the threshold criteria under s 31(2) of the Children Act 1989 established**, and subsequently approved the local authority's care plan for A's ultimate rehabilitation with his mother under a care order. **The public hearing of the care proceedings had been subject to a schedule of anonymisation covering all parties and witnesses**. ITV Wales attended throughout and subsequently made and transmitted a programme in which the requirements of anonymisation were strictly observed. **A further television programme was planned, and ITV Wales applied to have the anonymisation provisions relaxed**. This was **opposed by the grandparents, the guardian, the local authority** and the social worker who had been involved in the case and had been the subject of some criticism in the earlier judgment of Hedley J. **The mother, who wished to use publicity to highlight her complaints about the case, supported relaxation of anonymity**.

Held

Dismissing the application and continuing the anonymisation provisions indefinitely:

(1) **Since** *Clayton v Clayton*,[5] **the automatic restrictions of s 97 of the Children Act 1989 did not apply. The injunction could be continued only if justified on an analysis of the parties' competing rights under Arts 8 and 12 of the European Convention for the Protection of Human Rights and Fundamental Freedoms 1950:** *Re S (Identification: Restrictions on Publication)*.[6]

(2) **In this case, pre-eminence should be given to A's rights under Art 8, reinforced by the demands of his welfare**.

(3) A's welfare required the **continuation of the existing anonymisation** provisions, which were necessary to **preserve his privacy**.

---

4   [2008] EWHC 1773 (Fam), [2008] 2 FLR 1800.
5   [2006] EWCA Civ 878, [2007] 1 FLR 11.
6   [2004] UKHL 47, [2005] 1 FLR 591.

(4)   There were particular factors which rendered his **identification likely** if the **provisions were not continued**:
    (a)   his relatively **unusual** disability,
    (b)   the **lightly populated** rural area in which he lived, which had only two schools, and
    (c)   the risk that **not every organ** of the media would act as **responsibly** as ITV Wales in protecting his identity.

(5)   The **disclosure of the identity** of any person or body which might reasonably lead to the identification of A should be **refused**. This included family members, A's school and its staff, and the social worker and local authority.

MEDWAY COUNCIL V G AND OTHERS[7]

Family Division

Sir Mark Potter, President of The Family Division

18 July 2008

Headnote

A5.04   After the breakup of the parent's marriage the mother had applied for **non-molestation and occupation orders**, alleging domestic violence. During the course of residence proceedings initiated by the mother, **considerable concern had been expressed about emotional harm suffered by the child as a result of the conduct of both parents** over the years. Following a report from a psychologist about the family situation and its impact on the child, the judge found that **threshold criteria had been established for the making of interim care orders**. The child was taken into foster care, with regular contact with both parents. **Under a care order the mother was to have gradually increasing contact with the child, with the ultimate goal of a placement with the mother provided the mother achieved certain objectives.** However, aware that the assessment team had produced an unfavourable assessment, the **mother abducted the child from his foster placement, assisted by the child's stepfather, the mother's current husband**; the couple took the child to France. When the stepfather returned to the jurisdiction he was sentenced to 16 months' imprisonment for his part in the abduction. The 8-year-old child was currently believed to be living abroad with the mother; a search by the French authorities had been unsuccessful, although it was known that the mother had given birth to a second child, the stepfather's baby, in France. **The local authority obtained an injunction prohibiting the publishing or broadcasting of information that might result in the child's identification**. The injunction included a general non-solicitation provision, prohibiting anyone from seeking any information relating to the child or to the parents or to a carer. **The injunction was subject to a provision permitting**

---

[7]   [2008] EWHC 1681 (Fam), [2008] 2 FLR 1687.

publication of information relating to a public court hearing not itself covered by an injunction, plus the usual 'public domain' provision permitting publication of information already in the public domain, with a specific exception for references to the child's placement in foster care. The authority had issued an application for a placement order, but final orders had not yet been made in the care proceedings. **There had been considerable debate in the media as to the length of the stepfather's sentence, and the alleged secrecy of the family justice system.** The newspaper sought permission to interview the stepfather on certain matters, and at a later stage also sought publication of the care proceedings judgments to date, suitably anonymised. In the course of the hearing, the parties reached an agreement: **the local authority produced a summary of the facts in the proceedings in a form that the newspaper considered sufficient and satisfactory, and with which the other parties were content**. The newspaper therefore withdrew its application for publication of the judgments.

Held

Granting the newspaper permission to interview the stepfather concerning the criminal proceedings, and approving an order allowing use of the summary of the facts:

(1) **The newspaper required permission to interview the stepfather concerning the criminal proceedings, proceedings which related to his involvement with and abduction of the child; it was otherwise prohibited from doing so by the general words of the order's non-solicitation provision.**

(2) **There was no valid reason for prohibiting permission to interview the stepfather about his emotional state, his experience in prison or the support he had received from friends and family, as these issues were not covered by the injunction.**

(3) Provided that the newspaper took great care to avoid direct or indirect identification of the child when dealing with the support received from friends and family, **a human interest article dealing with such matters was plainly a permissible journalistic enterprise** (see para [45]).

(4) **The court approved the newspaper's use of the summary of facts, as agreed by the parties. Previous judicial encouragement of the publication of judgments in care cases, subject to anonymisation in the child's interests, had not anticipated publication of judgments before final orders had been made and the welfare interests of the child finally adjudicated.**

(5) Had the parties not reached agreement the rival arguments of both sides in this case, if fully deployed, would have involved a detailed weighing of the various human rights involved. Although the proceedings were not yet concluded, **the level of interest created by the imposition of a prison sentence made a very strong case for the background to be made more widely known, to enable the public to form its own view.**

(6) **Provided the child's anonymity was preserved, comment upon the care proceedings as set out in the agreed summary would not invade the child's Art 8 rights any more than the publicity to date had done.**

(7) The restricted content of the summary meant that the considerable and extensive references to intimate family matters and the child's welfare contained in the previous judgments would be sufficiently protected (see paras [55], [66], [67], [69]).

(8) **Identification of the local authority:**
   (i)   was **not** a matter prohibited by s 12(1)(a) of the Administration of Justice Act 1960,
   (i)   was not likely to lead to the identification of the child,
   (i)   did not represent a significant risk to the child, and
   (i)   would be permitted, not least because identification of the authority during the criminal proceedings meant that the authority's identity was already within the public domain (see paras [62], [63], [68]).

(9) **It was not in principle appropriate to exclude references to the child's foster care placement from the public domain provision unless it was very clear that the welfare interests of the child required such exclusion, and they did not.**

(10) If and insofar as the reference was simply a reference to the child having been in foster care, provided there was no publication of any details concerning the foster parents' identity or location, that was information made public during the criminal proceedings (see paras [65]).

Per curiam

At the stepfather's invitation, the court expressed the view that permitting him to contact the mother, which would currently be a breach of his prison licence conditions, would be a helpful development so far as the family court was concerned, provided such contact was limited to allowing him to communicate with her with a view to securing her return to the jurisdiction (see para [73]).

RE H (CARE PLAN)[8]

Family Division

Macur J

22 February 2008

---

[8]   [2008] EWHC 327 (Fam), [2008] 2 FLR 21.

Headnote

A5.05 In the course of the care proceedings the local authority failed to meet a number of deadlines for provision of a detailed interim care plan, failed to attend scheduled meetings, and provided conflicting information concerning contact. Following the fact-finding hearing the judge made strident findings against the mother, and the unchallenged expert psychological evidence suggested that great caution must be exercised in relation to the mother, who was only in the earliest possible stages of accepting these findings. However, the local authority's 'final' care plan advocated unsupervised contact between the mother and the child. Three social workers were associated with the care plan: the allocated social worker, her team manager and the service manager. **In the course of the welfare hearing it emerged that there had been an intractable dispute between the allocated social worker and the team manager as to whether the mother ought to have unsupervised contact, and that the team manager had substantially altered the care plan so that it advocated unsupervised contact without informing the social worker of the changes made, presenting the care plan as though it represented the social worker's views, while knowing that it did not.** Two versions of the care plan, one advocating supervised and the other unsupervised contact with the mother, had been emailed to the legal department, both signed. **The social worker alleged that she had been threatened with being deprived of a job reference if she persisted in challenging the team manager's preferred care plan. It further emerged that the service manager had not read the fact-finding judgment, or the expert reports, prior to signing off the care plan, or even before coming to court to give evidence.** After being required to read these documents by the judge, the service manager's proposals for contact changed significantly; her position on behalf of the local authority eventually shifted to the mother having only supervised contact for the foreseeable future. The court appointed an independent social worker and relisted the case. **At the resumed hearing the judge indicated an intention to record her findings concerning the stance taken by local authority personnel to the care plan in an addendum judgment; the guardian sought publication of this addendum judgment.**

Held

Permitting publication of a summary (and subsequently wider publication of the addendum):

(1) The court had disregarded the evidence of three social workers because of an inappropriate and uninformed stance taken by the senior social workers to matters concerning contact. **If not for the court process the local authority would have advanced a plan quite inconsistent with the welfare of a vulnerable child.** The social work team had been without coordination, focus or direction. **It seemed that the team manager had formulated a care plan from her own perspective of the case, quite divorced from any other opinion, proceeding on conjecture and personal prejudice against the father rather than on any finding of fact or professional opinion.** The service manager had failed to conduct any independent review of the

situation or to provide close managerial oversight. **The court had no jurisdiction to conduct a public enquiry, but an independent management investigation had reported, and its recommendations had been accepted, leading to a comprehensive overhaul of the local authority's preparation of care plans** (see paras [1]–[3], [5], [9], [10], [23]).

(2) If, as may have been the case, **the local authority's legal department** was aware of the conflict surrounding the issue of contact, and the existence of two different care plans, the department should have sought further and full instructions, **and considered the issue of disclosure to the other parties** (see para [21]).

(3) **Revised guidance** issued to all local authority staff as to the proper procedure to be adopted in the creation of and subsequent approval of care plans included:
   (a) **adequate investigation** by service managers of the background facts to the case, with review of all appropriate documentation;
   (b) the submission of one hard and **complete** copy of the care plan with attached **signatures**; and
   (c) a **closer scrutiny** of the timetable for submission of care plans by the legal department and managers (see para [26]).

(4) **Professional witnesses in family proceedings were not entitled to depend upon the cloak of confidentiality that covered their evidence during the proceedings to continue thereafter without more ado.**

(5) There was a **greater prospect** of publication of a family decision in the public interest now than there used to be.

(6) The remorse reflected by the prompt action of the local authority was to be recognised and applauded and might reflect in the balance of proportionate response, but the effectiveness of the new regime adopted by the local authority called for critical objective review. **There was an obvious public interest in informing 'clients' and other affected parties concerning the shortcomings that the new system was intended to redress.**

(7) **Arguments that publicity would adversely affect the authority's ability to meet its duties towards children and families had not been made out** (see paras [32], [33]).

RE B; X COUNCIL V B (NO 2)[9]

Family Division

Munby J

18 February 2008

---

[9]   [2008] EWHC 270 (Fam), [2008] 1 FLR 1460.

Headnote

A5.06 The original care proceedings, involving three of the family's four children, had **ended without any order being made**. The judgment had been reported, on the basis of strict anonymity, as *X Council v B (Emergency Protection Orders)*.[10] There had never been any injunction. Subsequently, in *Re B; X Council v B*,[11] at the mother's request and after consultation with the local authority, the **judge permitted identification of the authority involved. Shortly afterwards the judge received letters from two of the children, now aged 15 and 10, expressing their desire to speak out about their experiences of the care system**. A little later the judge received emails from the mother, including an email in which she explained that she had prepared an article on the family court system but had been told that it could not be published for legal reasons, even though the professionals involved had not been named. The judge proceeded on the basis that he was being asked for permission to identify the family publicly as the family involved in the original care proceedings.

Held

Ordering that the rubric on the cover sheet of the judgment be amended to allow the mother and two children to waive their anonymity:

(1) **The only relevant statutory restrictions were those imposed by s 12 of the Administration of Justice Act 1960.**

(2) **Section 12 did not prevent publication of the names of the parties, or of the children, nor did it prohibit discussion, within certain bounds, of the nature of the dispute**.

(3) **Section 12 did prevent, unless the judge otherwise directed: the publication of**:
   (a) accounts of what had gone on in front of the judge sitting in private,
   (b) of documents (or extracts or quotations from documents) filed in the proceedings, or
   (c) of transcripts or notes of evidence or submissions, and transcripts or notes of the judgment (see para [10]).

(4) **In this case permission had been given for the judgment to be published, but only in anonymised form and subject to the standard rubric as to anonymity of the family members**.

(5) **There was nothing to prevent the mother or the children** from identifying themselves in public as people who had been involved in the care proceedings brought by the local authority, or, **subject to compliance with s 12, discussing in public the nature of the dispute in the proceedings**.

---

[10]   [2005] 1 FLR 341.
[11]   [2007] EWHC 1622 (Fam), [2008] 1 FLR 482.

(6) **Nor was there anything to prevent them from making any use of the judgment in its anonymised form.**

(7) **However, assuming, without deciding the point, that the standard rubric was binding on anyone who sought to make use of the judgment, they could not link themselves with the anonymised judgment directly, as the mother and children referred to** (see paras [11]–[13]).

(8) **The standard rubric was to be amended to allow the three family members to waive their anonymity, if they wished to do so, given that;**
  (i) there was no ongoing state involvement with the family, and
  (ii) the eldest child, who was almost 16, was of an age at which he was entitled to speak of his own experiences.

(9) **This did not address the wisdom of individuals waiving their anonymity.**

(10) After such a waiver those individuals would be unable to control the media's use of information in the public domain, including all the matters in the original judgment, which contained references to a number of private and personal matters (see paras [14]–[18], [20]).

(11) **The local authority had not been consulted because the application had not concerned the authority.** Two other children had made no application, and were not covered by the order. No professionals were to be named (see para [20]).

RE LM (REPORTING RESTRICTIONS: CORONER'S INQUEST)[12]

Family Division

Sir Mark Potter: The President of The Family Division

16 May 2007

Headnote

A5.07 At the care hearing the cause of death of the child's younger brother was left undecided, but the judge concluded, on the civil standard of proof, that **the mother had caused the later death of the child's older sister through physical ill-treatment. The judge permitted the local authority to disclose various documents from the care proceedings to both the coroner and the police.** The coroner agreed, at the request of the child's guardian, to return the matter to the family court before taking any steps that might lead to the child being publicly identified. **The coroner now wished to resume the inquest, and sought directions as to how to proceed, given that whether or not the child's name was**

---

[12] [2007] EWHC 1902 (Fam), [2008] 1 FLR 1360.

mentioned, that of her dead sister and parents, whose surname was distinctive, would normally be mentioned and publicised, leading to possible identification of the child as a member of the family. The guardian, supported by the local authority and the parents, sought a reporting restriction order to prevent the media from reporting the names and addresses not only of the child, but also of the parents and of the children who had died. The media opposed the reporting restrictions insofar as they related to the parents and the dead children, but not in relation to the child. The child, now 5 years old, was living with foster parents. She was undergoing therapy and exhibited a number of serious problems: as a result of a strangling incident she had to have adult supervision whenever she was with a younger child. She was not yet aware that her sister's death had been attributed to the mother. Adoptive parents were being sought. The child's therapist had initially produced an impeccable report, addressing the issue of the potential effect upon the child of any publicity, but a further updating report, requested by the guardian in a letter of instruction, not seen or agreed by the other parties, addressed some inadmissible issues in response to questions that were tendentious in form.

Held

Permitting the media to report the names and addresses of the parents and of the two children who had died, but placing an embargo on publication of the name and the existence of the child, of her school or foster carers, or publication of her photograph or other information likely to lead to her identification:

(1)   Inquest proceedings were court proceedings subject to the principles of open justice and the remedies contained and limitations implicit in the Children and Young Persons Act 1933, s 39.

(2)   The principles stated in *Re S (Identification: Restrictions on Publication)* did not require modification or qualification in light of the fact that the relevant proceedings would be inquest proceedings as opposed to criminal proceedings: the *Re S* principles were broadly those applicable to all courts of record when an application was made by a party, not involved directly in the proceedings, who sought an order on the basis of an interference with his or her rights under the European Convention for the Protection of Human Rights and Fundamental Freedoms 1950. Although there were obvious differences between proceedings at an inquest and the criminal process, in this case the inquest was into the killing of a child, and of clear public interest and importance (see paras [39], [53], [54]).

(3)   It was clear that were the child's existence to be reported she and her carers would be likely to be the subject of identification within her circle, and also the subject of considerable media attention as the sole surviving child of the family. An order protecting the child's identity was proportionate and necessary to protect her Art 8 Convention rights (see para [56]).

(4)   **Precluding the media from identifying the parents and the children who had
died would be too substantial and undesirable an interference with the Art 10
rights of the media fully to report the proceedings and the circumstances
surrounding the inquest**. In this respect, the child's unhappy position did
not outweigh the rights of a free press and the interests of open justice.
**When a child had suffered from a homicide within the family, there were
inevitable difficulties to be faced in respect of the disturbance to that child's
life. This conclusion might have been different if the court had been satisfied
that publicising the mother's and the deceased sister's identity would operate
as a barrier to the child's future adoption or would result in a long term
stigma**. As it was, the undoubted possibility of additional, but uncertain,
difficulties with the child's therapy did not establish sufficient likelihood of
lasting harm referable to publicity as distinct from the general
circumstances of the case (see paras [55], [64])

(5)   **When experts reported in cases of this kind they should restrict themselves
to questions of fact, diagnosis and opinion, refraining from argument or the
expression of views that appeared to usurp the function of the court**. The
therapist had been asked, and had answered, questions that encroached to
a substantial degree on questions that it was appropriate for the court,
rather than the therapist, to answer (see paras [70], [73]).

RE R (IDENTIFICATION: RESTRICTION ON PUBLICATION)[13]

Family Division

Sumner J

22 November 2007

Headnote

A5.08   The four children, aged **5, 4, 2 and 1 years old**, had been removed from
the parents' care following the admission of the 4-year-old to hospital with
non-accidental injuries. The children went to foster parents and eventually
placement orders were made, as a preliminary to adoption. **The parents
appealed the placement orders, and their consent was dispensed with. During the
course of proceedings, the father breached an injunction, obtained by the local
authority because of his threatening and intimidating behaviour, was found guilty
of contempt and sentenced to a term of imprisonment**. The local authority were
concerned that the parents would seek to establish the whereabouts of the
children, and therefore provided the parents with only limited information
about the prospective adopters. There was evidence that the parents had
attempted to trace the children via the childrens' school, and the foster parents
reported that the father had visited their home and questioned their 17-year-old

---

13   [2007] EWHC 2742 (Fam), [2008] 1 FLR 1252.

son about the childrens' whereabouts. **The authority became aware that the parents were operating two websites containing photographs and the names of the four children, on which the parents stated that the children had been wrongfully removed from them, and warned that no one should attempt to adopt them.** The authority sought an order restricting the publication of the names and addresses of the children, their foster parents, their doctor, the childrens' school, any picture or video recording or any other particulars or information relating to the children, if such publication would lead to the identification of the children or establish that they were in the care of the local authority. Restriction was also sought on anybody seeking to obtain information relating to the children or their carer.

Held

Granting an order restricting publication relating to the children, and also granting a mandatory injunction requiring any persons served with an order to remove information relating to the children from any website under their control:

(1)   The parents did not accept the placement order and would do all within their power to prevent the children being adopted; **they were attempting to trace the children and to discourage anybody who might be minded to adopt them, frustrating the intentions of both the local authority and the court**.

(2)   **Without the prohibitory and mandatory orders there was a risk that the adoption would not go ahead as the parents intended; such orders were a proportionate remedy to the serious threat presented by the parents** (see paras [32], [34], [35]).

(3)   The parents were entitled to express their view that they had been the victims of a miscarriage of justice; they could air their grievances, and could probably identify the local authority. However, they were not entitled to:
(a)   interfere with the court adoption process by deterring prospective adopters, nor
(b)   could they identify evidence given at the hearings, the names of the children, or the doctors who gave evidence (see paras [39], [43], [44]).

RE X CHILDREN[14]

Family Division

Munby J

29 June 2007

---

[14]   [2007] EWHC 1622 (Fam), [2008] 1 FLR 589.

Headnote

A5.09 Care proceedings were commenced in respect of three children; a fourth was born during the course of the proceedings. **The threshold for the proceedings involved serious and very sensitive allegations that had rendered the children more than usually vulnerable.** The mother was also a victim. The children remained with the mother but the placement at home was fragile due to the emotional impact of the factors that led to the care proceedings. **Six months after proceedings were commenced, the father attempted to murder the principal social worker** by means of repeated stabbing, inflicting grave and life threatening injuries. He pleaded guilty to attempted murder. **Following his guilty plea, evidence emerged in the family proceedings indicating that the father had also committed very serious offences against one of the children.** This evidence was likely to lead to further criminal proceedings. Pending the father's sentencing for the attempted murder, **the Crown Prosecution Service (CPS) sought disclosure of papers from the care proceedings which had a bearing on intent and showed inconsistencies in his account within the criminal proceedings for attempted murder. The papers included letters written to the mother and children from prison.** The mother and guardian for the children supported the CPS application on the basis that the public interest in prosecuting serious criminal offences outweighed their privacy. **The defendant father, who was separately represented in the family and criminal proceedings, opposed disclosure on the grounds of privacy and the confidentiality of the care proceedings. The local authority also applied for an injunction to restrain publication of details that might identify the children and mother. The Press Association intervened to oppose this application.**

Held

Ordering disclosure of limited papers to the CPS for the criminal proceedings and making an injunction to restrain publication of identifying details:

(1) The factors to be considered when considering whether to order disclosure included:
    (a) The interests of the children in care proceedings and of other children, **although their welfare was not paramount.**
    (b) **There was also the need to maintain confidentiality and encourage frankness.**

(2) These factors were set against:
    (a) the public interest in the administration of justice and prosecution of serious crime,
    (b) the gravity of the offence and relevance of the evidence sought to be disclosed,
    (c) the co-operation of agencies working with children,
    (d) fairness concerning incriminating questions and fair trial of the defendant and any disclosure that had already taken place (see paras [24], [27] and [28]).

(3)   Sometimes it might be appropriate, indeed essential, to impose more or less stringent limitations or conditions on the use of documents. It might be appropriate for the family court to retain control over further dissemination of documents or disclose only parts of documents or disclose in an edited or redacted form. **In this case a cautious approach was required.** Once the CPS had the opportunity to examine the initial batch of documents, they might wish to seek disclosure of those parts which were edited or redacted. **It was clear that this was a case where the sensitivities and needs of the children were such that the family court must keep tight control over what use might hereafter be made of the documents to be disclosed.** Making an order containing conditions did not indicate a lack of confidence in those concerned in the criminal proceedings. But **those involved in the criminal proceedings saw things from that perspective. Not being immersed in the family proceedings they might not appreciate the implications for the children and the mother of the deployment in that context of some seemingly innocuous piece of information.**

(4)   **Against that, the family court's understanding of the criminal proceedings was necessarily far from complete, which was why the CPS and defendant should be free to return to the family court** for the purpose of obtaining further disclosure or relaxation of the conditions attached to the order (see paras [39], [41] and [42]).

(5)   **Notwithstanding that letters the defendant wrote to the mother and children from prison were especially private and sensitive, they should be disclosed as they were relevant and disclosure was not opposed by the mother and children** (see para [45]).

(6)   **Section 98(2) of the Children Act 1989 (the 1989 Act)** did not prevent the disclosure of certain items, even if they did contain any 'statement or admission' within the meaning of the section. **The protection was only against use of such statement 'in evidence' not to protect against use in a police inquiry.** In addition, **the limitations and conditions on the order for disclosure meant the documents could not be used in open court without prior sanction of the family court** (see paras [48], [49]).

(7)   **Putting inconsistent statements to a witness to challenge his evidence or credibility did not amount to using statements against him within the meaning of s 98(2) of the 1989 Act.** It was for the judge who was conducting the criminal proceedings to decide whether and to what extent s 98(2) applied in a particular situation. **There was therefore nothing in s 98(2) to prevent the ordering of the disclosure which would otherwise be appropriate** (see paras [50], [51], [52]).

(8)   **Because the children concerned were unusually and exceptionally vulnerable it was clear that they needed to have protected and kept confidential their identities, their connection with the defendant and his crimes and the fact that they have been involved in care proceedings** (see para [56]).

(9) **Furthermore although the media were free to report the criminal proceedings without being subjected to reporting restrictions imposed by the family court, this was subject to the proviso, namely, that the defendant's address, which is where the children were still living, should not be revealed** (see paras [69–73]).

RE B; X COUNCIL V B[15]

Family Division

Munby J

6 July 2007

Headnote

A5.10 In 2004, judgment was given in *X Council v B (Emergency Protection Orders)*[16], upon an application by the local authority to withdraw applications for interim care orders, without findings being made in respect of the original threshold criteria, so as to avoid the risk of alienating the parents who were by this stage working co-operatively with the local authority. Proceedings had begun by means of an application for an ex parte emergency protection order. **In that judgment, the local authority was criticised for its approach in seeking an emergency protection order and guidance was given as to the appropriate circumstances and considerations for issuing proceedings for ex parte emergency orders.** Three years later, Mrs B wrote to the judge asking for permission to make known the name of the local authority in the case, arguing that the guidance in the judgment had helped other families but did not help hers. **She wanted the opportunity to 'name and shame' the council in question by identifying the local authority criticised.** The contents of the letter were conveyed to the local authority, who, having taken advice from junior counsel involved in the original proceedings, wrote back to the judge. The local authority's reply conceded that as the council could be identified by means of the location of the solicitors' firms involved in the proceedings, they had no basis on which to resist the lifting of their anonymity and expressed commitment to transparency and openness. However, **they did express concerns about the risks of the children's privacy and welfare being jeopardised by any future publicity.** Concerns were also aired about the fact that findings were never made and that should the case become public the facts of the case and the local authority's conduct might be misrepresented. **It was also suggested that the views of other parties, particularly on behalf of the children, might be sought.**

---

15   [2007] EWHC 1622 (Fam), [2008] 1 FLR 482.
16   [2004] EWHC 2015 (Fam).

Held

Mrs B's letter should be treated as an application, the matter dealt with on paper and that the local authority's anonymity should be lifted:

(1) The **only matter raised** was the question of whether the local authority's name should continue to be anonymised. No ruling was made or view expressed on any other matter in the case.

(2) **Having reviewed recent authority and observed that local authorities were increasingly being identified, the approach adopted was whether there was some proper basis for continuing the local authority's anonymity** (see paras [10], [13], [14], [15]).

(3) **The local authority accepted that whatever anonymity it enjoyed was precarious, given the identification of the solicitors. There was no need to preserve the local authority's anonymity in order to protect the children's privacy** (see para [16]).

(4) If anonymity was lifted, the local authority might be exposed to ill-informed criticism, based on misunderstanding or misrepresentation of the facts. But, if criticism exceeded what is lawful, there were other remedies available. **The fear of criticism, however justified the fear or unjustified the criticism, was not of itself a justification for affording a local authority anonymity** (see para [18]).

(5) **Freedom of expression was instrumentally important inasmuch as it facilitates the exposure of errors in governance and administration of justice. Such errors could not be exposed or public authorities held accountable, if allowed to shelter behind a judicially sanctioned anonymity.** The balance came down clearly in favour of the local authority being identified (see paras [19], [20]).

(6) It was further observed that if local authorities which merit criticism are to be named, so too should those which deserve praise. **If the public interest is a reason for naming the incompetent, then the same public interest required the naming of the competent.** Otherwise the public may have a seriously distorted impression of the family justice system – and that was certainly not in the public interest (see para [23]).

Per curiam

Underlying the application was an important issue as to the effect of the rubric preserving anonymity where there was no injunction in place. The issue was not considered but the assumption was made that the rubric was binding on anyone seeking to make use of a judgment to which it is attached (see para [12]).

RE F (CHILDREN) (DNA EVIDENCE)[17]

Family Division

Anthony Hayden QC, sitting as a deputy High Court judge

16 October 2007

Headnote

A5.11 In care proceedings concerning eight children, it became necessary to clarify whether and to what extent each of the children was related to one another and who the respective parents might be. The judge ordered DNA testing. The solicitor for the children identified a company called DNA Diagnostics to undertake the work. The results provided were difficult to interpret, and a further order was made, clarifying the need for cross-referencing the children's results with the adult parties and any putative fathers. **Some of the results obtained were challenged by the adult parties, and on enquiry it emerged that DNA Diagnostics were unable to link donor and sample satisfactorily.** Without reference to the court, the company attempted to re-test, unsuccessfully sending an employee to the children's foster home. Counsel informed the court that this was not the first case in which DNA Diagnostics had been unable to link donor and sample. **A full audit of the company's cases revealed that 122 cases were affected by loss of data.** It further emerged that DNA Diagnostics was not an accredited company, indeed had not applied for accreditation. Another, accredited, company was therefore instructed; the second report revealed a 'likelihood ratio' that the parents of two of the children themselves shared a biological parent, said to be 'good evidence that two of the children were the product of an incestuous relationship'. A third company was instructed; its tests indicated that there was no likely relationship between the two adults concerned. The second company, asked to explain the discrepancy, confirmed that, faced with more specific questions, their results were entirely consistent with those reached by the third company.

Held

Issuing guidelines and accepting undertakings from DNA Diagnostics:

(1) Any order for DNA testing made by the family courts should be made, and specify that it was being made, pursuant to the Family Law Reform Act 1969 (the 1969 Act); it could not be made under s 38(6) of the Children Act 1989 or under the inherent jurisdiction.

(2) The order should either identify the company undertaking the testing, or direct that the company be selected in accordance with the 1969 Act. The

---

[17] [2007] EWHC 3235 (Fam), [2008] 1 FLR 348.

practice of drafting a direction in general terms had led to practitioners failing to appreciate the requirement to select companies on the Ministry of Justice's list.

(3)   While reports obtained from unaccredited companies by parties themselves prior to commencement of proceedings could be admitted, at the court's discretion, when the court made an order for DNA testing, only DNA experts on the accredited list could be instructed (see paras [19]–[22], [32]).

(4)   Taking samples from children should only be undertaken pursuant to the express order of the court; further samples might be taken only with court approval, following a written application to the judge. These requirements should be communicated to the identified DNA company in the letter of instruction (see para [32]).

(5)   Save in cases where the issue was solely confined to paternity testing, all requests for DNA testing should be by letter of instruction, which should:
   (a)   **emphasise that the responsibilities of DNA experts were identical to those of any expert reporting in a family case and that their overriding obligation was to the court;**
   (b)   **emphasise that if any test carried out in pursuance of their instructions cast any doubt on, or appeared relevant to the hypothesis set by their instructions, they should regard themselves as being under a duty to draw that to the attention of the court and the parties;**
   (c)   **set out in clear terms precisely what relationships were to be analysed and, where available, the belief of the parties as to the extent of their relatedness; and (d) make it clear that if the DNA experts considered there was any lack of clarity, or any ambiguity in their written instructions, or if they required further guidance, the DNA experts should revert to the solicitor instructing them, who should keep a note or memo of any such request. If an ambivalent question was asked of an expert in his written instructions, it was not remedied by an ambivalent answer within the body of the report; it was far better addressed by an insistence on a more focused question** (see paras [31], [32], [42]).

(6)   DNA experts preparing reports for court should bear in mind that they were addressing lay people; such reports should strive to interpret their analysis in clear language. Care should be taken to explain results within the context of identified conclusions, and particular care should be taken in the use of phrases such as 'this result provides good evidence'; such expressions should always be set within the parameters of current DNA knowledge and identify in plain terms the limitations as to the reliability of any test carried out. A 'likelihood ratio' by definition was a concept that had uncertainty inherent within it; the extent of the uncertainty would vary from test to test and the author of the report must identify and explain those parameters. Where any particular test and subsequent

ratio of likelihood was regarded as in any way controversial within the mainstream of DNA expertise, the use of the test and the reasons for its use should be signalled to the court within the report (see para [32]).

(7) The duty of the expert to draw to the court's attention anything he considered to be of relevance to the court, irrespective of the framework of his instructions, was, or ought to be, engraved in the practice of all who worked in the family justice system. Particularly in the area of medical science, experts had a heavy burden placed on them to identify issues that might not have been picked up by others, and to hone, refine or even re-frame the questions asked (see para [30]).

(8) **DNA Diagnostics was to be named, notwithstanding the norm of anonymity in care proceedings, because those potentially affected by the breakdown in the administrative systems of the company had a clear right to know both what had occurred and to take such steps as they considered right to reassure themselves. Their rights under Art 8 of the European Convention for the Protection of Human Rights and Fundamental Freedoms 1950 overwhelmed the Art 8 rights of the company director** (see para [41]).

BRITISH BROADCASTING CORPORATION V CAFCASS LEGAL AND OTHERS[18]

Family Division

Munby J

30 March 2007

Headnote

A5.12 Parents who had successfully resisted care proceedings begun by a local authority wished to tell their story to the BBC with a view to the BBC broadcasting a documentary about the case. The parents had recorded a video diary of their experiences using equipment and tapes supplied by the BBC. **The mother applied for an order that the judge's judgment be reported. The local Chief Constable applied for an order ensuring anonymity for a police officer referred to in that judgment.** The **BBC applied for an order that the mother and father be permitted to disclose the video footage to the BBC** and that the judgment be made publicly available. At the same time **the BBC was prepared to give an assurance that it would not disclose into the public domain or to third parties outside the BBC any of the video footage if and insofar as such disclosure would constitute a breach of s 12 of the Administration of Justice Act 1960.** The local NHS Foundation Trust **(the Trust) applied for an order that the names of the doctors employed by the Trust involved in the case should not be made public.** It emerged that no one was seeking to argue against either the publication of the

---

18 [2007] EWHC 616 (Fam), [2007] 2 FLR 765.

judgment or the disclosure to the BBC of the video footage. **The key issue was that various participants in the case wished to preserve their anonymity**. In light of this, the BBC further offered to give 14 days' notice in writing to all relevant individuals of any intention to take any steps which might lead to their public identification.

Held

(1) **There was no reason why the judgment should not be published in anonymised form. There was a general interest in the publication of judgments in care proceedings. The parents sought publication and no one opposed it. The balance of interests under the European Convention for the Protection of Human Rights and Fundamental Freedoms 1950 came down heavily in favour of publication of the judgment** (see paras [17]–[19]).

(2) The balance of interests also fell in favour of allowing, subject to the question of anonymisation, **the limited disclosure of the video footage sought by the BBC** (see paras [23]–[24]).

(3) **The safeguards to anonymity offered by the BBC were inadequate. Adequate protection of the anonymity of the individuals involved could only be achieved via a contra mundum injunction. Such an order should last only for so long as was necessary to achieve the purpose for which it was made. In this case the order should remain in effect until 28 days after the BBC had given written notice either of the first broadcast of a television programme based on the video footage or that it did not intend to proceed with the production of such a programme** (see paras [52]–[54] and [57]–[58] and [62]).

(4) **As a matter of principle anyone affected by a contra mundum injunction must be permitted to apply to the court to vary of discharge the order on short notice.** However, it would not be unreasonable in this case to require the BBC to give 28 days' notice of any intended publication or broadcast (see paras [65]–[67]).

Per curiam

The only principled approach to the question of whether a judgment delivered in chambers was to be released (either in anonymised or in non-anonymised form) was as follows:

- **First**: Everyone referred to in the judgment should be given an opportunity of considering, before the judgment was released, even in anonymised form, whether or not to apply for an order protecting their anonymity;

- **Second**: Anyone wishing to make such an application should make it in compliance with the requirements of s 12 of the Human Rights Act 1998 and the 2005 President's Practice Direction and the Practice Note; and

- **Third**: The court should not release the judgment (even in anonymised form) until after it has adjudicated on any application for anonymity (see para [44]).

RE R (SECURE EDITING OF DOCUMENTS)[19]

Family Division

Peter Jackson QC sitting as a deputy High Court judge

14 April 2007

Headnote

A5.13 The father of three young children had spent periods in psychiatric hospitals and prison. He was registered at Level 3 under the Multi-Agency Public Protection Arrangements (MAPPA) introduced by the Criminal Justice and Court Service Act 2000. **Level 3 registration was the highest and reserved for the critical few. Following separation, the mother and children moved to a refuge and subsequently to a supposedly secret addresses**. The father discovered the mother's whereabouts and made contact. She left the area and remarried. The father applied for contact. **An order was made permitting omission of the mother's address and contact details from any evidence and documents filed and served in the course of the proceedings**. The same order provided for a large volume of documentation held by the police and by medical and social services to be sent to the guardian's solicitors and distributed by them to the parties. **Due to inadequate editing of the documents by the various solicitors involved, the father discovered the mother's new name and he contacted her**.

Held

(1) **The careless distribution of documents gathered for the purposes of litigation amounted to a gross breach of the mother's right to respect for her private and family life. In order to avoid repetition of instances of this kind, the judge brought the matter to the attention of the President of the Family Division who approved the following guidelines** (see para [19]):
   (i) The court should identify a case falling into this category **and make a clear statement that special restrictions will apply**.
   (ii) A direction should be given that information **of a clearly specified kind shall not be contained in any document filed, gathered or circulated** in the proceedings. It was insufficient to allow the information to be withheld.

---

[19] [2007] 2 FLR 759.

(iii) In considering whether to order documentary disclosure, the court should bear in mind the risk **that confidential information may inadvertently be compromised, and avoid making unnecessarily wide orders. It is notoriously burdensome to edit large amounts of documentation accurately and mistakes are easily made**.

(iv) **The chain of possession should be spelled out**. The documents should in the first instance be gathered by one appropriately selected party and **only released once they have been carefully checked**.

(v) **Responsibility for the process should be given to one or more named individuals**. The **guardian's solicitor** may be the obvious candidate. **The solicitor for the party wishing to withhold** the information might well be given the opportunity to check the edited documents before they go to the party from whom the information is to be withheld. **A timetable can be imposed to avoid delay**.

(vi) There **should always be a second editor where there is a significant volume of materials to be edited**, or where the potential consequences of inadvertent disclosure are serious.

(vii) The editing/checking process should be carried out by someone who **knows the details of the case and the importance of the task. It is not an administrative task that can be delegated**. Where appropriate the persons carrying out the task should be identified by name (AB) rather than by title (the mother's solicitor).

(vii) **The editor(s) should know exactly what they are trying to protect**. It is obviously not sufficient to say 'the mother's name and address' if the editor does not know what they are.

(ix) The procedure should be **tailored to the circumstances** of the case.

RE K (ADOPTION: PERMISSION TO ADVERTISE)[20]

Family Division

McFarlane J

18 January 2007

Headnote

A5.14 The child's mother was addicted to **drugs**, and the **child was born with severe withdrawal symptoms**. Following his discharge from hospital the child was placed in **foster care**. At an interim hearing during the care proceedings, the **local authority applied for permission to advertise the child for adoption,** on the basis that the local authority's care plan was for adoption, and that the advertisement would be placed if:

(i) the permanency panel recommended that adoption was in the child's best interests; and

---

[20] [2007] EWHC 544 Fam, [2007] 2 FLR 326.

(ii)   a decision endorsing adoption followed.

The proposed advert was to contain a **photograph of the child,** together with his first name and other information that might identify him. The mother and grandmother opposed the application on the basis that it was premature. The child's guardian, who favoured a twin-track approach with the preliminary steps for both rehabilitation and adoption being progressed alongside each other, considered that any advert should be anonymous and without a photograph. The justices gave permission for an anonymised adoption advertisement. The local authority appealed the order on the basis that it was 'plainly wrong' to permit only **anonymous advertising.**

Held

Dismissing the local authority's appeal and setting aside the order below:

(1)   Within the context of the legislation, there **was no strict requirement upon a local authority with parental responsibility to apply to the court for permission to advertise**; advertising was simply a step that a local authority was entitled to take in the exercise of its parental responsibility. **The prohibition upon adoption advertising contained in s 123 of the Adoption and Children Act 2002 (the 2002 Act), did not apply to adoption agencies,** therefore its terms were not relevant to a proposal for advertising made by a local authority adoption agency. The effect of s 97(2) of the Children Act 1989 (the 1989 Act) was to prevent a child being identified in an adoption advertisement while proceedings were pending under the 1989 Act or under the 2002 Act, unless the court had dispensed with the requirements of s 97(2) by making an order which permitted such advertising to take place (at least where the advert contained reference to the fact that the child was subject to pending proceedings) (see paras [9], [10], [11]).

(2)   Any application for permission to advertise a child was, therefore, generated not by a provision within the statutory framework for child care law, but by the current adoption practice of the specialist adoption publications. Good professional practice required some authority, based either on parental consent or a court endorsement, for the presentation of a particular child as being available for adoption. **Where a child was subject to an interim care order and the local authority social workers wished to progress towards advertising for adoption, in the absence of parental consent, the agreement of the court to such advertising was likely to be required before any specialist adoption publication would accept the child's referral** (see paras [21], [22]).

(3)   As a matter of principle, it was not open to a local authority to advertise a child as 'available for adoption', or to seek permission to do so, until the authority had reached the stage of being 'satisfied that the child ought to be placed for adoption', which involved not only an adoption

recommendation by the panel, but also a decision favouring adoption by the appropriate officer taking into account that recommendation. **A court faced with a premature application made prior to the decision should refuse permission to advertise**. The court formulated guidelines as to the circumstances in which a court, prior to a final hearing in care proceedings, may give permission to advertise a child as available for adoption (see paras [34], [35], [36](i)–[36](ii), [37(i)]).

(3) At the time of the oral hearing, this case had not been to the adoption panel and there had consequently been no decision by an approved officer on the question of adoption for the child. **The local authority had not, therefore, been in a position to have been satisfied that the child ought to have been placed for adoption. The application for permission to advertise his availability for adoption had, therefore, been premature and should have been dismissed** (see para [46]).

RE WEBSTER; NORFOLK COUNTY COUNCIL V WEBSTER & ORS[21]

Family Division

Munby J

1 November 2006

Headnote

A5.15 The couple's three children had been taken into care and adopted, on the basis of, inter alia, allegations of **physical abuse** which the parents continued to **deny**. When the mother became **pregnant** with the **fourth child**, the parents moved to Ireland in an effort to **evade** further care proceedings, and publicised their story, arousing considerable media interest. **On the parents' return**, the local authority instituted care proceedings in respect of the fourth child. Severe reporting restrictions had been imposed. The **media** and the **parents** sought to lift many of those restrictions in respect of the fourth child, and also sought permission for the media to attend and to report on the care proceedings.

Held

Allowing the media access to the care hearing and lifting certain restrictions:

(1) **Section 97(4) of the Children Act 1989** had to be read as permitting the court to dispense with the prohibition on publication in s 97(2) if rights under the European Convention for the Protection of Human Rights and Fundamental Freedoms 1950 (the Convention) required such dispensation.

---

[21] [2006] EWHC 2733 (Fam), [2007] 1 FLR 1146.

(2)   In other words, the statutory phrase '**if ... the welfare of the child requires it**' should be read as a non-exhaustive expression of the terms on which the discretion could be exercised, so that the power was exercisable not merely if the welfare of the child required it but wherever it was required to give effect, as required by the Convention, to the rights of others (see paras [58], [62]).

(3)   **Rule 4.16(7) of the Family Proceedings Rules 1991, which provided that care proceedings, inter alia, be heard in chambers, also had to be read, construed and applied compatibly with the Convention.**

(4)   Once an issue had been raised as to whether a chambers hearing would be Convention compliant in a particular case, the judge had to balance all the various interests engaged, **not giving any special pre-eminence to the claim to privacy** (see paras [65], [77]).

(5)   **Having weighed the competing interests of open justice and confidentiality in children proceedings**, the court considered that not only the additional restrictions imposed in the case, but also the standard restrictions, constituted a disproportionate interference with the **rights of the parents and of the media**. Four factors in particular were significant:
(a)   the claim that the case involved a **miscarriage of justice**;
(b)   the **parents' own wish** for publicity;
(c)   the **very extensive publicity** there had already been; and
(d)   the need for the full facts and the **'truth'** to emerge in a way which would command public confidence.

(6)   The workings of the family justice system, and the views about the system of the mothers and fathers caught up in it, were **'matters of public interest which can and should be discussed publicly'**.

(7)   There was a pressing need for public confidence in the family justice system to be restored in relation to the present case, either by a public and convincing demonstration that there had been no miscarriage of justice, or by acknowledgment that there had been. **There had in any event been no justification for the prohibition on publishing anything at all about the case, which did not permit even that degree of discussion normally allowed by s 12 of the Administration of Justice Act 1960** (see paras [98], [99], [100], [104]).

(8)   **It was not clear what additional risks the child was likely to run if exposed to further publicity, given that the child's first name and his photograph were already in the public domain, and that many were already aware of the true identity of the parents.**

(9)   There was **no disproportionate interference** with the child's rights in permitting him and his parents to be identified by their real surname, **whilst any greater degree of restraint would involve a disproportionate interference** with the rights of the parents (see paras [113], [114]).

(10) It was not enough in the current case that there should be publication of the judgments, whether or not supplemented by judicially authorised press releases. **The rule of confidentiality facilitated the dissemination of false and tendentious accounts of proceedings in family courts**, which further undermined public confidence in the system.

(11) The media would be permitted access to the hearing; all the media would be given the same rights of access, not just those who had addressed the court on this issue.

(12) Although the general public would not be permitted, the hearing would not be 'in private' within the meaning of s 12 of the Administration of Justice Act 1960 because of the presence of the media, **however, s 12 would continue to apply to the care proceedings save in relation to any particular hearing which had been opened to the media**.

(13) **In principle, s 12 would apply to everything in the court bundle prepared for a particular hearing save insofar as either**:
   (a) particular parts of documents in the bundle had actually been read out or summarised during the course of the hearing (in which case, absent the imposition of further restrictions, the media would be able to report what had actually been said during the hearing); or
   (b) the judge authorised further disclosure.

(14) The trial judge would retain the ultimate right to control access by the media to any hearing and **it might be that there would be some particular part of the hearing during which it would be right to exclude them, perhaps, for example, while a particular witness was giving evidence**.

(15) There might also be questions which could only be resolved at the hearing as to whether some category of witnesses, or a particular witness, should be entitled to anonymity (see paras [105], [111], [119]–[121]).

Per curiam

Different issues might have arisen had it been suggested that the general public, not merely the media, should have had access to the care hearing (see para [124]).

And note the following dicta of Munby J in the follow-on hearing on 17 November 2006 reported at [2007] 2 FLR 415:

'[41] It will be seen that para 1(a) of my order permits the disclosure to the public of **Ms Langdale's position statement**. That order was required, if her position statement was to be made available to the media and to the public, because it was clearly a document to which the provisions of s 12 of the Administration of Justice Act 1960 applied and because, **although it had been extensively referred to during the course of the hearing, it had not been read**

out in full: see para [121] of *Re Webster*[22]. It was appropriate for me to make the order because it was **essential for me to do so if the media, and through the media the general public, were to understand what had gone on during the hearing on 3 November 2006**, and, in particular, to understand the basis upon which NCC was putting forward the interim care plan, which in the event I endorsed.'

LEEDS COUNTY COUNCIL & ORS V CHANNEL 4 TELEVISION CORPORATION[23]

Family Division

Munby J

6 July 2005

Headnote

A5.16 Channel 4 produced a **documentary about state schools** that included film shot **surreptitiously** in four schools, two in Leeds and two in the London Borough of Islington. The filming had been undertaken by a young female teacher who had obtained supply teaching jobs in those schools. One of the schools had been chosen to show how behaviour problems could be managed and prevented, but the footage from the other three schools showed **children who were very seriously out of control**, together with members of **staff** who appeared to be *utterly demoralized.* In addition, the covert filming seemed to show the senior staff of one of the schools **deliberately misrepresenting** the reality of life in the school to **OFSTED** inspectors. Channel 4 had alerted the two local authorities to the existence of the films, and in response to concerns expressed by Leeds Local Authority that children in its care might be identified, exposing some of them to risk, the **heads of all the children shown in the film had been obscured** to try to prevent identification of individual children. Notwithstanding this arrangement, two of the children who appeared in the film, appearing by their parents as litigation friends, **sought to injunct Channel 4 from broadcasting the film,** which was scheduled to go out on the following day. The children argued that the surreptitious filming was in breach of obligations of confidence enforceable at common law or equity and in breach of the Art 8 of the European Convention for the Protection of Human Rights and Fundamental Freedoms 1950 (the European Convention) right of privacy. The schools themselves were identified, as were year groups, and some children would be identifiable within the immediate locality. Channel 4 relied upon the right to freedom of speech under Art 10. Due to the urgency of the application there was no written evidence of any sort.

---

[22]   [2006] EWHC 2733 (Fam), [2007] 1 FLR 1146.
[23]   [2007] 1 FLR 678.

HELD

Refusing to grant the injunction:

(1) The **inherent jurisdiction survived** as a means of founding jurisdiction in those cases in which the jurisdiction would have existed before the decision in *Re S (Identification: Restrictions on Publication)* [2004] UKHL 47 (see para [16]).

(2) On the basis that the court was prepared to make every assumption in favour of the two applicants, there was **no benefit to be gained from granting a short-lived injunction** for the purpose of enabling further evidence to be gathered (see para [28]).

(3) **It was highly arguable that the relationship of parent or pupil and school in principle not merely engaged Art 8, but also gave rise to enforceable duties of confidentiality, based on both parents' and pupils' reasonable expectation of privacy in relation to the ordinary school day.** These children, although heavily obscured, were nonetheless highly likely to be identified by those who knew them. **There was on the face of it a compelling case to be made that there was, absent lawful justification, a breach of privacy and a breach of the duty of confidentiality** (see paras [18], [39]).

(4) A balancing exercise between the competing human rights had to be undertaken. The **Art 8 rights of the two applicant children were engaged**, as were the Art 10 rights of the broadcaster. **In addition the Art 8 rights of the other children, for example those whose education was being frustrated by the behaviour being displayed on film**, and the **Art 10 rights of other parents, and of the public in general**, to know what was going on in schools, had to be taken into consideration (see para [20]).

(5) **The balance came down heavily in favour of the broadcasters**. The particular problem which was being aired was one of very great public interest and concern, **capable of being brought to public attention only if surreptitious methods were used**. The film concerned what were alleged to be **very serious shortcomings in the state school sector**, amounting to 'incompetence that affects the public' within the **OFCOM Broadcasting Code** and the surreptitious filming had not gone beyond what was legitimate and permitted by the Code (see paras [22], [34], [35], [38], [39]–[41]).

(6) Although removal from the film of the two children who had brought the action would have only marginal impact upon the message and content of the film as a whole, **excluding footage of these two children alone was not appropriate**. There were no particular circumstances to justify protection of these two children, as opposed to the other children portrayed. **If removal of the two children who had brought proceedings were justified, removal of all the children would be justified**. Success for these two children

would almost inevitably lead to the grant of further injunctions, and might well lead to increasing numbers of children being excluded from the film, thereby emasculating it (see paras [45], [46] and [48]).

BRITISH BROADCASTING COMPANY V ROCHDALE METROPOLITAN BOROUGH COUNCIL & X & Y[24]

Family Division

Ryder J

24 November 2005

Headnote

A5.17 In *Rochdale Borough Council v A and Others*, **allegations of ritual and satanic abuse of 20 children were found not to have been made out**. The judge found that mistakes had been made and voiced criticism of the social workers involved. Judgment was delivered in open court. Injunctions were made to protect the identities of the children and of two social workers, X and Y. **The identities of X and Y were protected in order to protect the identities of the children**. In 2005, the BBC planned to produce a documentary on the case, and applied for orders, inter alia, permitting disclosure to the general public of the identities of X and Y, by broadcasting their names and video footage of their images. **By this time, the former wards were no longer minors and, as adults, wished to be identified and to relate their experiences to the public**. The local authority and X and Y cross-applied for injunctions to restrain the BBC from the proposed publication. **Following agreement between the parties as to certain disclosure and the court's approval thereof in response to the BBC's application, the only issue remaining was whether the identities of X and Y should remain unknown and barred from publication**.

Held

Dismissing the cross-applications of the local authority and X and Y:

(1)   **There was a legitimate public interest in the subject matter of the case, namely the workings of the family justice system.**

(2)   Equally, there was a public interest in encouraging the frankness which was essential in cases involving the welfare of children and in encouraging social workers to engage in difficult child protection work (see para [38]).

(3)   **Since the enactment of the Human Rights Act 1998, the proper approach to applications concerning media reports in relation to children was for the court to identify the various rights engaged and then to conduct the**

---

[24]   [2005] EWHC 2862 (Fam), [2007] 1 FLR 101.

necessary balancing exercise between competing rights, considering the proportionality of the potential interference with each right independently (see para [40]).

(a) The **interaction between Art 8 and Art 10** of the European Convention for the Protection of Human Rights and Fundamental Freedoms 1950 (the Convention) was **at the heart of the issue** in these proceedings. Neither Article had precedence over the other (see para [42]).

(b) The Art 8 Convention rights of the former wards were engaged. **An individual's right to communicate his or her story to fellow beings was protected not merely by Art 10, but also by Art 8** (see para [16]).

(c) **The Art 8 Convention rights of X and Y were engaged**. Article 8 protection extended to a person's name, identity and business or professional relationships. **In this case, X and Y sought to protect the integrity of their professional and family lives** (see para [47]).

(d) **The Art 10 Convention rights of the BBC were engaged. The exceptions to the right of freedom of expression had to be narrowly interpreted, and the necessity for any restriction convincingly established.**

(e) **The need for the court to be convinced of a pressing social need for restrictions on freedom of expression was given statutory effect** by s 12(3) and (4) of the Human Rights Act 1998 (see para [51]).

(f) **Article 6 of the Convention was intended, inter alia, to promote public confidence in the judicial process**. An important means by which such confidence was achieved and maintained was **permitting proper scrutiny of court proceedings** (see para [60]).

(4) **There was no longer any interest of any child in retaining the anonymity of X and Y**. The justification for the original anonymity no longer existed. **The evidence in support of the applications of the local authority and X and Y did not convincingly establish a pressing social need for the restraint sought.** Such restraint would be a **disproportionate interference** with the Art 10 Convention right. The evidence **did not establish an exceptional case for an interference with Art 10.**

(5) **Publication of the identities of X and Y would be an interference with their Art 8 rights, but one which was proportionate and in pursuit of a legitimate aim, namely informed and open discussion in the media of the public interest issues relating to the proceedings and family proceedings generally.** The Art 10 rights of the BBC, and the public interest, reinforced by Art 6, in enabling public scrutiny of court proceedings and family justice **should on the facts of this case prevail over the Art 8 rights of the applicants** (see paras [69], [70], [71]).

CLAYTON V CLAYTON[25]

Court of Appeal

Sir Mark Potter P, Arden and Wall LJJ

27 June 2006

Headnote

A5.18 Following the separation, the parents shared the care of the child. **Before the final hearing in the mother's proceedings for contact and residence, the father abducted the 4-year-old child, removing her to Portugal and living with her in a camper van. After 5½ weeks of concealment, the father was arrested, tried for abduction and sentenced to a prison term of 9 months, of which he served 6 months.** After his release, the father was able to resume contact with the child, by order of the court. **On the basis of an email from the father to the BBC, which indicated his intention to publicise and discuss his experiences of the family courts and to take the child to Portugal again so that he could document the abduction experiences, the mother sought and obtained an injunction** at an interim hearing of the contact and residence applications **which restrained the father from publishing various matters concerning the child.** The order was stated to be effective until the child's eighteenth birthday. At the final hearing the parents agreed to a shared care arrangement, but disagreed concerning the injunction. The judge ordered that the original injunction should continue until either the child's eighteenth birthday or sooner order of the court. The father appealed.

Held

Allowing the appeal, **discharging the injunction and substituting a prohibited steps order preventing the father from returning to Portugal with the child, or involving her in publication of information concerning the abduction**:

(1)   Section 97(2) of the Children Act 1989 prohibited publication of any material 'intended or likely to identify … any child as being **involved in any proceedings',** related to current proceedings, **and the prohibition ended once the proceedings were concluded** (see paras [48], [49], [50], [52], [102], [104]).

(2)   Section 12 of the Administration of Justice Act 1960, which was apt to prevent publication or reporting of the substance of or issues in proceedings (save in so far as permitted by the court or as revealed in any judgment delivered in open court), even after the conclusion of proceedings, was not thereby diluted. **Given the existence of s 12 it was not right, as a generality, to assume that identification of a child as having been involved in proceedings would involve either a failure to respect the child's family or private life or harm his or her welfare interests** (see paras [51], [53]).

---

[25]   [2006] EWCA Civ 878, [2007] 1 FLR 11.

(3)   Parents were not free to draw their children into an ongoing public debate after the conclusion of proceedings. **The court retained its welfare jurisdiction, enabling intervention in the form of an injunction or order prohibiting identification of a child where a child's welfare was put at risk by inappropriate parental identification for publicity purposes.**

(4)   However, **in deciding to make a long-term injunction** aimed at restricting the reporting and publication of proceedings involving children, the court was obliged in the face of challenge to conduct a **balancing exercise between competing human rights under Art 8 and Art 10** of the European Convention (see paras [54], [78], [114]).

(5)   **It would be appropriate for every tribunal, when making what it believed to be a final order in proceedings under the Children Act 1989, to consider whether or not there was an outstanding welfare issue which needed to be addressed by a continuing order for anonymity.**

(6)   **If there were no outstanding welfare issue, then it was likely that the penal consequences of s 97 of the 1989 Act would cease to have any effect, and the parties would be able to put into the public domain any matter relating to themselves and their children which they wished to publish, provided that the publication did not offend against s 12 of the 1960 Act** (see paras [54], [77], [115].

(7)   The judge had been wrong to continue the injunction. Bearing in mind the position of the father as an active campaigner for improvement in the processes and outcomes of the family justice system and his role as an advisor to others in that connection, as well as his views and interests concerning shared parenting arrangements, **the terms of the injunction were far too wide in their effect, preventing the father as they did from referring to his own case as one satisfactorily resolved by the particular shared parenting agreement approved by the judge.** The father should, however, **be restrained from involving the child in his campaigning or media activities, as that would be contrary to her welfare interests, exposing her to unsuitable and undesirable publicity** (see paras [72], [137], [138], [139], [141]).

Per Wall LJ: **Children were entitled to their privacy, and even if the law now allowed parents, after the conclusion of proceedings, to engage sensibly in public debate, and to identify their children in the process, they would be wise to think several times before doing so. Parents who breached their children's privacy might well pay a price in terms of their relationships with their children** (see para [116]).

See in this context the dicta of Munby J in *Webster: Norfolk County Council v Webster and Others*[26] at para [52]:

---

[26]   [2006] EWHC 2733 (Fam), [2007] 1 FLR 1146.

'The meaning and effect of s 97 has recently been considered by the Court of Appeal in *Clayton v Clayton*[27], where it was held that the prohibition in s 97(2) comes to an end when the proceedings are concluded. The common belief (which I confess I shared) that the statutory prohibition outlasted the existence of the proceedings has now been exploded for what it always was – yet another of the many fallacies and misunderstandings which have tended to bedevil this particular area of the law. **On the other hand, and as Sir Mark Potter P was at pains to point out (at para [53]), the fact that, following an end to the proceedings, the prohibition on identification under s 97 will cease to have effect does not of course mean that the provisions of s 12 of the Administration of Justice Act 1960 are diluted or otherwise affected**. The limitation upon reporting information relating to the proceedings themselves under s 12 of that Act will remain.'

RE H (FREEING ORDERS: PUBLICITY)[28]

Court of Appeal

Thorpe and Wall LJJ

18 October 2005

Headnote

A5.19   In October 2004, the county court made care orders in respect of two children and **removed them from their parents with immediate effect. The judge recognised the intervention as Draconian given that the parents were doing their best, but one child had already suffered, and the other was likely to suffer significant harm resulting from the parents' inability to provide an appropriate standard of parenting**. The judge had made plain that the local authority was to adopt concurrent planning and, after an unfavourable assessment of the paternal grandparents, a freeing application was lodged and an order was made in the High Court in August 2005 freeing the children for adoption. **Publicity in the national and local press in the interim period between the two judgments had largely promoted the idea that the children had been removed from their parents because their level of intelligence was insufficient to enable them to parent the children properly**. Release of the judgments did not result in corrective publicity and the parents sought permission to appeal on the ground, inter alia, that a full investigation would put the record straight.

Held

Refusing the application:

(1)   The need to put the record straight did not constitute a reason to grant permission to appeal for the very simple reason that **judgments given on a**

---

[27]   [2006] EWCA Civ 878, [2006] Fam 83, [2007] 1 FLR 11.

[28]   [2005] EWCA Civ 1325, [2006] 1 FLR 815.

permission application could themselves be made available for reporting either as a matter of public interest or as a matter of legal significance (see paras [12], [13]).

(2)   The removal of the children flowed from full and careful judgments in both courts. The High Court judge found that the local authority had made a proper assessment and reached the right conclusion, including the decision to terminate contact and the view that the hypothetical reasonable parent would have been that freeing the children for adoption was required to promote their welfare. At both trials the children were represented by a full litigation team, an experienced guardian ad litem and legal representation, and on both occasions they supported the local authority's position to the full (see paras [17]–[21]).

Per curiam

There was a strong argument for judges in controversial cases, or cases that had attracted media attention, to accompany delivery of their judgment with a short written summary of their conclusions and reasons which could be made publicly available (see para [30]).

RE Z (SHARED PARENTING PLAN: PUBLICITY)[29]

Family Division

Hedley J

26 July 2005

Headnote

A5.20   The parents of a 6-year-old child had been involved for more than 3 years in family proceedings primarily concerning the child's contact with her father. **At one point the father had abducted the child, as a result of which he had been subject to criminal proceedings and to a period of imprisonment. A non-publicity injunction had been made preventing publication of details of the proceedings.** The parents had been able to reach agreement as to the shared parenting of their daughter, but could not agree on the continuation of the injunction. The father wanted it lifted in its entirety, the guardian wanted it to continue as it stood, while the mother was content with a degree of publicity, provided that the child was not identified.

---

[29]   [2006] 1 FLR 405.

Held

Making an order by consent as to shared parenting of the child and making an order that the injunction should continue:

(1) **The question of the continuation of the non-publicity injunction required a balance to be struck between the father's right to freedom of expression under Art 10 of the European Convention for the Protection of Human Rights and Fundamental Freedoms 1950 (the Convention), and the child's right to respect for her private life under Art 8 of the Convention.**

(2) **The need to ensure that the child had peace and freedom from publicity outweighed the father's right to freedom of speech.** The father was free to use the present judgment as he wished, since open court proceedings were exempted from the injunction itself. This was sufficient to safeguard his interests under Art 10. The injunction should continue until the child reached the age of 18, in order to safeguard her interests under Art 8 (see paras [8]–[9]).

Per curiam

(1) **The shared parenting plan agreed by the parents in this case was to be commended and such an approach could be considered as a basis for discussion and negotiation in future cases** (see paras [5]–[6]).

(2) 'I am satisfied that the need to ensure that Z has peace and freedom from publicity should outweigh A's right to freedom of speech. That approach broadly reflects the policy of s 97 of the Children Act 1989. However, I believe that I can give adequate expression to my sympathies to A's position by **giving this judgment in open court. Provided the anonymisation is strictly adhered to, A is at liberty to use it as he wishes in that open court proceedings are exempted from the injunction itself – provided it is not used in such a way as would reasonably lead to the child's identification.'**

HER MAJESTY'S ATTORNEY GENERAL V PELLING[30]

Queen's Bench Division, Divisional Court

Laws LJ and Pitchford J

8 April 2005

Headnote

A5.21 The Attorney-General applied for an order of committal or other appropriate penalty in respect of what was said to be a grave criminal contempt

---

[30] [2005] EWHC 414 (Admin), [2006] 1 FLR 93.

of court, perpetrated by the defendant. **The alleged contempt was the publication by the defendant, in a journal and on the internet, of a judgment given in private in proceedings under the Children Act 1989.** The judgment in question was delivered in proceedings concerning an application by the defendant for a residence order in respect of his son. **At the time of publication of the judgment, the boy was 12 years old.** The judgment contained details of sensitive matters relating to the boy, including substantial extracts from a welfare officer's report. The defendant's publication of the judgment, the extent of the publication and the fact that it was intentional were all admitted by the defendant. **There was a history of attempts by the defendant through litigation to have the residence proceedings heard in open court and not in private.** This history encompassed decisions from the county court to the European Court of Human Rights, each agreeing that the defendant was not entitled to publish the judgment. The defendant called for one of the judges hearing the committal proceedings to recuse himself, on the basis of actual or perceived bias against the defendant. The defendant also objected to interlocutory orders made in the committal proceedings to the effect that none of the detail of the published judgment, nor the website address or addresses where it was available on the internet, should be published in the course of argument or otherwise in open court in the committal proceedings.

Held

Refusing the application for recusal and finding the defendant guilty of criminal contempt:

(1)   While it was uncomfortable and unsatisfactory for a judge to have to decide whether he or she was actually or apparently biased in proceedings, to adjourn the case for another judge to decide was likely to be much more injurious to the interests of justice, and had never been the practice. If it were the practice, the court's processes would be open to manipulation and contrived delay at the hands of disaffected litigants. There was no substance in the defendant's reasons for calling for Laws LJ to recuse himself and the application for recusal should be refused (see paras [5], [6]–[12]).

(2)   The defendant's objections to the interlocutory orders were essentially based on his claim that the common law, in conjunction with the European Convention for the Protection of Human Rights and Fundamental Freedoms 1950, entitled him to publish the judgment, and no rule of court or other measure could lawfully prevent him from doing so. This claim had already been concluded against the defendant by the Court of Appeal and the European Court of Human Rights and it was not open to the defendant to reopen the question in the current proceedings (see paras [34]–[37]).

(3)   **The essence of criminal contempt consisted in an intentional interference with the administration of justice.**

(4) In Children Act 1989 proceedings, as in wardship proceedings, **the protection of the interests of the minor was a function of the administration of justice, and publication of a judgment, which in the interests of the child the court had determined should be kept private, was an interference with the course of justice** (see paras [39], [42]–[43], [50]).

(5) **It was not possible to read s 12 of the Administration of Justice Act 1960, as amended by the Children Act 1989, as confining contempt in proceedings concerning minors to wardship proceedings only. Section 12, as amended, assimilated the Children Act 1989 jurisdiction with its predecessors for the purpose of contempt** (see paras [53]–[54]).

A LOCAL AUTHORITY V W, L, W, T AND R (BY THE CHILDREN'S GUARDIAN)[31]

Family Division

Sir Mark Potter P

14 July 2005

Headnote

A5.22 The mother of two children was awaiting sentence having pleaded guilty to a charge that she had knowingly infected the father of one of the children with HIV. The children were a girl and boy, aged 3 years and 6 months respectively. Both were the subject of care proceedings. The girl was in foster care, having been removed from her maternal grandmother's home. The boy was also in foster care, awaiting the assessment of the suitability of his father and paternal family as potential carers. It had been established that the girl was not HIV positive; the boy was too young to be reliably tested. After the mother's HIV status had become known in the community in which the family lived, she had been forced to leave her home due to abuse and harassment from neighbours. The 3-year-old girl was attending nursery away from the immediate area, where there was no knowledge of her mother's identity. **As there was a substantial level of ignorance in the area, the nursery staff and welfare officials feared that if publicity were given to the identity and HIV status of the mother or father that could give rise to a general outcry at the nursery, and also make the finding of alternative carers for the children more difficult.** The applicant council sought the renewal of an injunction prohibiting any newspaper, programme service or any media broadcast, including publication over the internet, from revealing the names and addresses or publishing any photographic images of the mother or father in connection with the criminal proceedings and the names, addresses or details of nursery placements, names of any carers, or any other particulars likely or calculated to lead to the identification of the children or any photographic image of either of them.

---

[31] [2005] EWHC 1564 (Fam), [2006] 1 FLR 1.

Held

Granting the injunction:

(1) Both Arts 8 and 10 of the European Convention on Human Rights and Fundamental Freedoms 1950 propounded a fundamental right which there was a pressing social need to protect. Each Article allowed for qualification of the right it propounded, so far as it may be lawful, necessary and proportionate to do so, in order to accommodate the other. **The exercise to be performed was one of parallel analysis in which the starting point was presumptive parity, in that neither Article had precedence over the other.**

(2) The court was required to examine the justification for interfering with each right and the issue of proportionality was to be considered in respect of each.

(3) **While the Art 10 right to freedom of expression was to be accorded great weight, the general rule that the press may report everything that took place in a criminal court might be displaced in unusual or exceptional circumstances** (see para [53]).

(4) The balance in this case fell in favour of the children's Art 8 rights for the following reasons:
   (a) given that there had been no previous publicity, and that the children were too young to be aware of the existence or significance of the criminal trial, there was a good prospect that they might be **isolated from its fallout**;
   (b) **were the injunction not be granted, the ensuing publicity may have an adverse or inhibiting effect upon the council's ability to find suitable carers for the children and so provide for their long-term stability and happiness**;
   (c) and the danger against which protection was sought in this case was not simply the burden of the knowledge that their mother might be a criminal, **but the attachment of the personal attribution of HIV** infection, falsely in the case of the girl and uncertainly in the case of the boy, with all the attendant consequences of such attachment (see paras [56]–[58]).

(5) **Furthermore, there was no danger that the grant of an injunction in this case would open up opportunities for adult non-parties faced with the possibility of damaging publicity to apply for similar injunctions, since the principal justification for the injunction in this case was the potential interference with the care and placement of the children under the court's care jurisdiction; a consideration which could not arise in the case of an adult non-party**.

(6) **The aim of the injunction here was to prevent the identity of the children from being linked with that of either parent; it was not designed to suppress**

the details or circumstances of the crime itself. The granting of the injunction would not inhibit the press from reporting the case and a **prohibition on revealing the identity of the parties should not impair well-informed debate on the issues it raised** (see paras [61]–[63]).

Per curiam

The **President's Direction (Applications for Reporting Restricting Orders)** (18 March 2005) and the helpful further advice afforded by the **Practice Note (Official Solicitor: Deputy Director of Legal Services CAFCASS Applications for Reporting Restricting Orders)** of the same date, were to be noted and followed in cases of this sort (see paras [80]–[84]).

BLUNKETT V QUINN[32]

Family Division

Ryder J

3 December 2004

A5.23 The two-year-old child lived with the mother and the mother's husband. The mother was **28 weeks' pregnant** and was suffering relatively severe complications of pregnancy. **The applicant, a senior politician, was seeking a parental responsibility order and a contact order, and described himself as the father of the child**. He made no other applications to the court. The mother disputed the applicant's claim to be the father of the child. **A judge refused the mother's application to adjourn the hearing until after the birth of the child she was now expecting**, and listed the proceedings for further directions before him on a specified date to consider: whether the mother's husband should be joined as a party; whether there should be scientific tests to determine the paternity of the child; and various case management issues. The mother appealed arguing that she could not obtain a fair trial without the adjournment.

Held

Dismissing the appeal:

(1) **Having regard to the quantity of material concerning this case that was in the public domain, some of it, even in the most responsible commentaries, wholly inaccurate, and having regard to the private and family lives of all concerned, it was right to hear the appeal in private, but to give this judgment in public, albeit excluding from the judgment unnecessary personal material**.

---

[32] [2004] EWHC 2816 (Fam), [2005] 1 FLR 648.

(2)   The ability to correct false impressions and misconceived facts would go further to help the rights of all involved under Art 6 and Art 8 of the European Convention for the Protection of Human Rights and Fundamental Freedoms 1950 (the European Convention) **than would the court's silence, which in this case would only promote further speculation and adverse comment that would damage both the interests of those involved and the family justice system itself**. It did not follow that future hearings would result in a public judgment (see para [22]).

(3)   The senior district judge had not failed to have sufficient regard to the mother's right to a fair trial, under Art 6 of the European Convention, in the light of her medical condition, as
   (a)   the evidence before the judge suggested that **the mother was not incapacitated from giving instructions nor, to a significant extent, from taking part in the proceedings**,
   (b)   delay would be damaging to the relationship between the putative father and the child; and
   (c)   **it was a proper consideration of the parties' Art 6 rights and their competing Art 8 rights to continue the proceedings by active case management, dealing with paternity as the first issue** (see para [28]).

Per curiam

It was not the case that the mother must necessarily attend all hearings, which was a matter for her to decide with her medical and legal advisers. There was considerable difference between (a) ensuring from hearing to hearing that the mother's right to a fair trial was secured by considering her health as against the instructions which she had given and the measures that could be taken to make her right of access to the court effective and (b) the abrogation by the court of its responsibilities to secure the rights of the child and the putative father for a period of at least 4 months (see paras [32], [33]).

RE S (A CHILD) (IDENTIFICATION: RESTRICTIONS ON PUBLICATION)[33]

House of Lords

Lord Bingham of Cornhill, Lord Nicholls of Birkenhead, Lord Steyn, Lord Hoffmann, Lord Carswell

28 October 2004

Headnote

A5.24 The guardian of the 8-year-old child **applied for an injunction restraining publication** of the identity of the child's mother, who was the

---

[33]   [2004] UKHL 47, [2005] 1 FLR 591.

defendant in a murder trial. **The mother had been charged with the murder of the child's older brother, who had died of acute salt poisoning**. At the time of the brother's death a number of newspaper reports had named the deceased brother, and where he lived. **The local papers in their earlier reports had named not only the deceased brother, but also the mother and father, the child and the child's school**. Following the death the child had been fostered, but, under the care plan approved by the court making the care order, **the child had been placed with the father, and returned to live at his old home and attended his old school**. The child continued to have **supervised contact** with the mother and maternal grandparents. An injunction was granted in the Family Division prohibiting publication of the child's, mother's and father's photograph, the child's name, address and school, or of any other information which might lead to the child's identification. The order was intended to prohibit publication of the name of the mother or of the deceased brother in any report of the criminal trial and to prevent publication of any photographs of the mother or brother. **On an application by a newspaper to modify the injunction, the judge altered the order so that newspapers would be able, in reports of the criminal trial, to publish the identity of the mother, or of the deceased brother or reproduce photographs of either of them**. The Court of Appeal, by a majority, dismissed the appeal against that decision. Through the guardian, the child appealed to the House of Lords, arguing that his right to respect for private and family life meant that he was entitled to protection against harmful publicity concerning his family. The mother had waived her right to a completely public trial and supported the child's appeal.

Held

Dismissing the appeal:

(1) **Since the coming into force of the Human Rights Act 1998, the preceding case-law about the existence and scope of inherent jurisdiction of the High Court to restrain publicity need not be considered in this or similar cases.**

(2) In a case such as the present the foundation of the jurisdiction to restrain publicity now derived from rights under the European Convention for the Protection of Human Rights and Fundamental Freedoms 1950 (the European Convention).

(3) **The case-law on the inherent jurisdiction was, however, not wholly irrelevant as it might remain of some interest in regard to the ultimate balancing exercise to be carried out under the European Convention provisions.**

(4) Although Art 8 of the European Convention was engaged, the **surviving child** would not be involved in the trial as a witness or otherwise; **it would not be necessary to refer to him, no photograph of him would be published, and the impact of the trial on the child would be essentially indirect**. The interference with Art 8 rights, however distressing for the child, was not of

the same order as that involved when juveniles were directly involved in criminal trials (see paras [24], [25], [27]).

(5) **The competing rights of freedom of the press under Art 10 were also engaged and were not, in these circumstances, outweighed by the rights of the child under Art 8. Full contemporaneous reporting of criminal trials in progress promoted public confidence in the administration of justice and promoted the values of the rule of law** (see para [28]).

(6) **Given the weight traditionally given to the importance of open reporting of criminal proceedings, it had been important for the judge, in carrying out the exercise required by the European Convention, to begin by acknowledging the force of the argument under Art 10 before considering whether the right of the child under Art 8 was sufficient to outweigh it,** although he went too far in saying that he would have come to the same conclusion if he had been persuaded that this was a case in which the child's welfare was the paramount consideration (see para [37]).

Per Munby J in *Re: Webster, Norfolk County Council v Webster and Others*;[34] in dicta which relate directly:

'[55] In *A Local Authority v W, L, W, T and R (by the Children's Guardian)*,[35] at para [53], Sir Mark Potter P summarised the effects of the judgment in *Re S* in this way:

"**There is express approval of the methodology in *Campbell v MGN Ltd*[36] in which it was made clear that each article propounds a fundamental right which there is a pressing social need to protect. Equally, each article qualifies the right it propounds so far as it may be lawful, necessary and proportionate to do so in order to accommodate the other. The exercise to be performed is one of parallel analysis in which the starting point is presumptive parity, in that neither article has precedence over or "trumps" the other. The exercise of parallel analysis requires the court to examine the justification for interfering with each right and the issue of proportionality is to be considered in respect of each. It is not a mechanical exercise to be decided upon the basis of rival generalities. An intense focus on the comparative importance of the specific rights being claimed in the individual cases is necessary before the ultimate balancing test in the terms of proportionality is carried out.**"

[56] It is clear from *In Re S* and *A Local Authority v W* that **in this context at least the interests of the child are *not* paramount**. Nor is there anything novel in this. As I said in *Re X (Disclosure of Information)*,[37] at para [23], summarising the relevant pre-Convention case-law:

---

[34] [2006] EWHC 2733 (Fam), [2007] 1 FLR 1146.
[35] [2005] EWHC 1564 (Fam), [2006] 1 FLR 1.
[36] [2004] 2 AC 457.
[37] [2001] 2 FLR 440.

"**The interests of the child (which ... typically point against disclosure) are a "major factor" and "very important" ... But ... it is clear that the child's interests are not paramount.**"

[57] In the present case, counsel have raised an important question as to how s 97(4) is to be construed. The point arises because, as will be recalled, the power to dispense with s 97(2) is, on the face of it, confined by s 97(4) to those situations where '**the welfare of the child requires it**'.

[58] **In my judgment, s 97(4) cannot be construed in this restrictive way.** In *Clayton v Clayton*, the Court of Appeal held that the effect of s 3 of the Human Rights Act 1998 was to require s 97 to be read in a Convention-compliant way, because s 97 constitutes a specific restriction on the media's rights under Art 10. **In the same way, s 97(4) must likewise be construed in a Convention-compliant way, not limiting the occasions on which s 97(2) is dispensed with to those where the welfare of the child requires it but extending it to every occasion when proper compliance with the Convention would so require.** In other words, the statutory phrase 'if ... the welfare of the child requires it' should be read as a **non-exhaustive** expression of the terms on which the discretion can be exercised, so that **the power is exercisable not merely if the welfare of the child requires it but wherever it is required to give effect, as required by the Convention, to the rights of others**. This is a process of construction which, in my judgment, comfortably satisfies the criteria identified in *Ghaidan v Godin-Mendoza*[38], and which is, therefore, required by s 3.

[59] This point was considered in *Clayton v Clayton* by Wall LJ, who set out (at paras [97]–[99]) the submission of Mr James Price QC to the effect that s 97(4) must be construed in such a way as to permit the court to lift the prohibition in s 97(2) where Convention rights required it. As I read Wall LJ's judgment (at paras [100]–[101]), he accepted Mr Price's submissions on this point, as more generally on s 97. Even if that is not so, and even if Wall LJ's observations on the point are purely obiter – and I do not accept either proposition – I am in no doubt that Mr Price's submission in relation to s 97(4) was correct. In my judgment, for the reasons given by Mr Price in his submissions in *Clayton v Clayton*, and repeated by Mr Warby, Mr Wolanski and Mr Hudson in their submissions before me, **s 97(4) has to be read as permitting the court to dispense with the prohibition on publication in s 97(2) where the right of free expression under Art 10 or other Convention rights require it**. To do otherwise would, as Mr Warby put it, place the child's interests on a pedestal in a way which is incompatible with the Convention. I agree.

[60] That this is the true view is, in my judgment, supported by two additional considerations. In the first place, as Mr Wolanski points out, s 97(2) is not confined to cases heard in private. **Unless s 97(4) can be 'read down' in this way, the power of the court to identify a child will be exercisable only in the rarest circumstances, even if the entirety of the proceedings has taken place in open court and in the glare of publicity.** And it would also mean that **the power of the Family Division to permit the identification of a child would be significantly more limited than the power of the Court of Appeal** (to which, as *Pelling v Bruce-Williams (Secretary of State for Constitutional Affairs*

---

[38] [2004] UKHL 30, [2004] 2 AC 557, [2004] 2 FLR 600.

Intervening)[39] shows, s 97(2) does not apply). Such undesirable anomalies would say little for a branch of the law already scarcely over-burdened with clarity and consistency.

[61] Secondly, as he points out, a narrow reading of s 97(4) does not accord with the practice. Mr Wolanski and Mr Warby draw attention to **Ryder J's** judgment in *Blunkett v Quinn*.[40] In the same vein. I might draw attention to my own judgment in *Harris v Harris; Attorney-General v Harris*.[41] In neither case is it easy to see how publication of the judgments in the form in which they were handed down could be justified on a narrow reading of s 97(4).

[62] **It follows, in my judgment, that s 97(4) must be construed in such a way as to permit the court to lift the prohibition in s 97(2) where Convention rights require it**.

[77] In short the judge must, as it seems to me, adopt precisely the same **'parallel analysis'** leading to the same **'ultimate balancing test'**, as described in *Re S (Identification: Restrictions on Publication)*[42] and *A Local Authority v W, L, W, T and R (by the Children's Guardian)*[43], which is applicable in deciding whether to relax on enhance reporting restrictions. I agree, therefore, with Mr Wolanski, when he submitted that **r 4.16(7)** is properly to be regarded simply as a 'default provision' but not as a provision indicating some heavy presumption in favour of privacy. In my judgment, **r 4.16(7)** must be read, construed and applied compatibly with the Convention. **Once the point has been raised, the outcome must be determined in accordance with the Convention, 'balancing' all the various interests which are engaged and *not* giving any special pre-eminence to the claim to privacy**. Moreover, and as Thorpe LJ pointed out, a judge must be alert to the dangers inherent in what he called the 'strong inherited convention of privacy' and **careful not to be 'prejudiced by the tradition or an unconscious preference for the atmosphere created by a hearing in chambers'**.

NOTE

Thus the s 97(4) power can be exercised in the discretion of the court also to give effect to the rights of others; the exercise of the discretion is not restricted to the welfare of the child.

RE RODDY (A CHILD) (IDENTIFICATION: RESTRICTION ON PUBLICATION)[44]

Family Division

Munby J

2 December 2003

---

[39] [2004] EWCA Civ 845, [2004] Fam 155, [2004] 2 FLR 823.
[40] [2004] EWHC 2816 (Fam), [2005] 1 FLR 648.
[41] [2001] 2 FLR 895.
[42] [2004] UKHL 47, [2005] 1 AC 593, [2005] 1 FLR 591.
[43] [2005] EWHC 1564 (Fam), [2006] 1 FLR 1.
[44] [2003] EWHC 2927 (Fam), [2004] 2 FLR 949.

Headnote

A5.25   The local authority sought a care order in relation to a **12-year-old girl who had become pregnant**. It was reported in the press that the **Roman Catholic church had given the girl money to dissuade her from having an abortion**. The local authority was granted an order protecting the identities of the girl and the baby's putative father, a boy of similar age. **Once the baby was born, the local authority began care proceedings; the mother was to remain in foster care, while the baby was to be adopted**. The mother was opposed to the adoption, but her consent was dispensed with and the baby was adopted. **Associated Newspapers Ltd applied to vary the terms of the order protecting the identities of the baby's parents**. The order was discharged and replaced with another, operative until the mother's eighteenth birthday, intended to protect the identities of the mother and father, and restraining the solicitation of information about the mother from a wide range of people. The care order in relation to the mother was later discharged and she returned to live with her parents. **The mother then approached The Mail on Sunday newspaper, saying that she was happy to be named and photographed for any ensuing article**. Associated Newspapers Ltd, owners of The Mail on Sunday, **sought a variation of the order prohibiting identification of the mother and father, to enable it to publish the mother's story, without identifying the father or the baby**. The local authority was prepared to agree to the proposed variation, but sought a further order explicitly protecting the identity of the baby.

Held

(1)   **The same principles as were applied in other areas of adolescent decision-making should apply to the question of whether a minor could exercise her right to freedom of expression under Art 10** of the European Convention for the Protection of Human Rights and Fundamental Freedoms 1950 (the European Convention), and choose to waive her right to privacy under Art 8. **It was the duty of the court to defend the right of the child who had sufficient understanding to make an informed decision, to make his or her own choice**. The court must recognise the child's integrity as a human being and acknowledge that, in order to respect the child's rights under the European Convention, the child must be allowed to make his or her own decision (see paras [50]–[58]).

(2)   The personal autonomy protected by Art 8 embraced the right to decide whether that which is private should remain private or should be shared with others. **Article 8 thus embraced both the right to maintain one's privacy and the right not merely to waive that privacy, but to share what would otherwise be private with others, or with the world at large** (see para [36]).

(3)   The court was first required to decide whether the child's rights were engaged, and then to conduct the necessary balancing exercise between the competing rights under Arts 8 and 10, considering the proportionality of the potential interference with each right considered independently.

The rights of Associated Newspapers Ltd under Art 10 and the mother's rights under Art 10 and Art 8 had to be balanced against the Art 8 rights of the father and the child. Since the mother's story raised important issues of public interest, **the public interest had also to be taken into account** in the balancing exercise (see paras [18], [21], [82], [83]).

(4) **A proper holding of the balance between the baby's father on the one hand, and the mother and Associated Newspapers Ltd on the other, required that there should be an injunction preserving the father's anonymity and restraining the solicitation of information about him either from the father or his family, but that there should be no injunction to prevent his story being told anonymously** (see para [43]).

(5) **A proper holding of the balance between the baby on the one hand, and the mother and the media on the other, required that there should be an injunction preserving the baby's anonymity and restraining the solicitation of information about her**. There was **insufficient** evidence that publication of the mother's story would harm the baby, however, to justify restraining the media from publishing altogether (see paras [64], [75], [76], [79]).

PELLING V BRUCE-WILLIAMS (SECRETARY OF STATE FOR CONSTITUTIONAL AFFAIRS INTERVENING)[45]

Court of Appeal

Thorpe, Sedley and Arden LJJ

1 July 2004

Headnote

A5.26   The father, a campaigner on family justice issues, had argued in a number of different forums that legal issues concerning his child should be heard in open court, with full access to the public at large. Ultimately, the European Court of Human Rights rejected his argument that the failure of English courts to hear family proceedings in public, with public pronouncement of judgments, was a breach of human rights under Arts 6 and 10 of the European Convention for the Protection of Human Rights and Fundamental Freedoms 1950 (the (European Convention), concerning right to a fair trial and freedom of expression. Nonetheless, **when the father subsequently made a joint residence application regarding his child, he included an application for a trial in open court with public pronouncement of judgment, and also moved for an order of certiorari to quash rr 4.16(7), 4.23(1) and 10.20(3) of the Family Proceedings Rules 1991,** so far as those rules prevented disclosure or inspection of Children Act 1989 judgments without leave of the judge, arguing that they were, in that respect, incompatible with Arts 6 and 10 of the European Convention. In a

---

[45]   [2004] EWCA Civ 485, [2004] 2 FLR 823.

judgment which was handed down in open court, but subject to the restriction that the anonymity of the child and adult members of the family be strictly preserved, the judge rejected the father's applications for a declaration of incompatibility and for certiorari. The judge also concluded that the hearing of the application for joint residence ought to be in chambers, and delivered his judgment on that issue in private. The father appealed. At the appeal hearing, the father objected to the notice on the door of the court which warned the public against identification of children within the proceedings, submitting that that was an unwarranted and illegal restriction on the father's and the public's entitlement to open justice; the father lodged an objection to any blanket imposition of reporting restrictions.

Held

Granting permission to appeal but dismissing the appeal:

(1) The father's arguments on the issue of open justice and Art 6 rights had already been rejected, by the court and by the European Court of Human Rights, and there had been no fresh development or argument to justify departure from the earlier decisions (see paras [35], [36]).

(2) **In connection with Art 6(1), it remained justifiable, in order to protect the privacy of the children and parties, and to avoid prejudicing the interests of justice, to hold residence proceedings in chambers and to limit the extent to which judgments were made available to the general public.**

(3) In connection with Art 10, the conduct of proceedings in chambers might properly be regarded as necessary in a democratic society for the protection of the rights of others, namely the rights of the respondent and the child under Art 8 (see paras [37], [38]).

(4) In the exercise of the judge's discretion to hear the particular case in chambers, and to refuse to pronounce the judgment in public, each determination of the judge had been sufficiently explained and was manifestly within the judge's discretionary ambit. **It was accepted that greater justification was required for the refusal of the pronouncement of judgment in public, given the almost universal practice of anonymising public judgments in Children Act 1989 cases** (see para [39]).

(5) Both the inherent jurisdiction and s 39(1) of the Children and Young Persons Act 1933 empowered the Court of Appeal to impose reporting restrictions, including the anonymisation of individuals concerned, in an individual case in the exercise of the court's discretion. **However, it was not evident that either the inherent or the statutory jurisdiction justified the imposition of an automatic restriction without the exercise of a specific discretion in the individual case.** It was, therefore, desirable for the Master of the Rolls and the President of the Family Division to review the standard practice of the court to reflect developments since *Re R (Minor)*

(Court of Appeal: Order Against Identification). **The time had come for the court to consider in each case whether a proper balance of competing rights required the anonymisation of any report of the proceedings and judgment following a hearing conducted in public and, therefore, open to all who cared to attend** (see paras [49], [54]).

Per curiam

Thorpe LJ:

> 'Policy questions do have to be addressed against this background: in reality, although the Family Proceedings Rules 1991 confer on the judge in any case the discretion to lift the veil of privacy, there is such a strong inherited convention of privacy that the judicial mind is almost never directed to the discretion, and, in rare cases where an application is made, a fair exercise may be prejudiced by the tradition or an unconscious preference for the atmosphere created by a hearing in chambers. Judges need to be aware of this and to be prepared to consider another course where appropriate.'

RE B (A CHILD) (DISCLOSURE)[46]

Family Division

Munby J

19 March 2004

Headnote

A5.27 The local authority began care proceedings in relation to a child who was then two-years old. **Its case was that the child's mother suffered from Munchausen's Syndrome by Proxy**. During the causation hearing the judge heard evidence from six medical experts, including two doctors. **The judge found that the mother had deliberately interfered with the child's medical treatment and had administered some unidentified infected substance causing rigors which were potentially life-threatening**. At the final outcome hearing the judge, accepting the findings made at the causation hearing, made a **final care order**. Following the Court of Appeal's decisions in a number of high-profile criminal cases on Munchausen's Syndrome by Proxy (notably, *R v Clark and R v Cannings*), the public debate was extended to possible miscarriages of justice in the family justice system. **The mother made a complaint to the Professional Conduct Committee of the General Medical Council (GMC) about the two doctors and a copy of that letter was sent to the Minister of State for Children**. The mother also provided an account of the child's story from the mother's viewpoint to the *Daily Mail* newspaper under a fictionalised name. The GMC invited the mother to provide further details of her complaint including the reports of the two doctors and copies of all documentation (including correspondence)

---

[46] [2004] EWHC 411 (Fam), [2004] 2 FLR 142.

relating to the legal proceedings. The mother sought permission to appeal to the Court of Appeal against the findings of fact made against her by the judge. **She also issued a notice of application for leave to disclose appropriately edited documents into the public domain.** The application was supported by a witness statement by her solicitor, who was also a sister of the Solicitor-General. **It eventually emerged that, without permission from the court, both the mother and her solicitor had already disclosed copies of the judgment, of the doctor's report, and the case summaries, variously to the mother's Member of Parliament, the Solicitor-General, the Minister of State for Children, the BBC and a newspaper journalist.** The local authority applied ex parte for injunctive relief against the mother, her solicitor and the BBC. Orders were made against the mother, but not against either her solicitor or the BBC. At the time of judgment, the Court of Appeal's decision was unknown.

Held

Restricting the public identification of the child, her mother, her carers and the two doctors; protecting the child and her carers from being approached by the media, whilst permitting the public identification of the local authority; permitting the mother to talk to and to be interviewed by the media if she wished and permitting the mother (but without identifying the doctor) to put into the public domain various facts and a suitable extract of the letter from the social worker:

(1) **There was a publication for the purpose of s 12(1)(a) of the Administration of Justice Act 1960 (the 1960 Act) whenever the law of defamation would treat there as being a publication. This meant that most forms of dissemination, whether oral or written, would constitute a publication.**

(2) **The only exception was where there was a communication of information by someone to a professional, each acting in furtherance of the protection of children.**

(3) Specifically, there was a publication for this purpose whether the dissemination of information or documents was to a journalist or to a Member of Parliament, a Minister of the Crown, a Law Officer, the Director of Public Prosecutions, the Crown Prosecution Service, the police (except when exercising child protection functions), the GMC, or any other public body or public official. The Minister of State for Children was not a child protection professional. Disclosure to the Minister of State for Children could not, therefore, be justified on the footing of the exception to the general principal (see paras [82](iii) and (iv)).

(4) **It was a contempt of court for the mother or her solicitor to disclose copies of the judgment, of the doctor's report and the other documents, and of the**

case summaries variously to the mother's Member of Parliament, the Solicitor-General, the Minister of State for Children, the BBC and other journalists.

(5) It was also almost certainly a contempt of court for the mother to disclose material published in the two paragraphs of the *Daily Mail*. Each of the various disclosures amounted to a publication prohibited by s 12 of the 1960 Act. Both had displayed a remarkable and disquieting lack of candour with the court and neither had made full and frank disclosure until after the hearing (see paras [109], [149]).

(6) **Permission should be given to disclose certain relevant papers to the GMC. Permission should also be given to the mother to disclose certain facts into the public domain to enable her to participate in the public debate both before, during and after the hearing of her appeal to the Court of Appeal** (see paras [113], [119]).

(7) **At this stage the balance came down in favour of permitting the mother to make her allegations in public whilst at the same time protecting the identities of the two doctors** (see para [131]).

Per curiam

To proceed on the blinkered assumption that there had been no miscarriages of justice in the family justice system would be deleterious. The issue had to be addressed with honesty and candour if the family justice system was not to suffer further loss of public confidence. **Open and public debate in the media was essential** (see para [103]).

'[13] I had to consider the question of a local authority's anonymity in the context of care proceedings *in Re B (a Child) (Disclosure)*[47]. At para [125] I said this:

"I do not agree with Mr Howard, however, that the identity of the local authority needs to be protected. He says that there is no public interest in naming the local authority. That may or may not be so, but it is, I think, largely beside the point. **It is for the local authority to establish a convincing case for an injunction to restrain the media publishing something which is prohibited neither by the general law nor by s 12 (of the Administration of Justice Act 1960). It cannot establish such a case merely by demonstrating – even assuming it can – that there is no public interest in the identity of the local authority, for that is to put the boot on the wrong foot.** His real case is that the local authority's identity needs to be protected in order to ensure that B's identity is protected. That argument, if it could be justified on the facts, might well weigh heavily in the balance. But, in my judgment, Mr Howard fails to make good the factual premise. **I do not accept his argument that identification of the local authority is likely to lead to the identification of**

---

either B or her carers. I do not accept his argument that a combination of the disclosure sought and 'tittle-tattle' will serve to identify B."
I subsequently adopted the same approach in *Re X; Barnet London Borough Council v Y and X*,[48] at para [173].

[14] There will, of course, be cases where a local authority is not identified, even where it has been the subject of stringent judicial criticism. A recent example is *Re X (Emergency Protection Orders)*.[49] **But current practice shows that local authorities involved in care cases are increasingly being identified**. In addition to the two cases I have already referred to, other recent examples can be found in *British Broadcasting Company v Rochdale Metropolitan Borough Council and X and Y*,[50] *Re Webster; Norfolk County Council v Webster and Others*,[51] *Oldham Metropolitan Borough Council v GW & PW*[52] and *British Broadcasting Corporation v CAFCASS Legal and Others*.[53] No doubt there are others.

[15] I propose to adopt the same approach here as that which I set out in *Re B (a Child) (Disclosure)*.[54] Is there some proper basis for continuing the local authority's anonymity? In my judgment there is not.

[16] In the first place, as the local authority very frankly accepts, whatever anonymity it enjoys is somewhat precarious, given the fact that the solicitors in the case have all been publicly identified. More importantly, however, I cannot see that there is any need to preserve the local authority's anonymity in order to protect the children's privacy and identities. **Disclosure of the name of the local authority is not of itself going to lead to the identification of the children**. In this respect the case is no different from *Re B (a Child) (Disclosure)*[55] and *Re X; Barnet London Borough Council v Y and X*.[56]

[17] **The real reason why the local authority seeks to perpetuate its anonymity is more to do with the interests of the local authority itself (and, no doubt, the important interests of its employees)** than with the interests of the children. That is not a criticism of the local authority's stance. It is simply a statement of the realities.

[18] I can understand the local authority's concern that if anonymity is lifted the local authority (or its employees) may be exposed to ill-informed criticism based, it may be, on misunderstanding or misrepresentation of the facts. But if such criticism exceeds what is lawful there are other remedies available to the local authority. **The fear of such criticism, however justified that fear may be, and however unjustified the criticism, is not of itself a justification for affording a local authority anonymity**. On the contrary, **the powers exercisable by local authorities under Parts IV and V of the Children Act 1989 are potentially so drastic in their possible consequences that there is a powerful public interest in those who exercise such powers being publicly identified so that they can be held publicly accountable**. The arguments in favour of publicity – in favour of openness, public scrutiny and public accountability –

---

48   [2006] 2 FLR 998.
49   [2006] EWHC 510 (Fam), [2006] 2 FLR 701.
50   [2005] EWHC 2862 (Fam), [2007] 1 FLR 101.
51   [2006] EWHC 2733 (Fam), [2007] 1 FLR 1146.
52   [2007] EWHC 136 (Fam), [2007] 2 FLR 597.
53   [2007] EWHC 616 (Fam), [2007] 2 FLR 765.
54   [2004] EWHC 411 (Fam), [2004] 2 FLR 142.
55   [2004] EWHC 411 (Fam), [2004] 2 FLR 142.
56   [2006] 2 FLR 998.

are particularly compelling in the context of public law care proceedings: see *Re X; Barnet London Borough Council v Y and X*,[57] at para [166].

[19] Moreover, and as Lord Steyn pointed out in *R v Secretary of State for the Home Department ex parte Simms and Another*[58], at 126, freedom of expression is instrumentally important inasmuch as it 'facilitates the exposure of errors in the governance and administration of justice of the country'. How can such errors be exposed, how can public authorities be held accountable, if allowed to shelter behind a judicially sanctioned anonymity? This is particularly so where, as in the present case, a public authority has been exposed to criticism. I accept, as the local authority correctly points out, that many – indeed most – of the matters in dispute in this case were never the subject of any final judicial determination, but the fact remains that in certain respects I was, as my judgment shows, critical of the local authority. And that is a factor which must weigh significantly in the balance: see *Re X; Barnet London Borough Council v Y and X*,[59] at para [174].

[20] In my judgment the balance here comes down clearly in favour of the local authority being identified.'

RE M (DISCLOSURE: CHILDREN AND FAMILY REPORTER: DISCLOSURE)[60]

Court of Appeal

Thorpe LJ and Wall J

31 July 2002

Headnote

A5.28 The parents of a girl born on 11 February 1997 were involved in a **private law dispute over the child's residence**. The parents had separated in April 1999 and the child had moved to live with her father in September 2001. On 10 February 2002 the mother attempted to remove the child from the father's care by retaining her at the end of a period of staying contact. On 25 February the mother applied for a residence order. On 28 February the district judge ordered the return of the child to the father's care by 1 March. A direction was given for a report to be prepared by a CAFCASS officer by 23 May. On 26 March the county court judge heard the mother's application for an interim residence order. Following a firm indication given during the course of the mother's evidence, a consent order was made confirming the status quo, ie that the child should live with the father. **On 30 April the CAFCASS officer appointed to report for the court interviewed the mother and her sister. They alleged that the father had behaved inappropriately in front of the child**. The CAFCASS officer contacted the judge and suggested there might

57 [2006] 2 FLR 998.
58 [2000] 2 AC 115.
59 [2006] 2 FLR 998.
60 [2002] EWCA Civ 1199, [2002] 2 FLR 893.

need to be an investigation under s 47 of the Children Act 1989 by the local authority. At a subsequent hearing the judge heard from the CAFCASS officer and counsel for both parties. **The judge refused leave for the CAFCASS officer to disclose the material to the local authority**. The judge granted the mother and CAFCASS permission to appeal his decision.

Held

(1) **Leave of the court is not required for the CAFCASS officer to disclose material** to the local authority as a matter of law. Rule 4.23 of the Family Proceedings Rules 1991 expressly protects the confidentiality of documents and it cannot be argued that the CAFCASS officer is prevented from reporting to the local authority concerns resulting from investigation simply because at a later date they will be recorded in the report to the judge (see para [19]).

(2) **Communication between two professionals exchanging information in the course of their respective functions, each acting in furtherance of the protection of children, does not constitute publication breaching the privacy of the contemporaneous Children Act proceedings** (see paras [21], [66], [67]).

(3) **The children and family reporter (CFR) is a member of a new statutory service, the success of which depends in part on the support of other disciplines including the judiciary**. The CFR acts independently and exercises an independent discretion as to the nature and extent of his investigations and inquiries. In the absence of any statutory prohibition on the discretionary communication from the CFR to the social worker the court was not prepared to find one in the common law or in the inherent nature of the functions of the CFR or in the inherent relationship between the CFR and the court (see paras [26], [96]).

(4) **The relationship between the judge and the CFR is a collaborative one. Both share the ultimate objective, namely, the protection of children and advancement of their welfare. The CFR executes that part of the judge's function which is inquisitorial. The judge should give due weight to the outcome of the CFR's investigations** (see paras [26], [85]).

(5) **There is a need for communication between the family justice system in private law proceedings and the local authority in discharging its statutory functions for the protection and care of children at risk of significant harm**. In exercising an independent discretion the CFR should be mindful of the judge's power within private law proceedings to order a s 37 investigation and in an emergency situation the power to intervene under s 44 of the Children Act 1989. **The CFR should always consider taking his concerns to the judge in the case rather than to the local authority**. Much may depend on the state of the proceedings – the later in the proceedings the more likely it is that the judge will have knowledge of the parties and insight built up over the course of previous hearings (see para [27]).

(6) Allegations from a party to the dispute of neglect or misconduct by the other party should be distinguished especially where they were made by an applicant for a residence order or an order for extended or defined contact. **It is the function of the judge to determine such allegations as a prelude to his conclusion and a CFR would be wiser to avoid direct involvement with the social services.** The party raising allegations has the opportunity to raise them in the proceedings before the judge but also has the right to approach the local authority director at any time (see paras [33], [35], [43]).

(7) Where the CFR's suspicions are raised by interview with the child alone or by a home visit he must exercise an independent professional judgment. There may be circumstances in which the decision will be to go immediately to the judge. Alternatively, his instinct may be to go to the social services without delay. **As a matter of practice the exercise of that discretion cannot be fettered by any rule of practice requiring prior referral to the court. Any such referral to the local authority should be reported to the judge at the earliest convenient opportunity to enable the judge, who controls the proceedings, to consider the impact of the development and the need for consequential directions.** Any decision to suspend an inquiry must be that of the judge and not the CFR (see paras [38], [43]).

Per Wall J: CFRs are not 'officers of the court'. They are officers of the service (CAFCASS) (see para [96]).

CLIBBERY V ALLAN[61]

Court of Appeal

Dame Elizabeth Butler-Sloss P, Thorpe and Keene LJJ

30 January 2002

Headnote

A5.29 The woman sought a **non-molestation order** against the man, and an **occupation order** in respect of a flat owned, indirectly, by the man. In accordance with common practice, the **hearing was conducted in chambers**. The judge found that the couple had never lived together as husband and wife, and that the flat had never been their home. He therefore concluded that he had no jurisdiction to make the occupation order. Newspaper articles appeared giving the woman's view of the facts, including direct quotations from the man's sworn written evidence. The man obtained ex parte injunctions to prevent the woman from disclosing: any part of any document filed in or disclosed in the proceedings; any part of the oral evidence given in the proceedings; or any part of the judgment. **The man argued, on his application for a continuation of the**

---

[61]   [2002] EWCA Civ 45, [2002] 1 FLR 565.

injunctions, that chambers proceedings in the Family Division were held in private for substantive and substantial reasons, and that matters relating to proceedings held in chambers should not be made public. The judge dismissed the application and discharged the injunction, concluding that there was, in principle, no difference in the procedures to be adopted in the Family Division from the other divisions of the High Court, and that the practice of hearing cases in chambers was largely for administrative convenience and did not denote privacy or confidentiality of the proceedings or the documents used in proceedings.

Held

Dismissing the appeal:

(1) The first issue which arose was whether proceedings held in chambers were private in the sense that the public could properly be excluded.

    (i) **In the interests of open justice, the exclusion of the public from proceedings had objectively to be justified in every case**.

    (ii) However, there was no statutory prohibition against providing for hearings in chambers; on the contrary there was a statutory basis for the Family Proceedings Rules 1991, which gave the court the power to exclude the public in family proceedings.

    (iii) **The chambers procedure under the 1991 Rules was designed to provide a measure of privacy, although not necessarily confidentiality, in family proceedings**.

    (iv) **There remained the power to allow the public in if the judge or district judge so directed**.

    (v) The judge below had expressed himself too broadly when he stated that family proceedings could not, with the exception of children cases, be heard in private. **The 1991 Rules were not ultra vires, and there was no objection to family courts hearing cases in private and excluding the public where the 1991 Rules permitted them to do so** (see paras [14], [16], [50]).

(2) **The second issue was in what circumstances proceedings held in private were to be treated as secret or confidential**.

    (i) **The hearing of a case in private did not, of itself, prohibit the publication of information about the proceedings, or information given in the proceedings**.

    (ii) **The Administration of Justice Act 1960, s 12 set out circumstances in which it would be a contempt of court to publish information given in private proceedings, but was not exhaustive, as any publication which substantially prejudiced the administration of justice would also be a contempt**.

    (iii) **The best known example of confidentiality based on potential prejudice to the proper administration of justice was the implied undertaking in compulsory disclosure of documents not to make use of such a document outside the action** (see paras [14], [51], [52], [54]).

(iii) **Classes of cases which manifestly required confidentiality were cases concerning children, and cases involving issues of ancillary relief.**

(iv) **Under the Administration of Justice Act 1960, s 12(1)(a), information relating to proceedings which related wholly or mainly to the maintenance or upbringing of a minor was indisputably private and secret.**

(v) **All cases involving issues of ancillary relief were also protected from publication by anyone without leave, because the duty on parties to ancillary relief proceedings to make full disclosure brought all information disclosed in such proceedings under the protection of the implied undertaking.**

(vi) **The implied undertaking extended to voluntary disclosure in ancillary relief proceedings, to the information contained in the documents, and to affidavits and statements of truth and witness statements, as all such information was required for the full and frank exchange of financial information and all the relevant circumstances.**

(vii) The implied undertaking would also be imposed in cases analogous to ancillary relief, such as those in Part III of the 1991 Rules (see paras [72], [73], [75]).

(3) However, other family proceedings were not automatically covered by secrecy, although heard in private. **Family proceedings were subject to the principle of open justice, and should not be seen as a separate category from other civil proceedings, other than in recognised classes of cases or in other situations which could be shown manifestly to require permanent confidentiality.**

(4) The court must look at each application before it, and come to a conclusion whether that application was covered by:
   (a) the Administration of Justice Act 1960, s 12,
   (b) or came within the recognised categories of cases, those of children and ancillary relief issues,
   (c) **or because of other factors there would be prejudice to the administration of justice if the proceedings were not to be treated as secret.**
   (d) It did not follow that an application under Part IV of the Family Law Act 1996, even one which was to some extent inquisitorial with the requirement that the court have regard to all the circumstances, would necessarily attract confidentiality (see para [77]).

(5) **It had not in the past been the practice of the family courts to prohibit publication of a name or matter in connection with the proceedings using the** Contempt of Court Act 1981, s 11, but there might be cases were its use would be appropriate, although the section ought not to be used as a blanket protection of non-publication in all hearings in private. It would, for example, be relevant in applications for occupation orders where children were involved. **The parties and the court must consider in each case**

whether the proper working of the administration of justice required there to be continuing confidentiality after the end of the proceedings (see para [79]).

(6) Nothing in the European Convention for the Protection of Human Rights and Fundamental Freedoms 1950 (the Convention), Art 6, required all cases to be heard in open court, **but there was a requirement that any private hearing or debarring of publication must be necessary in a democratic society, and proportionate to that necessity.** The practices set out above did not breach the Convention (see para [81]).

(7) On the present facts there was no ground upon which to prohibit publication of the proceedings. Even if the court had had jurisdiction to grant relief, it would not have exercised its discretion to do so (see paras [83], [84]).

Per Thorpe LJ: **Wherever the nature of proceedings not involving children was at least quasi-inquisitorial, there would be a discernible duty on the court to bring into account an extensive range of factors, many highly personal, which rested on an obligation to make full and frank disclosure, and a corresponding duty on the parties to refrain from ulterior use of the litigation material** (see paras [116], [117], [118]).

Per curiam

Butler-Sloss P:

'[71] **In each of the above cases, the obligation on the parties to make full and frank disclosure in their financial disputes was of such importance that it was in the public interest to preserve confidentiality of that information by means of the implied undertaking.** In order to achieve compliance with disclosure by the party under the obligation to do so, the party seeking the disclosure is required by the court only to use that information for the purposes of the proceedings. It is the protection provided by the court in cases of compulsion. Ancillary relief applications are appropriately heard in private in accordance with the 1991 Rules, see above. The public may not, without leave of the court, hear the evidence given in these applications. **It would make a nonsense of the use of an implied undertaking if information about the means of a party, in some cases sensitive information, could be made public as soon as the substantive hearing commenced.** Information disclosed under the compulsion of ancillary relief proceedings is, in my judgment, protected by the implied undertaking, before, during and after the proceedings are completed. Munby J, in his judgment, did not suggest to the contrary. He also pointed out that the 1926 Act (as amended in 1968) protects ancillary relief proceedings from press publication. This may be the case but we heard no argument on it.'

Thorpe LJ:

'[104] In civil proceedings restrictions on dissemination of litigation material for ulterior purposes are usually put on the basis of an implied undertaking not to do so. However it is plain that the concept of the implied undertaking is founded on the duty to the court. In *Prudential Assurance Co Ltd v Fountain Page Ltd and Another,*[62] Hobhouse J said at 774H:

> "It may be thought desirable to express the duty as an implied undertaking to the court. But whether it is so expressed or not, it is in my judgment a duty that is owed to the court and which can be enforced by the court ... Breach of the duty amounts to a contempt of court, which may be trivial or serious depending upon the circumstances. The court has the power wholly or partially to release the recipient from the duty, or undertaking, and to permit use to be made of the documents nevertheless."

[105] Accordingly I have no difficulty in concluding that in the important area of ancillary relief, where the table confirms that the volume of business is large all the evidence (whether written, oral or disclosed documents) and all the pronouncements of the court are prohibited from reporting and from ulterior use unless derived from any part of the proceedings conducted in open court or otherwise released by the judge.'

HARRIS V HARRIS; ATTORNEY-GENERAL[63]

Family Division

Munby J

27 April 2001

Headnote

A5.30 Following the parents' divorce, the three children resided with the mother under a residence order, with regular contact to the father. The father was dissatisfied, and sought increased contact and, ideally, residence. **He went to considerable lengths to see and speak to the children between agreed contact visits, and made repeated applications to the court to change the contact and residence arrangements**. Unhappy with the professionals involved in his case, **he staged public demonstrations against those of the lawyers, social workers and doctors** whom he felt were against him, pressuring them in a number of ways. Eventually **all three children refused to have further contact visits with the father, claiming that during contact he was placing unacceptable pressure on them, and was stalking and harassing them and the mother**. In the High Court, the husband stated that if he did not obtain the orders he wanted, he would: ignore all court orders; make every opportunity to see the children; **stage rooftop demonstrations at public buildings to attract maximum publicity; move into the children's street**; send messages by any means available; and *follow the children* wherever they went. The judge ordered indirect contact only and committed the

---

[62]   [1991] 1 WLR 756.
[63]   [2001] 2 FLR 895.

father to prison in respect of 30 breaches of injunctions. **The father was ordered not to seek publicity for his case in a way which identified the children, their address or their school, and an order prohibiting such publicity was made contra mundum. A further order prohibited the father from discussing the family circumstances with the media.** On release from prison there were a further 30 breaches of injunctions by the father within less than 5 months and he was given a suspended sentence. After a 6-month period, monthly contact sessions were re-introduced, supported by further injunctions including the setting up of an exclusion zone. The eldest child refused to attend. At the next **hearing the father's contact was reduced in response to expert reports which suggested that the father's continued questioning of, and pressure on, the children was causing them emotional harm.** The court rejected the arguments that the mother was sabotaging contact, noting that she obeyed all the contact orders, and that professionals observed no attempted manipulation of the children. **The father then began a series of serious and continuing breaches of the court's orders.** He entered the exclusion zone on a number of occasions, sent notes to the children, renewed his campaign of public protests, put pressure on the professionals involved, including **throwing a brick through the window of one expert**, and made a large number of applications to the courts. The fuel line on the mother's car was cut and her car vandalised, although there was no evidence to link these incidents with the father. **All three children now refused to attend contact.** The mother sought to have the father committed for contempt, and the father sought a new contact order, with discharge of the various injunctions in place.

Held

Reducing indirect contact, making a specific issue order dispensing with any requirement for the school to obtain the father's consent for school activities, restricting the father's right to make further applications, discharging the Official Solicitor, continuing the injunctions, but amending the injunction relating to publicity:

(1)   There was no implacable hostility on the mother's part, and the father's non-contact with his daughters had been directly brought about by his obstinacy, pig-headedness and blindness. The father's behaviour had caused the children such emotional strain that direct contact could not take place, and even indirect contact had to be significantly reduced. Any benefits which the girls derived from direct contact were heavily outweighed by the damage which such contact had inflicted upon them.

(2)   It was unacceptable that the father had to consider six different court orders in order to identify all the injunctions in place. The proper practice when drawing up an order amending an existing injunction was to express the new order as: (a) discharging the earlier injunction; and (b) granting a new injunction in the desired terms, incorporating the amendments. The need for these injunctions to remain in place was overwhelming in order to protect the mother and the children. A single order was required, setting out all the present injunctions with minor amendments.

(3) The father had continued to conduct the litigation in a wholly excessive, oppressive, unreasonable and abusive fashion, notwithstanding the s 91(14) orders which had been made. As a weapon of last resort, the court was entitled to act to prevent this abuse of process. No party was to commence any proceedings arising from these matters without leave, any application for leave was to be filed with the court only and would be dealt with on paper. This order imposed serious restrictions on the father's rights to bring proceedings, but the father had persisted in making groundless applications, and it was in the best interests of the children that there be a complete cessation of the litigation for the time being to end the quite intolerable and wholly unacceptable strain which the litigation was causing them.

(4) **The court should only exercise its powers to restrain publicity under the inherent jurisdiction, if and to the extent that:**
   (a) **the automatic restraints provided by the Administration of Justice Act 1960, s 12, the Contempt of Court Act 1981, s 2 and the Children Act 1989, s 97(2) were inadequate to protect the child from harm; and**
   (b) **if the interests of the child could not properly and adequately be protected by an order under the Children and Young Persons Act 1933, s 39.**

(5) **Given that s 97(2) of the 1989 Act now provided automatic protection of the child's identity in all cases where the child was involved in proceedings, in the future there would be fewer cases in which it was legitimate to exercise the inherent jurisdiction, particularly contra mundum.**

(6) **Those who sought to obtain an injunction contra mundum in the standard form, that is combining an injunction restraining identification and an injunction restraining solicitation, had to demonstrate:**
   (a) **that it was necessary for there to be an injunction protecting the identities of each of the categories of person referred to; and**
   (b) **quite separately, that it was necessary for there to be an injunction restraining solicitation in relation to each of the categories of person referred to.**

(7) It should not be assumed that, because there was a demonstrated need in relation to identification, that there was necessarily also a need to protect those persons from solicitation. **In this case, given the father's involvement with the media, there was ample evidence that the court needed to exercise its inherent jurisdiction to protect the children from the harassment to which they would otherwise be exposed.**

(8) **It was not a contempt of court to engage in reasoned criticism of the judicial system or the judiciary, even if the criticism was expressed in vigorous, trenchant or outspoken terms.** The court should not, even in a case involving children, exercise its inherent jurisdiction to prohibit such criticism. The contra mundum and in personam injunctions should be

qualified by appropriate words making it clear that, subject to appropriate safeguards, **the injunction was not of itself to prevent the publication or public display of information that the father, by name, had been involved in court proceedings concerning his contact with his daughters**.

(9)   **It was wrong in principle to prevent the media and the father from using his name and photograph in connection with his campaign of protest, and neither the use of the father's name, nor his photograph, would inflict on his children any damage such as could justify the extension of the court's protective powers over them to prevent it.**

(10) **The father was an unprincipled charlatan, but the remedy for his antics was not a futile attempt to gag him, but the truth, which was why the judgment was being given in public. The children's own best interests would be furthered by the public being told the truth.**

B V UNITED KINGDOM; P V UNITED KINGDOM[64]

European Court of Human Rights

Mr J.-P. Costa, President, Mr L. Loucaides, Mr P. Kuris, Mrs F. Tulkens, Sir Nicolas Bratza, Mrs H. S. Greve and Mr K. Traja, Judges and Mrs S. Dollé, Section Registrar

24 April 2001

Headnote

A5.31   Both applicants applied in the English courts for their **applications for residence orders in respect of their sons to be heard in public.** Both applications for a public hearing were dismissed at first instance and on appeal on the basis that the general practice of hearing child cases in private was reaffirmed **by r 4.16(7) of the Family Proceedings Rules 1991**. This provided that 'unless the court otherwise directs, a hearing of, or directions appointment in, proceedings to which this part applies shall be held in chambers', with the rule to be interpreted as applying to all children cases unless there were unusual features to the case. Both applicants applied to the European Court of Human Rights alleging a violation of their rights to a public hearing and public pronouncement of judgment under Art 6(1) of the Convention and of their right to freedom of expression under Art 10.

Held

Finding no violation of Art 6 (by 5 votes to 2) and finding unanimously that it was not necessary to examine separately the complaint under Art 10 of the Convention:

---

[64]   [2001] 2 FLR 261.

(1)   Article 6(1) of the Convention provided that, in the determination of civil rights and obligations 'everyone is entitled to a fair and public hearing'. However, as was apparent from the text of Art 6(1) itself, the requirement to hold a public hearing was subject to exceptions. **The present proceedings were prime examples of cases where the exclusion of the press and public might be justified in order to protect the privacy of the child and parties and to avoid prejudicing the interests of justice.** Moreover, it was not inconsistent with the general rule stated in Art 6(1) for a state to designate an entire class of case as an exception when considered necessary in the interests of morals, public order or national security or where required by the interests of juveniles or the protection of the private life of parties, although the need for such a measure must always be subjected to the court's control. The decision in each applicant's case to hold the hearing of his application for a residence order in chambers did not give rise to a violation of Art 6(1).

(2)   As regards the applicants' complaints that the county courts' residence judgments had not been pronounced publicly, long-standing case-law provided that the form of publicity given under the domestic law to a judgment must be assessed in the light of the special features of the proceedings and by reference to the object and purpose of Art 6(1). **In any event, copies of the full text and/or judgments in children cases were available to anyone who could establish an interest.** In the circumstances of the present case a literal interpretation of the terms of Art 6(1) concerning the pronouncement of judgments would not only be unnecessary for the purpose of public security but might even frustrate the primary aim of Art 6 to secure a fair hearing.

(3)   **In the light of the findings in connection with Art 6(1) that it was justifiable, in order to protect the privacy of the children and parties and to avoid prejudicing the interests of justice, to hold the residence proceedings in chambers and to limit the extent to which the county courts' judgments were made available to the general public, it was not necessary to examine the complaints under Art 10 separately.**

KELLY V BBC[65]

Family Division

Munby J

25 July 2000

---

[65]   [2001] 1 FLR 197.

Headnote

A5.32 After the **16-year-old boy** left home to join a religious group, his grandmother applied to make him a ward of court. The boy's whereabouts were not known, and the grandmother feared that he might leave the UK with members of the group. The court made the wardship order, and a **seek and find order, and enlisted the help of the media in tracing the boy**. A court order gave the Official Solicitor leave to give publicity about the boy, including the **disclosure of any photograph, to the press and broadcasting companies**. In response to the media campaign the boy communicated from time to time with members of the media and his grandmother, by way of email and telephone call, stating that he was happy. **The BBC approached the religious group, and obtained a telephone interview with the boy**. The BBC informed the boy's family, who obtained an injunction restraining publication of the interview with the boy. The BBC applied to discharge the injunction.

Held

Discharging the injunction, granting an injunction against solicitation, and making a statement in open court seeking the further assistance of the media:

(1) **So long as the media took care to avoid any breach of the restraints imposed by the Administration of Justice Act 1960, s 12, Children Act 1989, s 97(2) and Contempt of Court Act 1981, s 2, no contempt was committed by the media interviewing a child who was known to be a ward of court or publishing or broadcasting such an interview.**

(2) **An interview by the media was not an 'important' or 'major' step in a child's life**, however interesting or exciting, **therefore the media did not require the leave of the court either to interview a ward of court, or to publish or broadcast such an interview, although they could be injuncted from doing so by the court**.

(3) On the basis that the boy's participation in the interview did not raise any question with respect to his upbringing, **the boy's welfare was not the paramount consideration in this case**.

(4) **There was no burden on the media to establish why it should be allowed to publish.**

(5) The issues were:
(a) whether an injunction was necessary to protect the boy from clear and identifiable harm; and
(b) whether the injunction sought was proportionate to that aim and no wider than necessary.

(6) **No convincing case had been put forward** that broadcasting the interview or other further publicity was going significantly to harm the boy, and an

injunction framed as widely as that which the court was being invited to make would be wholly disproportionate to any aim that could legitimately be pursued on the boy's behalf.

(7) **There was a clear public interest in the boy's story, and in the interview, and a particular public interest in the media being encouraged to assist the court in cases such as this in which the court had itself sought to enlist the media's assistance**.

(8) In the circumstances, it would **not be appropriate to restrain the media** from publishing comments by other people about the boy.

Per curiam

(a) Even if some organs of the media were represented when an injunction contra mundum was granted, the injunction would necessarily still have been granted ex parte, or without notice, to all the other organs of the media upon whom it might eventually be served.

(b) **Every injunction contra mundum therefore had to be treated as if it were an ex parte injunction granted without notice**.

(c) **The following principles applied to all without notice injunctions, including cases relating to children in which injunctive relief was sought against third parties or the world at large**.
   - Any ex parte order containing injunctions should set out on its face, either by way of recital or in a schedule, a **list of all affidavits, witness statements and other evidential materials read by the judge**.
   - The applicant's legal representatives should, whenever possible, liaise with the associate with a view to **ensuring that the order as drawn contained this information**.
   - On receipt of the order from the court, the applicant's legal representatives should satisfy themselves that the order as drawn correctly set out the relevant information and, if it did not, should take **urgent steps** to have the order amended under the slip rule.
   - The applicant's legal representatives should respond forthwith to any **reasonable request from the party injuncted** or his legal representatives, either for copies of the materials read by the judge or for information about what took place at the hearing.
   - Persons injuncted ex parte were **entitled to proper information** about the hearing, and at the very least to be told, if they asked, exactly what documents, bundles or other evidential materials were lodged with the court either before or during the course of the hearing and what legal authorities were cited to the judge.
   - It would be prudent for those acting for applicants in such cases to keep a **proper note of proceedings**, lest they find themselves embarrassed by a proper request for information which they were unable to find.

- In urgent cases, such as the instant case, in which there was no time to prepare comprehensive evidence in proper form, the court must act upon the information provided by counsel, but in every such case there should be an **undertaking to swear and file an affidavit as soon as possible**.
- On the principles of natural justice, it would be wrong for a judge to be given material at a without notice hearing which would not at a later stage be revealed to the persons affected by the result of the application. In children cases this rule was qualified, **but there was no justification for not making full disclosure to the media of the material upon which an injunction contra mundum had been granted**.
- **If, as would often be the case it was not appropriate for the media to see the material in the form in which it was originally filed with the court, the solution was to set out the relevant material in a separate affidavit which could be shown to the media, and this should be done even if there appeared to be no immediate likelihood of there being an application to discharge the injunction.**
- **An injunction in rem or contra mundum should normally be qualified by a public domain proviso.**

RE G (CELEBRITIES: PUBLICITY)[66]

Court of Appeal

Swinton Thomas, Thorpe and Clarke LJJ

23 October 1998

Headnote

A5.33 The **divorce of the mother and father, both celebrities**, attracted much publicity. At the first hearing dealing with arrangements for the children, a judge made an order of her own motion designed to protect the children from unnecessary publicity, **including a paragraph which purported to restrain any person from taking or publishing photographs of the children**. Some time later, after the parents' private lives had attracted even greater publicity, the arrangements for the children broke down, and there were cross-applications for residence orders. **At the hearing the Official Solicitor, acting for the children, applied for tighter press restrictions**. A second judge confirmed the first order, and made a further order, with the consent of the mother and father, prohibiting both parents from (i) **speaking to or writing in the news media about each other or the children, or encouraging or instructing any other person to do so on their behalf,** and (ii) **disclosing the contents of the proceedings to any person not concerned in the proceedings as a legal representative or expert witness**. The judge also ordered that neither the text of the order nor a summary be

---

[66]   [1999] 1 FLR 409.

published. **The application by News Group Newspapers to discharge the second order and the paragraph relating to photographs was dismissed by the judge, and News Group Newspapers appealed**.

Held

Allowing the appeal in part:

(1)   The publicity which this family attracted made this an exceptional case, justifying the imposition of restrictions beyond those provided by the Administration of Justice Act 1960, s 12, which did not on its own prevent the media from reporting the comings and goings of the parties and witnesses outside the courtroom.

(2)   However, **given the emphasis in the authorities that any restraint imposed must be no wider than necessary and must be expressed in the clearest possible terms, the first order ought to be amended so that** (i) **it prohibited the taking of photographs of the children 'other than for private and domestic purposes'**, and (ii) **it was clear that publication of photographs taken before the order was made was not prohibited**.

(3)   The court undoubtedly had jurisdiction in personam to restrain any act by a parent that, if unrestrained, would or might adversely affect the welfare of the child the subject of proceedings. Neither parent sought release or variation from the reciprocal restraint on communicating with the media about each other or the children. **The element which prevented them from speaking about each other was relevant to the welfare of the children, and would not be deleted. Although the provision was intended primarily to impose a discipline on the family**, it was not possible, or desirable, to frame it in such a way as to protect a third party who knew of the order from being in contempt of court if he published information provided by the mother or father in breach of the order.

(4)   The provision preventing publication of even a summary of the order went too far. It meant that the news media had no way of knowing that they were not permitted to publish anything, rendering the entire order ineffectual and/or the subject of an unwitting breach. **The court should have adopted the conventional approach and issued a terse statement approved by the judge and agreed between the parties**. The Official Solicitor should now prepare and issue the briefest statement of outcome. **It was hard to conceive of circumstances which would justify preventing the media from publishing the bare outcome**.

Per curiam

The extent to which family proceedings were conducted in private hearings had been much criticised recently, and there were powerful arguments for more openness. **Those who were bound by contra mundum orders had no opportunity to make submissions as to where the boundary should be drawn, or to contribute their expertise to the drafting, and consideration ought to be given to developing a procedure to meet this deficit.**

PB (HEARINGS IN OPEN COURT)[67]

Court of Appeal

Butler-Sloss, Peter Gibson and Thorpe LJJ

20 June 1996

Headnote

A5.34   At the beginning of the hearing of the parties' residence applications, the father applied for the whole case to be heard in open court. The judge decided that all the proceedings should be heard in private and gave the father leave to appeal on that preliminary issue.

Held

Dismissing the appeal – although English law had not incorporated the European Convention on Human Rights, the present procedures in family proceedings were in accordance with the spirit of the Convention (see p 768D below). There was a long-established practice in the High Court and county court of hearing children applications in private. **Although appeals in the Court of Appeal were almost always heard in public it was the practice for the Court of Appeal to give a direction for non-identification of the child in child appeals (see p 768F below).** Other courts were bound to hear child cases generally in private and it was unlikely that judges would, other than rarely, hear the evidence relating to the welfare of the child in public. **The judgment was a different matter (see p 769B below).** The exercise of discretion remained in the hands of the trial judge. In the absence of an application to hear the case in open court and unusual circumstances, the normal position would remain and evidence would be heard in private. Matters of practice and procedure in the family justice system were the subject of constant interdisciplinary review. There were appropriate channels to express dissatisfaction (see p 771C–E).

RE Z (A MINOR) (FREEDOM OF PUBLICATION)[68]

Court of Appeal

Sir Thomas Bingham MR, Auld and Ward LJJ

---

[67]   [1996] 2 FLR 765.
[68]   [1996] 1 FLR 191.

31 July 1995

Headnote

A5.35   The child had **special educational needs**. She attended a unit which offered successful methods of treating such problems. The court in the exercise of its inherent jurisdiction granted an injunction in rem restraining the media from publishing information which would lead to the child's identity. **The mother subsequently breached the order by taking part in a broadcast which prompted sensational media reporting**. An injunction was later granted against the mother. At the time both injunctions were made, there were no other proceedings before the court. A company wished to televise the results of the unit and to identify the child to attract public attention. The mother was willing to co-operate in the making of the programme and sought the court's leave to proceed with the making and broadcasting of the film. The application was refused and the mother appealed.

Held

Dismissing the appeal:

(a)   it was necessary to examine the **source and extent** of the court's jurisdiction to prevent publicity (see pp 196C–D).

(b)   In wardship, there was the aspect of the jurisdiction which:
  (i)   sought to protect the welfare of the child and
  (ii)   **the court's power to protect its own proceedings in the interests of the administration of justice** (see pp 203G–H).

(c)   There was **a category of case where the freedom to publish information was set beyond the limit of the exercise of the wardship/inherent jurisdiction** (see pp 207E–208A).

(d)   However, **the jurisdiction would be exercised where the material was directed at the child or an aspect of the child's upbringing** (see pp 208C–D).

(e)   This child had the right of confidentiality in respect of her attendance at the unit.

(f)   The mother could waive the right to confidentiality in respect of her treatment (see p 210B below) **but this was an exercise of parental responsibility** and therefore a **prohibited steps order** under the Children Act 1989 could be made to control it (see pp 210F–211G below).

(g)   It was necessary to consider whether the paramountcy of the child's welfare governed the court's decision. **If the matter required the determination of a question with respect to the upbringing of the child, then**

the child's welfare was the paramount consideration and the child's welfare prevailed over the freedom of publication (see pp 212B–213G below).

(h) **If welfare was not paramount, then welfare must be balanced against freedom of publication** (see pp 213G–214C).

(i) Where a duty of confidentiality arose it could be absolute, although the right could be surrendered (see p 214D). **The question the court was being asked to determine was a question with respect to the upbringing of the child**.

(j) **The welfare of the child would be harmed and not advanced by her being involved in the making and publication of the film** (see pp 215A–B).

MRS R V CENTRAL INDEPENDENT TELEVISION PLC[69]

Court of Appeal

Neill, Hoffmann and Waite LJJ

February 1994

Headnote

A5.36 In 1992, the father was imprisoned following his conviction on **charges of indecency**. Part of the evidence against him consisted of a video film of **indecent acts** in the course of their commission. The **Crown Court** judge hearing the case imposed reporting restrictions to prevent the identification of the children concerned. In January 1994 **the respondent television company broadcast a trailer of a programme concerning the work of the Metropolitan Police Obscene Publications Squad**, to be broadcast later that month. In particular the programme related to the investigation and prosecution of the father and included pictures of him. **The applicant (formerly the wife of the father, by whom she had a child), who had seen the trailer, sought an order requiring the respondent to obscure pictures of the father so as to avoid the possibility of any identification of herself or her child**. Kirkwood J, sitting in the Family Division, granted the order sought. The respondent appealed.

Held

Allowing the appeal (per Neill and Hoffmann LJJ), the authorities showed that in a number of cases the court had exercised its statutory jurisdiction under the Administration of Justice Act 1960 in order to prohibit the publication of material relating to the upbringing of children over whose welfare the court was exercising its supervisory jurisdiction. In so doing, **the element of confidentiality belonged not to the child but to the court**. In the present case,

[69]   [1994] 2 FLR 151.

however, **the programme was in no way concerned with the care or upbringing of children**. If the threatened publication touched upon matters which were of direct concern to the court in its supervisory role, following *Re X (A Minor) (Wardship: Jurisdiction)*, it would be necessary to balance the interests of the child against the rights of free speech. **Since, however, the programme had nothing to do with the care and upbringing of the child concerned, there was nothing to weight in the balance against the freedom to publish**. It followed that there was **no jurisdiction** on this case to restrain the respondent from publishing pictures of the father. The appeal would be allowed accordingly.

Per Waite LJ: The exercise of the prerogative jurisdiction parens patriae was theoretically unlimited. It followed that the court in the present case technically had jurisdiction to protect the child by preserving the father's anonymity. **However, such an order should only have been made if the effective working of the court's own jurisdiction was threatened or potentially threatened by the publicity**. The judge below had sought to balance the welfare of the child against the public interest in the freedom of publication. **He should, however, have declined to make the order sought as there was no question of any threat to the exercise of the court's jurisdiction, and consequently no such balance to be struck.**

Per curiam

Per Hoffmann LJ: in the area of human rights such as the exercise of the freedom of speech, the wisdom of creating judge-made exceptions, particularly when they required a judicial balancing of interests, was doubtful. **No freedom was without cost, and the judiciary should not whittle away freedom of speech with ad hoc exceptions. The principle that the press was free from governmental and judicial control is more important than the particular case.**

RE E (A MINOR) (CHILD ABUSE: EVIDENCE)[70]

Family Division

Scott Baker J

27 March 1990

Headnote

A5.37 On 18 August 1989, the local authority commenced wardship proceedings in respect of a four- year-old boy, **E, on the basis of allegations that he, together with three other boys of approximately the same age had been subjected to sexual abuse by the boy's parents and the father's brother. The case against the boy's parents and uncle depended wholly upon the evidence of the three other children.** The children lived in the same housing estate in a Midlands town and frequently played together in each other's houses until 9 August 1989

---

[70]   [1991] 1 FLR 420.

when one of them, **D**, **questioned by his mother who had heard rumours about E's household, told her about sexual activity there. He made specific allegations of buggery and other forms of sexual abuse. The social services were informed and D was interviewed by a social worker together with two women police officers, when he made similar disclosures. D's mother told the mother of another of the children, Z, who was also interviewed. Z made no disclosures, but a police surgeon who examined both D and Z, though he found no evidence that D had been abused, found 'clear evidence of penetration of the back passage' with regard to Z. Z then made disclosures both to his mother and to a social worker and two women police officers. He was examined again on 14 August by a paediatrician who found nothing abnormal. After making further allegations to his mother, some bordering on fantasy, he was interviewed for the third time on 15 August, so that his previous disclosures could be recorded on video. Despite considerable pressure he did not repeat his allegations. E's parents were arrested and a place of safety order was obtained for E, who lived thereafter with his maternal grandparents. E said nothing to indicate he had been abused, and a medical examination revealed no sign of injury.** The third child, R, when asked by his mother, denied that anything unusual had happened, **but 5 days later implied to the social worker and a woman police officer that there had been sexual abuse by the father's brother against E.** On 13 September the police informed the parents that no charges would be brought for lack of corroboration, but that they were 95% certain of their guilt. On 29 September the social services held a case conference at which it was decided that the NSPCC would work with Z, and that if evidence of further sexual abuse was discovered that evidence would be directed to the police department with the recommendation that they reconsider their decision not to prosecute. Over the next few months seven interviews with Z took place, four being video-taped. **The President of the Family Division gave leave for E to be interviewed by a well-known child psychiatrist, who concluded that E was a normally healthy boy and that there were no clinical signs of sexual abuse.** At the hearing, it was clear that the mothers of the children and the two social workers concerned had been completely convinced from an early stage that all that the children said was true. That view was reinforced by, and based upon, the police surgeon's diagnosis with regard to Z. **However, the police surgeon admitted in evidence that he had neither the knowledge nor the experience to reach the conclusion that he had reached, and conceded that his findings with regard to penetration could not be relied on.**

Held

The evidential value of what the children were reported as having said was very limited for the following reasons:

(1)   The mothers of D and Z, who were crucial as to their children's earliest disclosures, were unreliable in that they were so consumed from the first by certainty about the parent's guilt that they were unable to be objective. **Their evidence was at times conflicting and factually inaccurate.**

(2) **All three children had inevitably been influenced by the climate in which they made their disclosures, in which both parents and social workers were disposed to accept uncritically what they said and were convinced of the parent's guilt.**

(3) The interviews of the children were deficient, because:
  (a) **inadequate records were kept;**
  (b) **anatomically correct dolls were introduced at too early a stage and allowed to play too dominant a part;**
  (c) **leading questions were asked;**
  (d) **the interviewers were convinced that the children had been abused; and**
  (e) **there were too many interviews, particularly in Z's case, which were bound to have diminishing value besides being potentially damaging to the children.**

  One carefully planned and video-recorded interview of each child would have had far greater evidential value. The vast majority of recommendations with regard to conducting child interviews set out in para 12.34 of the Cleveland report had been ignored.

(4) There were inconsistencies in the children's accounts, both between the children and in accounts by the same child on different occasions. Some accounts were undoubtedly fiction.

(5) Each child's behaviour during the summer of 1989, when they played happily together and visited E's house willingly, was inconsistent with the truth of the disclosures.

(6) The alleged abusers had appeared to be reliable witnesses whose evidence must be given due weight, and the evidence as to E from expert witnesses and other did not support the disclosures of the other children.

It must be concluded from the above and from all the evidence that neither parent had abused E or any of the children in the case; that the parents were loving and caring parents, and that E's best interests would be met by living in their house unsupervised by the court or any public authority; and that the parents had been subjected to a considerable injustice in having unsubstantiated allegations made and pursued against them. The wardship proceedings would be discharged.

In the interests of justice, the court would give leave for the judgment to be reported, directing that the injunction made during the currency of the wardship proceedings restraining national newspapers and others from identifying the parties should be continued.

Appendix 6

CASES REFERRED TO BY LORD STEYN IN *RE S (IDENTIFICATION: RESTRICTIONS ON PUBLICATION)*[1]

(Note that font emphasis is that of the author's)

CONTEXT IN WHICH LORD STEYN REFERRED TO THESE CASES

A6.01

'[23] The House unanimously takes the view that since the Human Rights Act 1998 came into force in October 2000, the earlier case-law about the existence and scope of inherent jurisdiction need not be considered in this case or in similar cases. The foundation of the jurisdiction to restrain publicity in a case such as the present is now derived from convention rights under the European Convention. This is the simple and direct way to approach such cases. In this case the jurisdiction is not in doubt. **This is not to say that the case-law on the inherent jurisdiction of the High Court is wholly irrelevant. On the contrary, it may remain of some interest in regard to the ultimate balancing exercise to be carried out under the European Convention provisions**. My noble and learned friend Lord Bingham of Cornhill invited the response of counsel to this approach. Both expressed agreement with it. I would affirm this approach. Before passing on I would observe on a historical note that a study of **the case law revealed that the approach adopted in the past under the inherent jurisdiction was remarkably similar to that to be adopted under the European Convention**. Indeed the European Convention provisions were often cited even before it became part of our law in October 2000. Nevertheless, it will in future be necessary, if earlier case-law is cited, to bear in mind the new methodology required by the European Convention as explained in *Campbell v MGN Ltd*.'[2]

WHAT ARE THE DICTA IN *CAMPBELL*?

A6.02 See para [19] in *Campbell*:

'[18] In reaching this conclusion it is not necessary to pursue the controversial question whether the European Convention itself has this wider effect. Nor

---

[1] [2005] 1 FLR 591.
[2] [2004] UKHL 22, [2004] 2 WLR 1232, [2004] UKHR 648.

is it necessary to decide whether the duty imposed on courts by section 6 of the Human Rights Act 1998 extends to questions of substantive law as distinct from questions of practice and procedure. **It is sufficient to recognise that the values underlying articles 8 and 10 are not confined to disputes between individuals and public authorities**. This approach has been adopted by the courts in several recent decisions, reported and unreported, where individuals have complained of press intrusion. A convenient summary of these cases is to be found in Gavin Phillipson's valuable article "Transforming Breach of Confidence? Towards a Common Law Right of Privacy under the Human Rights Act",[3] at 726–728.

[19] In applying this approach, and giving effect to the values protected by article 8, courts will often be aided by adopting the structure of article 8 in the same way as they now habitually apply the Strasbourg court's approach to article 10 when resolving questions concerning freedom of expression. **Articles 8 and 10 call for a more explicit analysis of competing considerations than the three traditional requirements of the cause of action for breach of confidence identified in** *Coco v A N Clark (Engineers) Ltd.*[4]

[20] I should take this a little further on one point. Article 8(1) recognises the need to respect private and family life. Article 8(2) recognises there are occasions when intrusion into private and family life may be justified. One of these is where the intrusion is necessary for the protection of the rights and freedoms of others. Article 10(1) recognises the importance of freedom of expression. But article 10(2), like article 8(2), recognises there are occasions when protection of the rights of others may make it necessary for freedom of expression to give way. **When both these articles are engaged a difficult question of proportionality may arise. This question is distinct from the initial question of whether the published information engaged article 8 at all by being within the sphere of the complainant's private or family life.**

[21] Accordingly, in deciding what was the ambit of an individual's 'private life' in particular circumstances courts need to be on guard against using as a touchstone a test which brings into account considerations which should more properly be considered at the later stage of proportionality. **Essentially the touchstone of private life is whether in respect of the disclosed facts the person in question had a reasonable expectation of privacy.**

[22] Different forms of words, usually to much the same effect, have been suggested from time to time. The second Restatement of Torts in the United States (1977), article 652D, p 394, uses the formulation of disclosure of matter which "would be highly offensive to a reasonable person". In *Australian Broadcasting Corporation v Lenah Game Meats Pty Ltd*,[5] para 42, Gleeson CJ used words, widely quoted, having a similar meaning. This particular formulation should be used with care, for two reasons. First, the "highly offensive" phrase is suggestive of a stricter test of private information than a reasonable expectation of privacy. Second, the "highly offensive" formulation can all too easily bring into account, when deciding whether the disclosed information was private, considerations which go more properly to issues of proportionality; for instance, the degree of intrusion into private life, and the extent to which publication was a matter of proper public concern. This could be a recipe for confusion.'

---

3   (2003) 66 MLR 726.
4   [1969] RPC 41.
5   [1969] RPC 41, (2001) 185 ALR 1, 13.

RE M AND N (MINORS) (WARDSHIP: PUBLICATION OF INFORMATION)[6]

Family Division

Thorpe J

22 March 1989

Court of Appeal

Donaldson MR, Butler-Sloss and Stuart-Smith LJJ

11 July 1989

Headnote

A6.03 Two children were placed with a foster-mother. The foster-mother remarried and had two children. A social worker became aware of difficulties between the children and the foster-father and inquiries were made. **One of the children made allegations of a sexual nature against the foster-father to a social worker in confidence.** The social worker promised not to breach this confidence. The local authority considered that they had the right and duty to remove children whom they considered to be at risk or whose welfare otherwise required them to act where necessary without prior consultation with, or even notification to, the foster-parents even though the placement with the foster-parents had been long established. **The children did not return home after school one day and were placed elsewhere. The local authority informed the foster-parents by letter as to some of the reasons for the removal but the sexual allegations were omitted.** A provincial newspaper desired to publish information about the removal of the wards from the foster-parents. **Although the newspaper did not wish to act to the children's detriment, it considered that it had a public duty to inform the public in their area of the way in which the local authority had exercised their power and to put the spotlight on a possible abuse of such power.** The local authority considered that any publicity was likely to identify the children to their disadvantage and it sought and was granted a widely termed injunction against press publicity by the newspaper, which subsequently applied for the discharge of the injunction. This application was dismissed. The newspaper appealed.

Held

(1) Allowing the appeal to the limited extent of substituting a narrower form of injunction for that ordered by the judge – the correctness of the removal from the foster-parents would be in issue in subsequent wardship proceedings but present proceedings concerned the appropriateness of the injunction.

---

[6]   [1990] 1 FLR 149.

(2) **There were two opposing considerations for the court: the children's welfare and the freedom of the press to publish**. The main issue was the form and scope of the injunction to be granted.

(3) **The scope of s 12(1) of the Administration of Justice Act 1960 was limited in that the statutory prohibition and indeed the common law prohibition related solely to the publication of details of the actual proceedings.** The protection in the Contempt of Court Act 1981 did not fit easily into the wardship jurisdiction. **Any protection of a child from publication outside the restricted statutory scope therefore required an express prohibition by way of injunction.**

(4) **The power of the courts to impose restrictions on publication for the protection of children was derived from the inherent jurisdiction of the High Court exercising the powers of the Crown as parens patriae. The sole question was whether the children's interests should prevail over the freedom of the press. The children's welfare was not the paramount consideration.**

(5) A balancing exercise had to be carried out whereby the courts had to give proper balance between the wards' protection and the right of free publication. **There had been an upsurge in investigative journalism into situations affecting children. The courts must move with the times and might be obliged to grant injunctions, the terms of which should be no wider than was necessary to protect the children's welfare.**

(6) Certain factors were important on the facts. **The interest of the newspaper was not curiosity but public interest in the exercise of the power of a local authority**. They recognised that uninhibited publicity would be to the children's detriment and accepted that some restriction on publication was required. **The scope of the restriction must be scrutinised with care. A formula was required which gave as much protection from identification as was reasonably possible.**

(7) There might be circumstances where, for the welfare of the child, no information at all should be divulged. **However, the present case was one where the newspaper should have the right to publish the story with certain safeguards: the identity of the children, foster-parents, parents, schools, current foster-parents and any relevant addresses should not be disclosed.**

(8) Some protection should be granted against the doorstep intrusion type of interviewing, but the local authority did not require that protection. In cases of legitimate public interest, judges might consider the desirability of giving judgment in open court, making suitable adjustments to protect the parties' identity.

Per curiam

Criticism about the absence of evidence before the judge on an ex parte application for an injunction was misconceived. To require evidence on affidavit before urgent applications could be made would impede the judge's function in acting swiftly. The suggestion for the production of specific evidence of psychological harm to the child by the publication was also misconceived and was not normally necessary. **The enormous difficulties for those who were recipients of confidences of children was acknowledged.** The following observations were made. **Once a serious allegation was made, it could not be ignored. The fact and contents of the allegation would eventually have to be revealed to others.** Depending on the circumstances, it might be premature and unwise to tell the foster-parents or other carers while the child remained in their care. **But, as soon as the child was protected, justice to the foster-parents must involve a right to be told as soon as possible.** A child had to be told that at some stage (unless the allegation was ignored) the carers would have to be told. Any other approach would be unjust to the child as it would be to the adults concerned.

RE C (A MINOR) (WARDSHIP: MEDICAL TREATMENT) (NO 2)[7]

Court of Appeal

Lord Donaldson of Lymington MR, Balcombe and Nicholls LJJ

26 April 1989

Headnote

A6.04 A judge, in wardship proceedings brought by a local authority authorised the **withholding of certain forms of medical treatment** from a female child, C, aged 4 months who was severely brain damaged and terminally ill. **There being a legitimate public interest in such a case, the judge delivered a detailed and reasoned judgment in open court and in order to protect the privacy of those involved in the case sought to put a 'ring fence' around C and all connected with her.** An injunction was granted restraining any person from making any inquiry directed to ascertaining the identity of C, her parents, the local authority, the area health authority, hospital, medical practitioners, or staff having or having had care of C. It was further ordered that the media be restrained from publishing any material which would identify or assist in identifying any person or body mentioned in the injunction.

The Official Solicitor, acting on behalf of C, appealed to the Court of Appeal in order to question parts of the judge's order relating to the treatment to be given to C. **The Court of Appeal also gave judgment in open court and in so doing**

---

[7]   [1990] 1 FLR 263.

quoted extensively from a report which had been written by a professor of paediatrics. The Court of Appeal confirmed the injunctions granted by the judge and extended them by prohibiting publication of the names of the solicitors for the parties, since this would have identified the district where they were practising and hence the local authority and the area health authority.

Mail Newspapers plc (the applicants) applied to the Court of Appeal to review the width and terms of the injunctions. **The applicants accepted that neither C nor, without their consent, her parents should be identified. However, they submitted that they ought to be free to publish photographs of all who were or had been involved in the care and treatment of C, to make inquiries of them and others as to her care and treatment and as to the circumstances which had led to her being made a ward of court, and to publish the results of those inquiries.**

The applicants relied on the fact that, by reason of her condition, C was not, and never would be, capable of understanding anything written about her. The applicants also drew to the attention of the Court of Appeal the difficulties faced by the media in complying with a non-identification injunction, if neither the order nor the notification identifies the ward whose identification is prohibited.

Held

Allowing the application and substituting a new injunction which restrained identification of C, her parents, any hospital at which C was being or had been treated, or any natural person who was caring or who had cared for C and the solicitation of any information relating to C and her parents from her parents themselves, any staff employed at any such hospital, or any of C's carers or former carers and the publication of any information so obtained:

(1) **The information disclosed in open court by the judge and the Court of Appeal in the main appeal provided all necessary material for discussion and comment on the sole issue of genuine public interest, namely the vitally important question of how a baby should be cared for and treated in the tragic situation of C, and in particular, there was no public interest that required the disclosure of the circumstances which had led to C becoming a ward of court.**

(2) The exercise of the jurisdiction to grant injunctions in wardship cases having a high degree of public interest involved holding **a sensible balance between the protection of the ward and her rights and the rights of outside parties and, in particular, their right of free publication**.

(3) **C's welfare required that those caring for her should be protected from any pressure, attack, interference or harassment which might occur if they were publicly identified or solicited for information in order that they should be free to make awesome decisions about her future care and treatment solely in her interests.**

(4)   C's carers, former carers and the staff employed at hospitals where she was being or had been cared for owed her a duty of confidentiality in relation to information acquired by them in such capacities. The court was entitled and bound to safeguard C's rights by creating an obstacle to third parties' possible attempts to induce and exploit breaches of that duty of confidentiality.

(5)   Although C's parents were not involved in her care, any identification of, or pressure, upon them could well indirectly affect her professional carers and a restraint upon the solicitation of information from them about C or themselves was justified as being in support of the wardship jurisdiction. Many parents would not willingly make or agree to a child being made a ward of court, if they thought that this might lead to their being identified and singled out for special attention by the media.

(6)   The injunction order should be entitled (by reference to a schedule) with the real name of the ward, and not just as in 'In the Matter of Baby C' and should name the district registry and the parties (the defendants being named only in the schedule), otherwise the persons to whom the order is addressed will not know whom it is they are restrained from identifying or soliciting.

RE W (A MINOR) (WARDSHIP: RESTRICTIONS ON PUBLICATION)[8]

Court of Appeal

Neill, Balcombe and Beldam LJJ

24 July 1991

Headnote

A6.05   A boy, aged 15, received into council care in 1989 and made a ward of court in 1990, had a disturbed background and had been involved for several years in **homosexual activities with men much older than himself**. His mother was unable to care for him. In December 1990 the council, without informing the wardship court, **placed him with foster-parents who were both men who had had a stable homosexual relationship with each other for many years. On learning that a newspaper intended to publish an article about the matter, the council applied for, and was granted, an injunction restraining publication, on the ground that it was likely to cause the boy serious harm, both because readers of the article might identify him and also because, if he read the article himself, he would be adversely affected by its terms and by his fear of the reaction of others to it**. Furthermore, the placement was going well and might be put in jeopardy. The newspaper appealed, contending that the placement of a ward who had been subjected to

---

[8]   [1992] 1 FLR 99.

homosexual abuse in the past with male homosexual foster-parents was a matter of public interest and concern of which the public should be informed, in particular where the placement had been made without the knowledge of the court and, as was claimed, against the wishes of the mother.

Held

Allowing the appeal:

(1)   The freedom of the press to publish matters of genuine public concern, as opposed to matters of mere curiosity, should not be restricted by the exercise of the court's jurisdiction in wardship **any more than was essential to protect the ward from clear and identifiable harm.**

(2)   **In most cases, the public interest in favour of publication could be satisfied without identification of the ward, but, occasionally, some wider identification might have to be accepted, and only in exceptional cases should publication be prohibited in order to prevent the ward being harmed by reading an article in which he could identify himself.**

(3)   In his performance of the balancing exercise in the present case, the judge had attached undue weight to the risk to the ward of possible identification and wholly insufficient weight to the fact that he was dealing with a matter of great public interest and concern. In that regard, he had been plainly wrong and, accordingly, the court would substitute its own direction. **The newspaper, while doing its best to avoid any risk of identification, should be free to publish the story, detailing all the ingredients of public concern, including the identity of the council.**

RE H-S (MINORS) (PROTECTION OF IDENTITY)[9]

Court of Appeal

Neill LJ and Ward J

21 December 1993

Headnote

A6.06   There were three children now aged 17, 13 and 10. The parents had been unhappily married due to the father's sexuality. In divorce proceedings in 1984, the mother was granted custody of the children. **The father regularly dressed as, and sought to pass himself off as, a woman.** In 1987 the mother could no longer cope with the children and they subsequently lived with the father. In 1989 the mother sought the return of the children. **At that stage, the father stated that he wished to be addressed in the feminine and undergo a sex-change**

---

[9]   [1994] 1 WLR 1141, [1994] 1 FLR 519, [1994] 3 All ER 390, CA.

operation. An order was made that the children remain with the father, subject to the supervision of the local authority. The father had indicated a wish at some future time to write a book, but he denied any intention to exploit the situation to earn money by selling the story to the press. **Within a week of the hearing, the father participated in a programme about transsexualism. The father was then deluged by the media and, as a result of the publicity which ensued, the identity of the father and the children was revealed**. One year later there was a further blaze of publicity and the mother applied again for a variation of the custody order. In 1990 an injunction was granted against the father, preventing him from taking or permitting any act likely to expose the children to any form of publicity arising from his custody of the children, his transsexuality, and the sex-change operation, until the wife's application for custody was heard or further order. Within days of this order, two more articles appeared in the press, identifying the father and the children. The mother applied for the father's committal but no order was made. The father subsequently applied to discharge the injunction. Both parents' applications were refused. The judge continued the injunction in the same terms until the youngest child was 18. The father appealed.

Held

Allowing the appeal:

(1) **The order would be varied to ensure that the father did not pursue dealings with the media from the property at which he and the children lived or elsewhere in their presence, to respect the children's privacy**. The present form of the injunction was obscure in its meaning and too wide. It would prevent the father informing the school that the children were being cared for by another person while he had his operation. **The purpose of the application was to prevent publicity in the intended book and by the media**.

(2) **There was ample evidence before the judge to satisfy his finding that the children would be adversely affected by such publicity, and expert evidence of the harm was not necessary. The important question was whether the father's freedom to publish and the media's freedom to publish matters of public interest outweighed the risk of harm to the children**.

(3) **The financial rewards did not assuage the hurt that would flow from the family being in the public eye and subject to taunting from their peers. The welfare of the child was not the paramount consideration because it was more than a question of the court's determination of the upbringing of the child**. The freedom of the press was in issue. The facts of the case did disclose a matter of public interest which the media were entitled to publish and about which the public might legitimately debate, namely the fact that the court, with the support of the local authority, had approved of young children being and remaining in the care of a parent who was transsexual and who had undergone a change of sex. **Public interest turned**

to public curiosity when information was sought as to the identity of the parties. The interest of the particular child then became the more important factor.

(4) Where an injunction was sought, the effect of which was to impose a restraint upon the freedom of the press, and the media generally, then such a matter should be transferred to the High Court, and the Official Solicitor should be invited to represent the children concerned.

R V CENTRAL INDEPENDENT TELEVISION PLC[10]

Court of Appeal

Neill, Hoffmann and Waite LJJ

February 1994

Headnote

A6.07 In 1992 the father was imprisoned following his conviction on charges of indecency. **Part of the evidence against him consisted of a video film of indecent acts in the course of their commission.** The Crown Court judge hearing the case imposed reporting restrictions to prevent the identification of the children concerned. In January 1994 the respondent television company broadcast a trailer of a programme concerning the work of the Metropolitan Police Obscene Publications Squad, to be broadcast later that month. **In particular the programme related to the investigation and prosecution of the father and included pictures of him.** The applicant (formerly the wife of the father, by whom she had a child), who had seen the trailer, **sought an order requiring the respondent to obscure pictures of the father so as to avoid the possibility of any identification of herself or her child.** Kirkwood J, sitting in the Family Division, granted the order sought. The respondent appealed.

Held

Allowing the appeal (per Neill and Hoffmann LJJ):

(1) The authorities showed that in a number of cases the court had exercised its statutory jurisdiction under the Administration of Justice Act 1960 in order to prohibit the publication of material relating to the upbringing of children over whose welfare the court was exercising its supervisory jurisdiction.

(2) In so doing, the element of confidentiality belonged not to the child but to the court.

---

[10]   [1994] 2 FLR 151.

(3) **In the present case, however, the programme was in no way concerned with the care or upbringing of children.**

(4) **If the threatened publication touched upon matters which were of direct concern to the court in its supervisory role, following Re X (A Minor) (Wardship: Jurisdiction), it would be necessary to balance the interests of the child against the rights of free speech.**

(5) Since, however, the programme had nothing to do with the care and upbringing of the child concerned, there was nothing to weigh in the balance against the freedom to publish. **It followed that there was no jurisdiction in this case to restrain the respondent from publishing pictures of the father.** The appeal would be allowed accordingly.

Per Waite LJ: The exercise of the prerogative jurisdiction parens patriae was theoretically unlimited. It followed that the court in the present case technically had jurisdiction to protect the child by preserving the father's anonymity. **However, such an order should only have been made if the effective working of the court's own jurisdiction was threatened or potentially threatened by the publicity. The judge below had sought to balance the welfare of the child against the public interest in the freedom of publication. He should, however, have declined to make the order sought as there was no question of any threat to the exercise of the court's jurisdiction, and consequently no such balance to be struck.**

Per curiam

Per Hoffmann LJ: in the area of human rights such as the exercise of the freedom of speech, the wisdom of creating judge-made exceptions, particularly when they required a judicial balancing of interests, was doubtful. No freedom was without cost, and the judiciary should not whittle away freedom of speech with ad hoc exceptions. The principle that the press was free from governmental and judicial control is more important than the particular case.

RE R (WARDSHIP: RESTRICTIONS ON PUBLICATION)[11]

Court of Appeal

Sir Thomas Bingham MR, Henry and Millett LJJ

14 April 1994

Headnote

A6.08 In 1989 care and control of a ward, then aged 2, was granted to the ward's mother with staying access to the father on condition that the father complied with a direction issued by the court. **The father failed to comply with**

---

[11] [1994] 2 FLR 637.

the condition and contact ceased accordingly. The father abducted the ward and took her eventually to Israel. The father was extradited to the UK and was arrested and charged with the abduction. **Considerable publicity surrounded both the abduction and the subsequent extradition, and an order was made in the wardship proceedings in the Family Division preventing the publication, inter alia, of any material from which the ward could be identified.** The father made an application to the Family Division for the discharge of the order, so as to permit publicity regarding his forthcoming criminal trial. The judge held that further publicity regarding the case would be detrimental to the welfare of the ward, and, on the basis that an order made in the wardship proceedings would afford a greater degree of protection than an order made in the criminal proceedings under the Children and Young Persons Act 1933, s 39, made an order in the wardship proceedings prohibiting further publicity regarding the ward, including publicity concerning the father's impending trial. The father appealed, on the basis that reports of the criminal proceedings against him should have been excepted by proviso from the order made.

Held

Allowing the appeal:

(1)   It was obviously very desirable, in the interests of the ward, that publicity concerning her upbringing, abduction and family situation should be as limited as possible. **However, in the absence of a statutory restriction, the starting-point was that reports of proceedings in public courts should only be restrained where and to the extent that restraint was shown to be necessary to protect the proper administration of justice.** In the present case, there was no statutory provision which automatically restrained the reporting of the criminal trial. **Nevertheless, as the ward (being the victim of the abduction) was the person in respect of whom the proceedings were taken, the judge in the criminal proceedings did have the power under the Children and Young Persons Act 1933, s 39, to direct that information from which the ward might be identified should be excluded from reports of those proceedings.**

(2)   Whether a judge sitting in the Family Division had jurisdiction to impose restraints upon the reporting of the criminal proceedings was severely doubted; however, even if the judge was technically able to do so by virtue of the theoretically unlimited wardship jurisdiction, that power should never in practice be exercised.

(3)   **The provisions of s 39 of the 1933 Act were specifically directed at this situation, and it was obviously preferable that the decision as to whether it was necessary to derogate from the normal principle of open justice and impose reporting restrictions in the criminal proceedings should be taken not by the wardship judge, but by the trial judge** (see pp 645–646, 648–649, 651 below). *Attorney-General v Leveller Magazine Ltd* considered.

Appendix 7

EXAMPLE OF A JUDICIAL BALANCING EXERCISE

(Note that font emphasis is that of the author's)

INTRODUCTION

A7.01 This Appendix offers an example of a judicial balancing exercise post *Re S* with particular reference to the importance of judicial detachment, objectivity openness and the public interest.

A7.02 See dicta of Munby J in *Webster; Norfolk County Council v Webster & Ors*;[1] such dicta embrace many of the authoritative cases and give a shape to the overall decision-making process. (Note that in the following text, the emphasis by way of font is the author's).

THE BALANCING EXERCISE – DISCUSSION

A7.03

'[97] Subject to one important point, I accept the general thrust of the submissions by Mr Warby, Mr Wolanski and Mr Hudson.

[98] With all respect to His Honour Judge Curl, the extremely wide order he made is clearly too wide. Even if all the guardian's concerns were fully justified, that could not in my judgment justify the prohibition of publishing anything at all about the case: compare *Re B (A Child) (Disclosure)*,[2] at para [144]. **It does not permit even that degree of discussion normally allowed by s 12 of the Administration of Justice Act 1960**.

[99] Four factors in particular weigh heavily in my judgment in favour of the view that any greater degree of restraint than that which is being proposed by the applicants will indeed constitute a **disproportionate** – a significant and heavily disproportionate – interference with their rights: **the claim that the case involves a miscarriage of justice, the parents' own wish for publicity, the very extensive publicity there has already been, and the need, in the circumstances, for the full facts and the "truth" – whatever it may be – to emerge, and, moreover, to emerge in a way which will command public confidence**. Two of these factors require a little elaboration.

---

[1] [2006] EWHC 2733 (Fam), [2007] 1 FLR 1146.
[2] [2004] EWHC 411 (Fam), [2004] 2 FLR 142.

[100] As I observed in *Re B (A Child) (Disclosure)*, at para [99], parents – like the mother in that case and the parents in the present case – often want to speak out publicly. I repeat in this context the point I made in *Re Roddy*, at para [83]. **In my judgment, the workings of the family justice system and, very importantly, the views about the system of the mothers and fathers caught up in it, are, as Balcombe LJ put it in** *Re W (Wardship: Discharge: Publicity)*[3], **at 474, 'matters of public interest which can and should be discussed publicly'.** Many of the issues litigated in the family justice system require open and public debate in the media. **I repeat what I said in** *Harris v Harris,*[4] **at paras [360]–[389], about the importance in a free society of parents who feel aggrieved at their experiences of the family justice system being able to express their views publicly about what they conceive to be failings on the part of individual judges or failings in the judicial system. And I repeat in this context what I said in the same case, at para [368]:**

"The freedom to publish things which judges might think should not be published is all the more important where the subject of what is being said is the judges themselves. Any judicial power to punish such publications requires the most cogent justification. Even more cogent must be the justification for giving the judges a power of prior restraint."

[101] The fact that the parents may not be the martyrs they claim to be – something which I am in absolutely no position to assess and on which I express no views at all – **the fact that it may turn out that there was no miscarriage of justice, is not of itself any reason for denying the parents their voice**.

[102] In the first place, and in the very nature of things, the initial "official" response to any allegation that there has been a miscarriage of justice is likely to be one of scepticism or worse. But that, it might be thought, is all the more reason why there should not be restraint, why the media should not be hindered in their vital role. I repeat what Lord Steyn said in *R v Secretary of State for the Home Department ex parte Simms and Another*[5]: **"In principle it is not easy to conceive of a more important function which free speech might fulfil"**.

[103] **Moreover, freedom of speech is not something to be awarded to those who are thought deserving and denied to those who are thought undeserving.** As Lord Oliver of Aylmerton robustly observed in *Attorney-General v Guardian Newspapers Ltd and Others; Attorney-General v Observer Ltd and Others; Attorney-General v Times Newspapers Ltd and Another*[6], at 1320:

"… the liberty of the press is essential to the nature of a free state. The price that we pay is that that liberty may be and sometimes is harnessed to the carriage of liars and charlatans, but that cannot be avoided if the liberty is to be preserved."
It is, after all, the underdog who is often most in need of the help afforded by a fearless, questioning and sceptical press.

---

3   [1995] 2 FLR 466.
4   [2001] 2 FLR 895.
5   [2000] 2 AC 115.
6   [1987] 1 WLR 1248.

[104] The other element of great importance, as it seems to me, in the present case, is what I have referred to as the public interest in maintaining the confidence of the public at large in the courts and, specifically, in the family justice system. This is not merely a point of general application. It has, at it seems to me, a particular resonance in this particular case. Rightly or wrongly, correctly or otherwise – and for present purposes it matters not which – **the media have suggested that the parents and their children A, B and C have been, and that the parents and Brandon are at risk of being, the victims of a miscarriage of justice. In these circumstances there is a pressing need for public confidence to be restored – either by the public and convincing demonstration that there has *not* been a miscarriage of justice or, as the case may be, by public acknowledgement that there has been.** That is not, of course, the purpose of the current proceedings, and it is very possible that the outcome of the judicial process, whatever it may be, will not be a clarity and certainty that all will accept. But as few obstacles as possible should be placed in the way of the media doing their job. For in the proper exercise by the media of their investigative and other functions there exists perhaps the best chance of the truth, whatever it may be, emerging at the end of the day. And that, at least in the circumstances of this case, points to the media having access not merely to more information than His Honour Judge Curl's order would permit them but access also to the forthcoming hearing.

[105] As a number of judges have pointed out, there is another important aspect of the problem that has to be taken into account: **the unfortunate fact that the rule of confidentiality facilitates the dissemination of false and tendentious accounts of proceedings in family courts, which in turn tends to further undermine public confidence in the system.**

[106] In *Re B (A Child) (Disclosure)*,[7] at paras [133]–[134], I commented that:

> "One of the disadvantages of the "curtain of privacy" to '[133] which Balcombe LJ referred – what some campaigners would prefer to characterise as the cloak of secrecy surrounding the family courts – has become apparent. Those who without justification attack the family justice system can all too easily do so by feeding the media tendentious accounts of proceedings whilst hypocritically sheltering behind the very privacy of the proceedings which, although they affect to condemn, they in fact turn to their own advantage. It is all too easy to attack the system when the system itself prevents anyone correcting the misrepresentations being fed to the media: see *Harris v Harris; Attorney-General v Harris*,[8] at para [386]. ... I make the point for two reasons. In the first place it [134] suggests that too relentless an enforcement of the privacy of family court proceedings may be counter-productive and **that the courts should perhaps in future be more willing than they have been in the past to exercise the disclosure jurisdiction so as to permit matters such as these to be put into the public domain.** Secondly, if disclosure is to be permitted, the person seeking disclosure – here the mother – may have to be prepared to take the rough with the smooth. The mother is not necessarily entitled to set the media agenda. If she wants to put some parts of the case into the public domain, then she may have to accept that other less appealing parts of the case are also put into the public domain."

---

7   [1987] 1 WLR 1248.
8   [1987] 1 WLR 1248.

[107] In *Blunkett v Quinn*,[9] at para [22], **Ryder J** said:

"In considering the competing rights [under Articles 6, 8 and 10], **I have come to the clear conclusion that having regard to the quantity of material that is in the public domain, some of it even in the most responsible commentaries wholly inaccurate, it is right to give this judgment in public.** The ability to correct false impressions and misconceived facts will go further to help secure the Art 6 and Art 8 rights of all involved than would the court's silence which in this case will only promote further speculation and adverse comment that will damage both the interests of those involved and the family justice system itself."

[108] In *Re H (Freeing Orders: Publicity)*,[10] at paras [31] and [33], **Wall LJ** said:

"Cases involving children are currently heard in private [31] in order to protect the anonymity of the children concerned. However, the exclusion of the public from family courts, and the lack of knowledge about what happens in them, easily lead to the accusation of **'secret justice' ... What is manifestly unacceptable is the unauthorised and [33] selective leakage of one party's case or selective, inaccurate and tendentious reporting in breach of the rules relating to the confidentiality of the proceedings. This, in my experience, invariably leads to unbalanced misreporting of the difficult and sensitive issues with which the courts have to grapple. In my judgment, therefore, the best way to tackle that problem is by greater openness in the decision-making process.**" He indicated what he had in mind, at para [26]:

"In my judgment, this case provides a strong argument for those who, like myself, take the view that the judgments of circuit and Family Division judges hearing care and adoption proceedings should, as a matter of routine, be given in an anonymised form and in open court."
He returned to the same theme in *Clayton v Clayton*,[11] at paras [85]–[89].

[109] In *Re X, London Borough of Barnet v Y and X*[12] at paras [166]–[167], I said:

"... In my view the public generally, and not just the [166] professional readers of law reports or similar publications, have a legitimate – indeed a compelling – interest in knowing how the family courts exercise their care jurisdiction. Moreover, if leave is confined in practice to those cases which are, for some reason, thought to be worthy of reporting in a law report, the sample of cases which will ever come to public attention is not merely very small but also very unrepresentative."

[167] **My own view, and I make no bones about this, is that, subject of course to appropriate anonymisation, the presumption ought to be that leave should be given to publish any judgment in any care case, irrespective of whether the judgment has any particular interest for law reporters, lawyers or other professionals. It should not be necessary to show that there is some particular reason to justify why leave should be given in the particular case, let alone any**

---

9   [2004] EWHC 2816 (Fam), [2005] 1 FLR 648.
10   [2005] EWCA Civ 1325, [2006] 1 FLR 815.
11   [2005] EWCA Civ 1325, [2006] 1 FLR 815.
12   [2006] 2 FLR 998.

need to justify leave on the basis that the judgment deals with some supposedly interesting point of law, practice or principle. For my own part, I should have thought that the proper approach ought to the other way round. It is not so much for those who seek leave to publish an anonymised judgment to justify their request; surely it is for those who resist such leave to demonstrate some good reason why the judgment should not be published even in a suitably anonymised form.

[110] In the present case there are, I think, overwhelmingly strong reasons for authorising the disclosure – perhaps subject to some degree of necessary anonymisation – of His Honour Judge Barham's two judgments. And in many cases adoption of the practice recommended by Wall LJ will be sufficient to meet the needs of transparency and to facilitate appropriate public debate. **But cases of alleged miscarriage of justice seem to me to stand on a somewhat different footing. After all, what is being alleged in such cases – what is being asserted in this case – is that there has been a failure of the** *judicial* **process. Sometimes it may be said that that is the fault, the responsibility, of the judge. Here, as it happens, responsibility seems to be attached more to deficiencies in the evidence and what are said to have been failings on the part of the local authority.** But on either basis, if what is being said is that there has been a failing in the *judicial* process, **it might be thought – and certainly will be thought by some – to be less than satisfactory that the only accounts of what has happened, the only explanations to be given to the public, are those which a judge thinks it appropriate to include either in a judgment or in a judicially approved press release.** After all, the complaint may be that the judge has misunderstood the evidence, overlooked some vital piece of evidence or gone against the weight of the evidence – and how can that case be made if the only material available to the public is the very judgment whose alleged deficiencies are under challenge? How can the media properly assess things if denied access to the hearing?

[111] **In the present case it is not enough that there should be publication of the judgments, whether or not supplemented by judicially authorised press releases. To confine the parents and the media to that extent is, in my judgment, to interfere disproportionately with their rights under Arts 6, 8 and 10.**

[112] I have of course considered very carefully all the points made both by NCC and by Brandon's guardian. I do not doubt the strength of the guardian's views, and in particular the concerns she has as to the possible effect on Brandon if the applicants achieve what they desire. But after anxious consideration I have come to two conclusions which, in the final analysis, are determinative of the ultimate balancing test.

[113] The first is that the risks to Brandon are in significant measure speculative and, in any event, not as large as the guardian would have it. Given all the publicity there has already been – and it is not said that it has been in any way damaging to Brandon – one has to ask, taking a realistic view, what additional risks he is likely to run if exposed to further publicity. Moreover, one has to bear in mind that even if His Honour Judge Curl's order were to remain in place, there can be no assurance that there will not be continuing publicity, and continuing publicity which, however much anonymised, those "in the know", including, it may well be, many in the local community, will readily appreciate is about Brandon and his parents. The media, after all, are adept at working their way – quite lawfully, I might add – around even the most drastic restraints.

[114] **My second conclusion is that the restraints being sought by the guardian go further – much further – than is required to protect Brandon's rights**, whilst at

the same time involving, as I have said, a quite disproportionate interference with the applicants' rights. **In the particular circumstances of this particular case, an intense focus on the comparative importance of all the various rights which are in play leads in the final analysis to an ultimate balancing which satisfies me that, subject to one important qualification, the outcome contended for by the applicants involves no disproportionate interference with Brandon's rights, whilst any greater degree of restraint would indeed involve a disproportionate interference with the applicants' rights.**

[115] I appreciate that the effect of the order I am proposing to make is that the family's true name – Webster – will for the first time be publicly known. But it seems to me that this alone will have little if any discernible impact upon Brandon. **His first name and his photograph are already in the public domain, and those 'in the know' and, I suspect, many in his local community are well aware that Mr and Mrs Hardingham (as they have hitherto been referred to) are in fact Mr and Mrs Webster.** There is, in my judgment, no disproportionate interference with Brandon's rights in permitting him and his parents to be identified by their true name. On the other hand, and in the particular circumstances of this case, it would, in my judgment, be a disproportionate interference with the parents' rights to deny them what they want, the right not merely to argue their case in public but to do so under their true name and not under a pseudonym.

[116] The qualification I have mentioned arises out of the fact that the applicants' submissions have paid small attention to, and their analysis has attached what I believe is insufficient weight to, the various rights and interests which **I referred to in para [80], subparas (v), (vi) and (vii)**, above. This is a matter which, as will be appreciated, troubles NCC. It also troubles me.

[117] This is not, in my judgment, any reason to refuse the media all access to the proceedings, let alone any reason sufficient to justify His Honour Judge Curl's order. But there are important public interests involved here – see the analysis in para [45], above – just as there are the important interests of the social workers, of Brandon's children's guardian and of the other witnesses to be borne in mind. And these interests require to be carefully considered and appropriately protected. (I do not agree with Ms Langdale that the same goes for NCC's legal team).

[118] These are issues which I considered in *Re B (Disclosure to Other Parties)*[13] and, with particular reference to expert witnesses, in *Re B (A Child) (Disclosure)*.[14] The position of social workers is the subject of consideration by the Court of Appeal in *Re W (Children) (Family Proceedings: Evidence)*,[15] and more recently by Ryder J in *British Broadcasting Corporation v Rochdale Metropolitan Borough Council*[16] – authorities to which I was not referred and on.

[119] I cannot resolve these issues today, but I must put appropriate interim protective measures in place:

    (i)   In the first place, the trial judge must have the ultimate right to control access by the media to any hearing. It may be that even though the media should, in principle, be able to attend the hearing, there will be

---

13   [2001] 2 FLR 1017.
14   [2004] EWHC 411 (Fam), [2004] 2 FLR 142.
15   [2002] EWCA Civ 1626, [2003] 1 FLR 329.
16   [2005] EWHC 2862 (Fam), [2007] 1 FLR 101.

some particular part of it during which it would be right to exclude them, perhaps, for example, while a particular witness is giving evidence.

(ii)   There may be questions as to whether some category of witnesses, or a particular witness, should be entitled to anonymity. That is not a matter I can resolve today.

It is for these reasons that I have included in the draft order prepared by the applicants the provisions in paras 1(b) and 8(c).

[120] **There are two final matters I should mention. In the first place, if the media are to be permitted access to the forthcoming hearing that access cannot properly be confined to the particular organs of the media who are before me. It is not for a judge to licence the media, preferring one over another. If the media are to be permitted to attend, then all the media must be given the same rights of access. Hence the additional words I have inserted in para 1**.

[121] The other relates to the effect of my order permitting media access to the forthcoming hearing. The general public will not be able to attend the hearing. **But since the media will be entitled to be present, the hearing will not, as it seems to me, be "in private" within the meaning of s 12 of the Administration of Justice Act 1960.** Section 12 will therefore not apply in relation to that hearing. But this does *not* mean that s 12 ceases to apply altogether to the care proceedings. Save in relation to any particular hearing which has been opened to the media, s 12 will continue to apply. Hence para 10 of the order. Moreover, the effect of the order I am proposing to make is *not* to permit the dissemination of the entire contents of the court bundle prepared for a particular hearing merely because that hearing is not "in private", *nor* to permit the publication of any or every part of a document merely because passing reference has been made to it during the course of the hearing. In principle, s 12 will continue to apply to everything in such a bundle save insofar as either: (a) particular parts of documents in the bundle have actually been read out or summarised during the course of the hearing (in which case, absent the imposition of further restrictions, the media will be able to report what has actually been said during the hearing); or (b) the judge authorises further disclosure.'

PUBLIC DOMAIN: THE CANUTE PRINCIPLE

A7.04   As to '**public domain**' see the following dicta of Eleanor King J in *East Sussex County Council v Stedman and Others*.[17]

'[74]   Evidence has been produced on behalf of NGN Ltd in the form of a statement by Mr Benjamin Beabey, the solicitor representing NGN Ltd. The statement aims to demonstrate to the court the quite extraordinary amount of press and internet coverage that there has been about these three children. **The story has been reported all over the world, it has been the subject of TV programmes and of comment in Parliament.**

[75]   It is accepted by the Local Authority that literally millions of people have seen and read about the story. To quote but a few examples from the statement of Mr Beabey: a Google search of the name Alfie Patten on 28 March 2009 produced *about 359,000* results, a search term of Alfie's name in

---

17   [2009] EWHC 935 (Fam).

Google Images produced *25,100 images* (which inevitably include pictures of Chantelle and Maisie as well). During the course of the hearing a Google Image search of Chantelle Stedman produced 5,660 images of her often including Maisie as well. Prior to the order of 26 March 2009 requiring the removal of the story from the internet, *The Daily Mirror* story, which revealed the results of the DNA tests, had resulted in 84,000 page views.

[76] **The original articles, many of which are not only pejorative of but deeply hurtful to Alfie and/or Chantelle, are still readily available on the internet.** Some articles in print and on line include speculation as to the paternity of Maisie and include the names and photographs of other potential putative fathers.

[77] It is accepted that all these articles, photographs and images are in the public domain and may well be unaffected by the proposed Reporting Restrictions Order. **Even if the court makes the order sought it is simply unrealistic to imagine that all the website proprietors all over the world will get notice of the injunction and will act upon it.**

[78] When conducting the balancing exercise between Article 8 and Article 10, where one outcome would affect freedom of expression, the court has to consider s 12(4)(a)(i) Human Rights Acts 1998, that is to say the extent to which:

(i)   the material has, or is about to, become available to the public.

[79] In *Mosley v News Group Newspapers Ltd*,[18] Eady J said:

"The extent to which material is truly "in the public domain" will ultimately depend upon the particular facts before the Court. In *Attorney-General v Greater Manchester Newspapers Ltd*[19] the test was applied as to whether certain information was "realistically"accessible to members of the public or only "in theory"."

[80] Mr Lord referred me to an unreported case *Re C (A Minor)*[20] where Sir Stephen Brown P said:

"... It would be taking a very strong line indeed if a court were to seek to restrict the media from publishing information which they have lawfully published in the past and which remains on their files and is readily available to members of the public ..."

[81] Mr Lord submits, whilst that may hold true in confidentiality cases, **that may not be so in privacy cases involving vulnerable children who are wards of court.** He points to *Re X, Y (Children)*[21] and to *A v M*[22] where, on the particular facts of the case and having carried out the balancing act, the court decided that there would be no "public domain qualification". **Further publication would it was decided in each case be damaging and the overall public interest required that further publication should be restrained.** In my judgment each of those cases was decided on their own particular facts, **the requirement under s 12(4)(a)(i) of the Human Rights Act to consider the extent to which the**

---

[18]   [2008] EWHC 687 (QB).
[19]   [2001] All ER (D) 32 (Dec).
[20]   15 March 1990.
[21]   [2004] EMLR 29.
[22]   [2000] 1 FLR 562.

material has become available to the public applies equally whether the
material is confidential or private and whether it relates to adults or children.

[82] Mr Lord further suggests that the *Daily Mirror* article of 26 March 2009 was
not "lawful"as required by Sir Stephen Brown P in *Re C (A Minor)* and was
in breach of the injunction of 18 February 2009. **There is therefore authority
for the proposition that the court can, contrary to normal practice, order that
there be no public domain qualification when making an injunction.**

[83] Mr Lord also submits that, in considering the weight to be placed on the fact
that material is within the public domain, a distinction needs to be made
between confidentiality and privacy; once confidentiality is lost it is lost for
all time, a photograph on the other hand is capable of being a fresh intrusion
on the subject's privacy with every fresh publication; this was considered by
Sedley LJ in *Douglas v Hello Ltd (No 3)*[23] at [105]:

> "**In general, however, once information is in the public domain, it will no longer
> be confidential or entitled to the protection of the law of confidence, though
> this may not always be true**: see *Gilbert v Star Newspaper Co Ltd* [24] and
> *Creation Records Ltd v News Group Newspapers Ltd.*[25] The same may
> generally be true of private information of a personal nature. Once intimate
> personal information about a celebrity's private life has been widely
> published it may serve no useful purpose to prohibit further publication. **The
> same will not necessarily be true of photographs**. Insofar as a photograph
> does more than convey information and intrudes on privacy by enabling the
> viewer to focus on intimate personal detail, there will be a fresh intrusion of
> privacy when each additional viewer sees the photograph and even when one
> who has seen a previous publication of the photograph is confronted by a
> fresh publication of it. To take an example, if a film star were photographed,
> with the aid of a telephoto lens, lying naked by her private swimming pool,
> we question whether widespread publication of the photograph by a popular
> newspaper would provide a defence to a legal challenge to repeated
> publication on the ground that the information was in the public domain.
> **There is thus a further important potential distinction between the law relating
> to private information and that relating to other types of confidential
> information**."

[84] Mr Nicklin rightly emphasises that the "naked film star" example used in the
Hello! case is an example of a photograph that is intrinsically intrusive
namely a covert picture taken of a person whilst naked; the intrusion on her
privacy with each repeated publication is obvious. In the present case, he
submits, the photographs in question are not intrusive per se; they merely
show a young boy or girl or baby whether together or separately. The
photographs, Mr. Nicklin says, do not therefore fall into the "naked film
star" category (another example of which are the *Mosley* images), rather, he
says, they fall within the category whereby the information, in the form of
the photographs, has been widely published and it therefore serves no useful
purpose to prohibit further publication.

[85] It is right that the photographs are not of themselves offensive but that does
not mean they are not capable of causing distress and being an invasion of

---

[23] [2005] EWCA Civ 595; [2006] QB 125, 162.
[24] [1894] 11 TLR 4.
[25] [1997] EMLR 444, 456.

privacy each and every time they are published showing, as many of them do, Alfie as "father" with Chantelle and his "daughter" Maisie.

[86] **During the course of his submissions, Mr Lord emphasised that one of the considerations for the court under Article 10(2) is maintenance of the authority of the judiciary. NGN Ltd should not be able to bolster their case by relying on the fact that** *The Daily Mirror* **has already published the story in relation to the DNA tests to their readership of about 5 million.** That publication was, he submits, if not a flagrant breach of the order of Baron J of 18 February 2009 at the very least wholly contrary to the spirit of an order which was quite clearly designed to prevent the reporting of "new" information about the children. To allow NGN Ltd to rely on the publication of the DNA test results in support of their "public domain" argument would, the Local Authority say, undermine the authority of the judiciary.

[87] I have considerable sympathy with the Local Authority's frustration in this respect and most courts would feel stung by the advantage which was taken by *The Daily Mirror* of what was arguably a lacuna in the drafting of the order of the 18 February 2009. **Looking forward it seems to me that there is another aspect of the maintenance of judicial authority to be considered and that is that the courts must not be seen to make an order which would appear to the public to be ludicrous or absurd and which is unenforceable.** In *Attorney-General v Guardian Newspapers (No 2)* (the "Spycatcher" case)[26] Lord Goff of Chieveley said (p 289D–E):

"I nevertheless take the view in the present case that to prevent the publication of the book in this country would, in the present circumstances, not be in the public interest. It seems to me to be an absurd state of affairs that copies of the book, all of course originating from Peter Wright – imported perhaps from the United States – should now be widely circulating in this country, and that at the same time other sales of the book should be restrained. To me, this simply does not make sense. I do not see why those who succeed in obtaining a copy of the book in the present circumstances should be able to read it, while others should not be able to do so simply by obtaining a copy from their local bookshop or library. In my opinion, artificially to restrict the readership of a widely accessible book in this way is unacceptable: if the information in the book is in the public domain and many people in this country are already able to read it, I do not see why anybody else in this country who wants to read it should be prevented from doing so."

The *Spycatcher* case was a case about confidentiality, but for the purposes of this point it seems it seems to me that there is little or no difference whether one is considering the dissemination of confidential material or private material.

[88] In *Mosley v News Group Newspapers Ltd* Mr Justice Eady, having considered the passage from *Douglas v Hello! (No 3)* I have quoted above, went on to say:

"[33] **Nevertheless, a point** *may* **be reached where the information sought to be restricted, by an order of the Court, is so widely and generally accessible "in the public domain" that such an injunction would make no practical difference.**

---

26   [1990] 1 AC 109.

[34] As Mr Millar has pointed out, if someone wishes to search on the Internet for the content of the edited footage, there are various ways to access it notwithstanding any order the Court may choose to make imposing limits on the content of the *News of the World* website. **The Court should guard against slipping into playing the role of King Canute. Even though an order may be desirable for the protection of privacy, and may be made in accordance with the principles currently being applied by the courts, there may come a point where it would simply serve no useful purpose and would merely be characterised, in the traditional terminology, as a *brutum fulmen*. It is inappropriate for the Court to make vain gestures**.

[35] ...

[36] **In the circumstances now prevailing, as disclosed in the evidence before me, I have come to the conclusion that the material is so widely accessible that an order in the terms sought would make very little practical difference. One may express this conclusion either by saying that Mr Mosley no longer has any reasonable expectation of privacy in respect of this now widely familiar material or that, even if he has, it has entered the public domain to the extent that there is, in practical terms, no longer anything which the law can protect. The dam has effectively burst**. I have, with some reluctance, come to the conclusion that although this material is intrusive and demeaning, and despite the fact that there is no legitimate public interest in its further publication; the granting of an order against this Respondent at the present juncture would merely be a futile gesture. Anyone who wishes to access the footage can easily do so, and there is no point in barring the *News of the World* from showing what is already available."

[89] The court refused the application and the video remained available on the internet.

[90] When assessing the words of Eady J, I bear in mind that in *Re X, Y (Children)*[27] the public domain material was old and had been published only in local newspapers. In *A v M*[28] the information in the public domain was information from court proceedings concerning the children which proceedings had been held in private. Although the mother had approached the media, there had been no widespread publicity of the type in either the *Mosley* case or the present case. In both cases the injunction was capable of enforcement.

[91] **I have to deal with the reality of the situation regardless of whether or not the *Daily Mirror* article was published lawfully. There are not just hundreds of public domain photographs of Chantelle, Maisie and Alfie in existence, there are tens of thousands all over the world and largely on the internet**.

[92] The Local Authority says that it is the print medium which will be particularly damaging to Chantelle and that the injunction they propose can be enforced so far as the print media is concerned. I feel unable to reach any such conclusion: print may appear to be the most immediate medium but it is a matter of public record that newspaper circulation is suffering as a consequence of the large number of (particularly younger) people reading the news online. **If the fear is that it is printed stories which will render**

---

27   [2004] EMLR 29.
28   [2000] 1 FLR 562.

Chantelle vulnerable to abuse it should not be overlooked that young people can be every bit as cruel and thoughtless as every other age group.

[93] In taking a pragmatic view about the publication of public domain photographs of Alfie, Mr Inglis said that it is **"simply anachronistic to assert that the net is a less accessible medium than the printed press"**. I agree. If that were the case why, for example, would "No 10" set up its own "YouTube" channel upon which the Prime Minister has appeared?'

Appendix 8

RECENT CASE LAW

(Note that font emphasis is that of the author's)

RE CHILD X – 'FAMILY LAW' SUMMARY

A8.01   *Re Child X (Residence and Contact; Rights of Media Attendance*; FPR Rule 10.28(4))[1] (Family Division; Sir Mark Potter P, 14 July 2009).

A8.02   There was media interest in residence and contact proceedings because the father was a celebrity; the proceedings concerned a child who was old enough to read about and follow references to her parents or herself. The case had hitherto been heard in private; the county court judge had required both parents to give undertakings that nothing should be disclosed concerning the proceedings, save to legal advisers. A Cafcass officer had interviewed the father, mother and child, and a consultant child and adolescent psychiatrist had been jointly instructed to report on questions relating to the child's welfare. The Judge had made certain findings of fact at the conclusion of a four-day hearing, and in response to the urgent application of the parties had also made an order contra mundum prohibiting publication of the child's name, address or school, or any information likely to identify the child, including the names and addresses of the parents. There was no application to discharge or vary the terms of this injunction.

A8.03   However, some time later, on the day on which changes to the Family Proceedings Rules 1991 came into force, opening private family hearings to accredited representatives of the media, the media applied to the judge for admission to the next hearing, which was to involve questioning the psychiatrist on the contents of his latest report, and evidence from the Cafcass officer.

A8.04   In the course of the hearing detailed reference was bound to be made to the Judge's earlier fact-finding judgment, and to previous evidence given by both the expert and the Cafcass officer. Under the new r 10.28, duly accredited media representatives were permitted to be present during 'private' hearings, subject to the court's power to direct their exclusion during all or part of the proceedings, for one of a number of reasons specified in para 4 of the new rule.

A8.05   In accordance with the President's Guidance issued on 22 April 2009, the Judge referred the question of press access and reporting restrictions to the High Court. Both the expert and the Cafcass officer supplied statements to the

---

[1]   [2009] EWHC 1728 (Fam).

High Court, and both were concerned about the child's welfare if the media were admitted; in addition, the expert raised a variety of concerns about revealing to the media information given to him in confidence by a child who had understood that the information would be shared only with the court and the parents.

A8.06 The combined effect of Administration of Justice Act 1960, s 12(1) and Children Act 1989, s 97 was that, while the press were entitled to report on the nature of the dispute in proceedings involving children, and to identify the issues in the case and the identity of participating witnesses (save those whose published identity would reveal the identity of the child in the case), they were not entitled to set out the content of the evidence or the details of matters investigated by the court. Whereas the media were now able to exercise the role of 'watchdog' on the part of the public at large and to observe family justice at work for the purpose of an informed comment on its workings and the behaviour of its judges, they were unable to report the identity of the parties or the details of the evidence that were likely to catch the eye and engage the interest of the average reader or viewer. This distinction was recognised as a valid one when balancing Art 8 and Art 10 considerations under the European Convention on Human Rights.

A8.07 In this case, despite procedural deficiencies, the contra mundum order should remain in place, including the provision that information should not be solicited. Further, the media should be excluded from the proceedings, in the interests of the child concerned in the proceedings, and also upon the basis that justice would otherwise be impeded.

A8.08 Reporting restrictions were not sufficient to protect the child in the instant case because: (a) press presence would be a betrayal of the trust built up between the child and the expert and Cafcass officer; and (b) foreign media representatives were present, and if they published information they were beyond the reach of the court so far as contempt proceedings were concerned.

A8.09 While there were no transitional provisions, the fact was that matters had to date proceeded in the case on the basis of the privacy of the proceedings and the confidentiality of the exchanges between the child and the expert and the Cafcass officer. In deciding whether or not to exclude the press in the welfare or privacy interests of a party or third party, the court had to conduct a balancing exercise between Art 8 and Art 10, and to decide whether exclusion was 'necessary'.

A8.10 The grounds for excluding the media under r 10.28(4) were, in broad terms Art 6 compliant. Although nothing was included in r 10.28 to provide for exclusion of the press where the Art 8 interests of the parties (as opposed to those of the child) so required, Art 8 interests of the parties could properly justify exclusion of the media under ground (b) to prevent the press from hearing and/or reporting allegations of an outrageous or intimate nature before the court decided whether or not they were established, as it might well constitute a serious and irredeemable invasion of the privacy and/or family life of an adult party if the press were not excluded.

A8.11 No special rules applied to the children of celebrities, but the need for protection of a child of a celebrity from intrusion or publicity, and the danger of leaking of information to the public, would, like the interest of the press in such children, be more intense. In deciding whether or not the grounds advanced for exclusion were sufficient to override the presumptive right of the press to be present and in particular whether or not an order for total exclusion was proportionate, it would be relevant to have regard to the nature and sensitivities of the evidence, and the degree to which the watchdog function of the media might be engaged, or whether its apparent interest lay in observing and reporting on matters relating to the child that might well be the object of interest, in the sense of curiosity, on the part of the public, but which were confidential and private and did not themselves involve matters of public interest properly so called.

A8.12 However, the burden remained on the applicant to demonstrate that the matter could not be appropriately dealt with by allowing the press to attend. The comment in *Spencer v Spencer* that, if a proper case for excluding the media was demonstrated on the basis that there was a significant risk that a witness would not give full or frank evidence in the presence of media representatives, the order requiring the media to remove themselves should apply only to the evidence of that witness, was not of universal application, and did not apply in this case because the evidence of the relevant witnesses was likely to be the only 'live' evidence before the court, and the matters to be dealt with were all matters of high sensitivity and importance to the welfare of the child. In making the original contra mundum order the Judge had been in breach of the relevant President's Direction (18 March 2005).[2] The terms of the order had gone beyond the scope of Administration of Justice Act 1960, s 12(1) and Children Act 1989, s 97, in particular in prohibiting any person from soliciting any information relating to the child from key individuals. Such orders could only be made by the High Court.

A8.13 Further, the order should not have been made without the person against whom the application was made being present or represented, unless satisfied that the applicant had taken all reasonable steps to notify the respondent or that there were compelling reasons why the respondent should not be notified. The press had been deprived of their opportunity to argue against the grant of the injunction, and any opportunity to see informative material upon which to base any decision. This must not happen again.

A8.14 When injunctions founded upon Convention rights were contemplated, applicants must bear in mind the provisions of s 12(2). If it was not possible to draft explanatory documentation in the time available before the hearing, the court should require the applicant to file it at the earliest opportunity, and to

---

2   [2005] 2 FLR 120.

make it available on request to any person affected by the order. If the need for an order arose in existing proceedings in the County Court, judges should either transfer the application to the High Court or consult their Family Division Liaison Judge. Where the matter was urgent, it could be heard by the Urgent Applications Judge of the Family Division.

A8.15 The President's Direction of April 2009 also contained provisions for service of the application on the National News Media. Although the Practice Direction did not expressly so provide, it was incumbent upon an applicant who wished to exclude the media from a substantive hearing ab initio to raise the matter with the court prior to the hearing for consideration of the need to notify the media in advance of the proposed application and, if that was done, the court should require the applicant to notify the media via the CopyDirect service. The Press Association was willing for its CopyDirect service to be used for the purposes of notification to the media on the basis that such notification was supported by the same documentation as was provided for in the Practice Note of 18 March 2005. In cases in which the justification needed to refer to confidential and sensitive information, it would be sufficient for the justifying statement, without revealing the detail of the matter, to outline and make clear the nature of the matters and issues covered in such reports in a manner sufficient to enable the media to make an informed decision as to whether they wished to attend the hearing. Where the reports or other documents containing sensitive matters were already in the possession of the applicant's solicitors, these should be brought to the hearing of the application in a convenient bundle to enable the Judge to refer to such documents as seemed to him necessary for the purposes of his decision. It was not practical or necessary for such a procedure to be adopted in cases in which an application was made for temporary exclusion of the media during the course of the proceedings.

RE CHILD X – SELECTED DICTA

A8.16 The following text offers selected paragraphs from the transcript of Sir Mark Potter's judgment in *Re Child X*.

'[11] In making the *contra mundum* order the Judge was in breach of the President's Direction dated 18 March 2005[3] which, regrettably, appears not to have been drawn to her attention by counsel in the case (not Mr Spearman QC) who it appears, were unaware of it. Nor was it referred to in the skeleton argument prepared by the solicitors. Despite the fact that the order was headed with a reference to s 12(1) of the *Administration of Justice Act 1960* ("AJA") and s 97 (2) of the Children Act 1989, the terms of the order, and in particular paragraph 6, went beyond the scope of those statutory provisions. As such the application required to be founded on Convention rights. This being so, it was subject to the provisions of Section 12(2) of the *Human Rights Act 1998* ("HRA") which states that an injunction restricting the exercise of the right to freedom of expression must

---

3   [2005] 2 FLR 120.

not be granted where the person against whom the application is made is neither present nor represented unless the Court is satisfied (a) that the applicant has taken all practical steps to notify the respondent or (b) that there are compelling reasons why the respondent should not be notified. In relation to this provision, paragraph 3 of the President's Direction makes clear that:

"The Court retains the power to make without notice orders, but such cases will be exceptional, and an order will always give persons affected liberty to apply to vary or discharge at short notice."

[12] More importantly, however, paragraph 2 of the President's Direction provides that such orders can only be made in the High Court and are normally dealt with by a Judge of the Family Division. If the need for an order arises in the existing proceedings in the County Court, Judges should either transfer the application to the High Court or consult their Family Division Liaison Judge. Where the matter is urgent, it can be heard by the Urgent Applications Judge of the Family Division. Paragraph 3 sets out provisions for service of the application on the National News Media via the Press Association's CopyDirect Service. Paragraph 4 of the direction refers applicants for guidance to the joint Official Solicitor/CAFCASS Practice Note, also dated 18 March 2005 and states that such guidance should be followed.

[13] The importance of observing the President's Direction in cases of high media interest has been judicially emphasised in *Local Authority v W*.[4] It should be well known to practitioners in the field.
***

[18] In adjourning for that purpose, the Judge was acting in accordance with the *President's Guidance in Relation to Applications Consequent Upon the Attendance of the Media in Family Proceedings* dated 22 April 2009 and issued in anticipation of Rule 10.28 coming into force. Under paragraph 20 of that Practice Direction, County Courts and Magistrates Courts were advised that, … if injunctive relief were sought restraining publication based on Convention rights rather than statutory provisions, the matter should in any event be transferred to the High Court to be dealt with under the President's Direction dated 18 March 2005 to which reference has already been made.
***

[21] For the purposes of assisting the parties' Rule 10.28 application and the Court's consideration, Dr C and Miss E have supplied statements specifically directed to the question of the welfare of X and the damaging effect upon the progress and outcome of the processes in which she is currently participating, should the media be permitted to attend the proceedings. Dr C also addressed the question of his personal position and a variety of ethical considerations which arise in relation to the work of medical experts such as himself.

[22] He raises an issue which may well not have been foreseen by government (it is certainly not mentioned), in its Response to the Consultation conducted prior to the Rule change (see further at paragraph 42 below). However, it lends considerable substance to the recognition by government in that

---

4   [2006] 1 FLR 1.

Response of the need to safeguard and protect children and their families. Dr C explains that when a specialist such as himself interviews children for public or private law proceedings, they explain to them according to their age and understanding, the process in which they are involved and what is going to happen to what they say to the specialist. Hitherto specialists have explained that what the children say will be written down and put in a report which will be seen by the Judge, their parents and, according to circumstance, a CAFCASS or other social worker. Hitherto children have not been informed that the media will be given access to what they have said. That is the position in this case in relation to X who has spoken frankly and in confidence to Dr C and Mrs M, a colleague working closely with him, on the basis that matters would only be disclosed to the Judge the parties their legal advisors and the CAFCASS officer. Dr C considers, and has been so advised by the Medical Protection Society, that if he were to disclose to the Court in the presence of the media the information which he possesses concerning X it would be a clear breach of confidentiality. Furthermore, if he or Mrs M were to inform X now that the information they possessed were to be so disclosed it would undermine the trust which X has placed in Dr C and the work undertaken by him. She would also be highly likely to assume, regardless of explanations to the contrary, that their attendance was at the invitation and instigation of one of her parents. Dr C considers that, if the media are admitted to the hearings in this matter, X will not have sufficient trust in the ongoing process to be able to participate in it and the work initiated as a result of these proceedings will be unable to continue. Dr C also makes clear that, quite apart from that unfortunate effect, he would himself be inhibited and in considerable difficulties in relation to giving evidence about X if the media were to be admitted to the hearings.

[23]   Miss E states that X is already aware of some of the reporting of her circumstances in the media and, in a recent conversation, told Miss E that reading about herself in the papers made her feel horrid and she became upset. She further asserts that the information and assessments contained in the Court documents (which will be the subject of evidence and submissions before the Judge) are of a highly sensitive nature and, if the media were present during the Court hearing she would have grave concerns that it would not be possible to maintain the level of anonymity required to safeguard X from emotional harm.

[24]   It is in those circumstances that, in relation to this hearing, and indeed all subsequent hearings, the parties seek an order excluding representatives of the media from attending under the provisions of Rule 10.28 and, in particular, sub-rule (4) (a) (i) and (4) (b).
***

[After the Judge recited Rule 10.28 and gave its history]

[38]   The net result of all this is that, while the press are entitled to report on the nature of the dispute in the proceedings, and to identify the issues in the case and the identity of the participating witnesses (save those whose published identity would reveal the identity of the child in the case), they are not entitled to set out the content of the evidence or the details of matters investigated by the Court. Thus the position has been created that, whereas the media are now enabled to exercise a role of "watchdog" on the part of the public at large and to observe family justice at work for the purpose of

informed comment upon its workings and the behaviour of its judges, they are unable to report in their newspapers or programmes the identity of the parties or the details of the evidence which are likely to catch the eye and engage the interest of the average reader or viewer.

[39] It is of course in the context of disputes over children between "celebrities" in private law proceedings such as these that the media find the current statutory limitations most irksome. The line drawn is nonetheless one recognised as valid when balancing Article 8 and Article 10 considerations as between the privacy rights of individuals and the watchdog role of the press: see *Von Hannover v Germany*[5] at para 63:

> "A fundamental distinction needs to be made between reporting facts – even controversial ones – capable of contributing to a debate in a democratic society reacting to politicians in the exercise of their functions, for example, and reporting details of the private life of an individual who, moreover, as in this case, does not exercise official functions. While in the former case the press exercises its vital role of "watchdog" in a democracy by contributing to "imparting information and ideas on matters of public interest" it does not do so in the latter case."
>
> ***

[45] Put in terms of the Convention, the position seems to me to be as follows. The restrictions i.e. the grounds for exclusion under Rule 10.28 (4) are in broad terms Article 6 compliant. Paragraph (a) (i) is within the legitimate aim of protecting the interests of juveniles and grounds (a) (ii) (iii) and (b) are legitimised under the heading of "special circumstances where publicity would prejudice the interests of justice". It is to be noted in passing that nothing is included in the Rule to provide for exclusion of the press where the Article 8 interests of the parties (as opposed to those of the child) so require. However, one can envisage a situation where a ground for exclusion, at least for part of the proceedings, might be required to protect the Article 8 interests of the parties which could properly justify exclusion of the media under ground (b) to prevent the press from hearing and/or reporting allegations of an outrageous or intimate nature before the Court's decision as to whether or not they were established. This might well constitute a serious and irredeemable invasion of the privacy and/or family life of an adult party if the press were not excluded.

[46] The task faced by the Court in deciding whether or not to exclude the press in the welfare or privacy interests of a party or third party is to conduct the balancing exercise and process of parallel analysis first considered by the House of Lords in *Campbell v MGN Limited*[6] and further elaborated in *Re S (A Child)*[7] in respect of the interplay between Articles 8 and 10 of the Convention. At paragraph [17], Lord Steyn observed that four propositions emerged clearly from the decision in *Campbell*:

> "First, neither Article has as such precedence over the other. Secondly, where the values under the two articles are in conflict, an intense focus on the comparative importance of the specific rights being claimed in the individual case is necessary. Thirdly, the justifications for interfering with or restricting

---

5   [2005] 40 EHRR 1.
6   [2004] 2 AC 457.
7   [2005] 1 AC 593.

each right must be taken into account. Finally, the proportionality test must be applied to each. For convenience I will call this the ultimate balancing test."

[47]   The structure of Articles 8 and 10 are both the same; accordingly, the same considerations apply to the rights protected by each and to the grounds for restricting those rights. In relation to the interference with either right it is necessary to consider whether the interference complained of corresponds to a pressing social need, whether it is proportionate to the legitimate aim pursued, and whether the reasons given by the National Authority to justify it are relevant and sufficient. All cases are, to an extent, fact specific and, in relation to press freedom, the question to be asked is that articulated by Lord Hoffman in the *Campbell* case at para [56]:

"When press freedom comes into conflict with another interest protected by the law, the question is whether there is sufficient public interest in *that particular publication* to justify curtailment of the conflicting rights." (emphasis added)

In that respect, the positive obligations which are imposed on the state under Article 8 are to respect, and therefore to protect the interests of private and family life which embrace right of autonomy, dignity, respect, self esteem, to control the dissemination of private and confidential information and to establish and develop relationships with other people. In relation to the question of confidentiality, as Lord Phillips CJ stated in *HRH The Prince of Wales v Associated Newspapers Ltd*[8] at para [68]:

"The test to be applied in considering whether it is necessary to restrict freedom of expression in order to prevent the disclosure of information received in confidence is not simply whether the information is a matter for public interest but whether, in all the circumstances, it is in the public interest that the duty of confidence should be breached. The Court will need to consider whether, having regard to the nature of the information and all the relevant circumstances, it is legitimate for the owner of the information to seek to keep it confidential or whether it is in the public interest that the information should be made public."

[48]   While the task for the Court to perform in relation to Rule 10.28 (4) is to apply the same process as the House of Lords in *Re S*, the outcome in terms of the hegemony accorded to the Article 10 rights of the press over the Article 8 rights of the child is by no means necessarily the same. In *Re S*, the Court was concerned with an application to restrain the right of the press freely to report criminal proceedings and, in particular, to report the identity of the adult defendant in those proceedings in order to protect the identity and privacy of the defendant's child who was not involved in the proceedings in any way. The dispositive feature in the decision of the House of Lords was (a) the emphasis it placed upon the importance of the public and media interest in enjoying the uninhibited right both to attend and report on all criminal proceedings; (b) the fact that the child who was sought to be protected was not the subject of or involved in the proceedings in any way; (c) the fact that the provisions of s 39 of the *Children and Young Persons*

---

8   [2007] 3 WLR 222.

Act 1933 directed to the question of child protection in relation to criminal proceedings limited the Court's powers to any child or young person concerned in the proceedings as a party or a witness; thus, the right not to be identified which the child was asserting was contemplated but not recognised by domestic legislation. None of those considerations applies to the issues in this case. Whilst the principle of open justice is important in civil proceedings concerning children, the need for the protection of children from publicity in the course of proceedings which concern them, was long ago recognised at common law in *Scott v Scott*, and is provided for in the statutory provisions as to identification to which I have referred at paragraphs 29–31 above.

[49] Nonetheless, it is important to keep one's eye on the ball of the parties' application, which is not to limit the media's reporting rights, but to exclude the media altogether from their presumptive right under Rule 10.28 to be present for the purpose of exercising a watchdog role, albeit with limited reporting rights under the terms of the AJA.

[50] I therefore now turn at once to the application of the parties to exclude the press. I will then deal with the question of the *contra mundum* relief earlier granted and currently in force, and then with certain procedural issues which have arisen and upon which the media seek guidance under the new regime.'

The application to exclude

'[51] By way of general observation it is important to make the following matters clear. First, private law family cases concerning the children of celebrities are no different in principle from those involving the children of anyone else. An application by a celebrity who happens also to be a parent who is unable to agree with a former spouse or partner over the appropriate arrangements for their child(ren) is not governed by any principle or assumption more favourable to the privacy of the celebrity than that applied to any other parent caught up in the court process. In this respect, and in very different circumstances concerning the publication of the identity of a barrister who had been convicted of criminal offences, (*Crawford v CPS*[9]), Thomas LJ rejected the submission that, in conducting the *Re S* balancing exercise there involved the Court should have regard to the public profile of the appellant:

"[34] That is because it is fundamental that all persons are equal before the law of England and Wales, as embodied in our common law, our legislation and the Conventions to which this party (*sic*) has subscribed.

[35] No person in this country can enjoy a different status because he holds a public position. It is important to stress that."

[52] However, in considering whether or not to exclude the press under Rule 10.28 (4) (a) (i), the focus is upon the interests of the child and not the parents. It is almost axiomatic that the press interest in and surrounding the case will be more intense in the case of children of celebrities; and the need for protection of the child from intrusion or publicity, and the danger of leakage of information to the public will similarly be the more intense.

---

[9]   [2008] EWHC 854 (Admin).

[53]   Second, Rule 10.28 provides that, in order to exclude the press on any of the grounds stated, the Court must be satified that it is *necessary* to do so. That is wording which picks up and reflects the provisions of the Convention relevant to the balancing act which the Court has to perform as set out in Articles 6 (1), 8 (2) and 10 (2) of the Convention. We are here concerned with a restriction on the freedom of expression of the media under Article 10 (1), (namely the right to receive and impart information and ideas without interference) for the purpose of the protection of the rights of the child to respect for her private and family life.

[54]   So far as necessity is concerned, as stated in *R v Shayler,*[10] *per* Lord Bingham at para [23]:

> "Necessary" has been strongly interpreted; it is not synonymous with "indispensable", neither has it the flexibility of such expressions as "admissible", "ordinary", "useful", "reasonable" or "desirable": *Handiside v United Kingdom*[11] at para 48. One must consider whether the interference complained of corresponds to a pressing social need, whether it is proportionate to the legitimate aim pursued and whether the reasons given by the national authority to justify it are relevant and sufficient under Article 10 (2): *The Sunday Times v United Kingdom*[12] at para 62."

[55]   Third, since the ECHR has already held FPR Rule 4.16(7) to be Convention-compliant in a form which effectively excluded the press from admission, the introduction of a provision which gives the media the clear *prima facie* right to be present during the proceedings, subject only to exclusion on limited grounds is plainly Convention compliant from the point of view of the media's Article 10 rights. In the light of the wording of Rule 10.28 (4) and the Convention jurisprudence, the question of necessity in respect of the derogations from those rights must be approached on the basis set out by Lord Bingham above, in the context of the particular facts of the case, and with an eye to the question whether any information received in confidence is involved and therefore at risk by reason of press attendance, as to which see the observations of Lord Phillips CJ quoted at paragraph 47 above.

[56]   Fourth, so far as the Practice Direction of 20 April 2009 is concerned, its reference to the exercise of the Court's *discretion* to exclude media representatives from all or part of the proceedings is, strictly speaking, not accurate. In *Interbrew SA v Financial Times*[13] at para [58] Sedley LJ made clear that where the Court has a duty to apply a test of necessity in relation to a series of questions as to legitimacy and proportionality the duty of the Court is to proceed though the balancing exercise making a value judgment as to the conflicts which arise rather than to regard the matter simply as an exercise of discretion as between two equally legitimate courses. Thus references to the Court's discretion in paragraph 3.1 and in the heading to paragraph 5 in the Practice Direction dated 20 April 2009 are a misnomer. Nonetheless, the balancing act involved in the weighing of the conflicting but interlocking rights and restraints embodied in Article 10 and Article 8 of the Convention are highly fact sensitive from case to case. Thus, in

---

[10]   [2003] 1 AC 247, 268.
[11]   (1976) 1 EHR 734, 754.
[12]   (1979) 2 HER 245, 277–278.
[13]   [2002] EWCA Civ 274 [2002] 2 Lloyd's Rep 229.

performing the necessary balancing act, and in particular the ultimate test of proportionality, it is the Judge dealing with the case who is the person best placed to make the necessary decision.

[57] Fifth, the burden of satisfying the Court of the grounds set out in Rule 10.28 (4) is upon the party or parties who seek exclusion, or the Court itself in a case where it takes steps of its own motion, to exclude the press. This will be an easier burden to satisfy in the case of temporary exclusion in the course of the proceedings, in order to meet concerns arising from the evidence of the particular witness or witnesses.

[58] Sixth, in deciding whether or not the grounds advanced for exclusion are sufficient to override the presumptive right of the press to be present and in particular whether or not an order for total exclusion is proportionate, it will be relevant to have regard to the nature and sensitivities of the evidence and the degree to which the watchdog function of the media may be engaged, or whether its apparent interests lie in observing, and reporting on matters relating to the child which may well be the object of interest, in the sense of curiosity, on the part of the public but which are confidential and private and do not themselves involve matters of public interest properly so called. However, while this may be a relevant consideration, it in no sense creates or places any burden of proof or justification upon the media. The burden lies upon the applicant to demonstrate that the matter cannot be appropriately dealt with by allowing the press to attend, subject as they are to the statutory safeguards in respect of identity and under the provisions of s 12 of the 1960 Act.

***

[65] While it is true that an exclusion order will deprive the media of their strong *prima facie* to attend the proceedings, they will not thereby be deprived of attending a case in which the issues raised matters of public interest or of particular importance from the point of view of the watchdog role of the press. It has been argued by Mr Millar QC for the media that the interests of X can be sufficiently catered for by the protections as to identity and on reporting imposed by the current statutory regime. I do not consider that is so for a number of reasons. The first is that which I have already articulated, namely that the intrusion of the press into the proceedings in relation to this particular child and the particular matters investigated in Court would constitute a betrayal of the trust already built up between X and Dr C and Mrs E and would present a grave danger to a successful outcome for the welfare and family issues on the case.

[66] Finally, this case is one in which there is a very high degree of interest on the part of the English media and an even greater interest in the media of a particular country who have already been active in approaching the parties for comment on the proceedings, on one occasion by the press, and on another by the presence of a foreign television crew outside the Court. The reason for the Judge's granting of the *contra mundum* order was the presence of press photographers outside the Court throughout the hearing. Shortly after the grant of the injunction, a foreign magazine published an article identifying the parents and speculating upon the outcome of the proceedings. Upon the day the matter was transferred to me by the Judge, a member of the press of that country was taking photographs in the Court corridors and of the door of the Court. Upon appearing before the Judge, she said that she was intending to publish the pictures to illustrate a report of the proceedings in a foreign magazine.

[67] In these circumstances, and with this level of curiosity, as it seems to me, if the press are admitted to the proceedings at this stage at least, there is inevitably a danger of details of the case as explored and discussed in Court leading to a wider audience and, in the case of the foreign media, being published in a country beyond the reach of this Court so far as proceedings for contempt of court are concerned. If this happens, there is an obvious danger that the contents of the article may come to the attention of X via her own access to the internet or via her friends.

[68] In all the circumstances, I am satisfied it is necessary to exclude the media from the imminent hearing before the Judge on the grounds set out in paras 4 (a) (i) and 4 (b) of Rule 10.28.'

The *Contra Mundum* Injunction

'[71] It is the submission of the media, that there should be no restrictions in this case which go beyond the extensive reporting restrictions already provided by s 12 of the 1960 Act and s 97 (2) of the Children Act. I propose to deal with that question quite shortly because, subject to certain prior comments upon the form of the injunction, I am satisfied that it remains necessary for the protection of X, at least so long as these proceedings last, given the matters spoken to by Dr C and Mrs E.
***

[73] The paragraph which plainly does depend upon an assertion of the Article 8 rights of the child rather than upon any statutory protection available is paragraph [6] prohibiting the solicitation of information from X, her school staff, fellow pupils etc, from any carer or from her parents. This is similarly designed to prevent harassment of the child by representatives of the media seeking to acquire, with a view to publication information about X not already in the public domain. In the light of the evidence of Dr C and Mrs E, such approaches and/or publication of such information would plainly cause distress to the child, be corrosive of her current regime and would be likely to cause her to perceive herself as having been placed in the limelight by one or other of her parents in an unwelcome manner.

[74] In the course of argument before me, Mr Millar QC at no stage felt able to suggest that paragraph [6] of the injunction imposed a fetter upon the media in respect of any purpose which they might legitimately wish to pursue. Indeed, Mr Millar recited and relied upon the terms of the Press Complaints Commission Editor's Code of Practice which variously provides that "editors must not use the fame, notoriety or position of a parent or guardian as the sole justification for publishing details of a child's private life"; "Pupils must not be approached or photographed at school without the permission of the school authorities"; and "In cases involving children under 16, editors must demonstrate an exceptional public interest to over-ride the normally paramount interests of the child". That being so, I do not regard the provisions of paragraph [6] of the injunction as constituting an oppressive or unjustified fetter upon the Article 10 rights of the media, whereas I do regard its provisions as an essential part of the protection to be afforded within the circumstances of this particular child in the course of these particular proceedings.

[75] The second issue raised by the media for consideration in relation to the granting of the injunction is the significance and consequences of the parties' and/or the Judge's failure to comply with the provisions of the

President's Direction dated 18 March 2005. Mr Millar also complains that there was a failure to respect the provisions of s 12 (2) of the *Human Rights Act*. So far as the Practice Direction is concerned, there is now available to the media and the Court a copy of the skeleton argument presented to the Judge in support of the application for the judgment and extracts from the transcript of the proceedings on that day which show that the Judge retired to read the skeleton argument and came back into Court confirming that she was satisfied as to the correctness of its contents.

[76]   Unfortunately, while the Judge was fully and properly referred to the terms of s 12 (3) of the HRA ("No such relief is to be granted so as to restrain publication before trial unless the Court is satisfied that the applicant is likely to establish that publication shall not be allowed") and s 12 (4) which requires the Court to have particular regard to the importance of the Convention right to freedom of expression, she was not referred to paragraph 12 (2) which states that, if the person against whom the application for relief is made is neither present or represented, no relief shall be granted unless the Court is satisfied that the applicant has taken all practical steps to notify such person or that there are compelling reasons why such person should not be notified.
***

[79]   The upshot of all this was that the media were also deprived of the opportunity to see any informative material upon which to base any decision they might take to seek an application to vary or discharge the order. This is not a position which should occur again. Practice Directions issued for the purpose of giving important procedural protections to the media should be observed. Where injunctions founded upon Convention rights are contemplated, applicants must bear in mind the provisions of section 12(2) which the procedure provided for in the President's direction is designed to support. If (as does not appear to have been the case here) it is not possible to draft explanatory documentation in the time available before the hearing, the Court should require the applicant to file it at the earliest opportunity and to make it available on request to any person who is affected by the order: see para 3 of the Official Solicitor's Practice Note.'

Procedural Issues

'[81]   The important procedural question which these proceedings have highlighted and upon which guidance is also sought by the media is the question by what machinery may the media, for the purposes of their submissions as to their proposed exclusion, be apprised of the materials upon which an applicant bases his application to exclude, when the protection of the confidentiality and/or sensitivity of the details contained within those materials constitutes the very reason for the application to exclude.
***

[82]   In the course of their submissions, Mr Millar QC for the media and Mr Wolanski as *amicus curiae* pointed out that the machinery is available in the methodology and procedure set out in the President's Direction of 18 March 2005 relating to Reporting Restrictions, coupled with the further guidance in the Official Solicitor/ CAFCASS Procedural Note of the same date. Its terms are readily applicable to the case where an applicant intends

at the outset of the proceedings to seek from the Judge an order excluding the press altogether (see para 2 of the Practice Note).

[83] Following completion of the parties' submissions, I have received a communication from the Press Association Injunction Alert Service confirming that the Press Association is willing for its CopyDirect service to be used for the purposes of notification to the media on the basis that such notification is supported by the same documentation as is provided for in the Practice Note of 18 March 2005. This seems to me to be a welcome development which I propose to adopt.

[84] As previously noted, the Practice Note provides for service of a witness statement justifying the need for an order which may be, and frequently is, a statement by the parties' solicitor. This may or may not exhibit documents or opinions referred to in the statement which support the grounds of justification advanced. Where, as here, the grounds are based upon the confidentiality and sensitivity of material contained in medical and social work reports which will be deployed and referred to in the course of the proceedings from which it is sought to exclude the media, it would obviously defeat the object of the application for those reports to be supplied or that detailed contents be revealed in advance. In those circumstances it is sufficient for the justifying statement, without revealing the *detail* of the sensitive or confidential matter, to outline and make clear the *nature* of the matters and issues covered in such reports in a manner sufficient to enable the media to make an informed decision as to whether they wish to attend the hearing of the application and/or the proceedings to which it relates (cf paragraph 4 of the Practice Note). I would add that where the reports or other documents containing sensitive matters are already in the possession of the applicant's solicitors, they should be brought to the hearing of the application in a convenient bundle to enable the Judge to refer to such documents as seem to him necessary for the purposes of his decision. Such a procedure is fully in accordance with the principles discussed and applied by Lord Mustill in *Re D (Minors) Adoption Reports: Confidentiality)*[14] and it is a procedure sufficient to make disclosure to the media of the case they have to meet where application is made to exclude them from the proceedings altogether.

[85] This procedure is not one required by the Practice Direction of 20 April 2009 made by me and approved on behalf of the Lord Chancellor in conjunction with the Rule change. Paragraph 6 of the Practice Direction contemplates and provides for a system whereby applications to exclude media representatives should be dealt with as and when the occasion arises in the course of the proceedings by way of oral representations. It does not require prior notification to media interests unless the Court so directs (see para 6.4). All that is required of a party who intends to apply for the exclusion of the media is that, where practicable, advanced notice should be given to the Court and the other parties, including any childrens' guardian (para 6.3), and that, when an application has been made to the Court and is "pending" the applicant must where possible notify the relevant media organisations (para 6.4)

[86] The terms of the Practice Direction are conditioned by the anticipation that, up and down the country and at all levels of Court, applications under the provisions of Rule 10.28 (4) may arise in cases being heard daily and should

---

[14] [1996] AC 593.

in their ordinary way simply be dealt with on the spot, subject to the provisions of para 6.4 in respect of pending applications. A general mandatory requirement to go through the processes provided for in the President's Direction and CAFCASS Practice Note of 18 March 2005 would introduce unacceptable interruption and delays into court processes already hard pressed by the rising volume of work nationwide.

[87] In the light of the media interest to be anticipated in cases involving the children of "celebrities", whether national or local, I do not consider the provisions of paragraph 6.4 to be an adequate provision to protect the interests of the press and I am of the view that it requires to be reconsidered. Meanwhile, although the Practice Direction does not expressly so provide, I consider that it is incumbent upon an applicant who wishes to exclude the media from a substantive hearing *ab initio* to raise the matter with the Court prior to the hearing for consideration of the need to notify the media in advance of the proposed application and that, if this is done, the Court should require the applicant to notify the media via the CopyDirect service in accordance with the procedure provided for in the CAFCASS Practice Note. The Court should at the same time make directions for the hearing of the application whether by way of special appointment or consideration at the outset of the next substantive hearing. It is of course not necessary for the matter to be dealt with by a High Court Judge and it should, wherever possible, be dealt with by the trial judge. In the light of the view I have expressed, I consider that para 6.4 of the Practice Direction of 20 April 2009 should be read as if there were added at the end of the final sentence in that paragraph the words "and should do so by means of the Press Association CopyDirect service, following the procedure set out in the Official Solicitor/CAFCASS Practice Note dated 18 March 2005".

[88] It has been suggested on behalf of the media that a similar procedure is necessary or appropriate even in respect of cases where, although the parties do not challenge the right of the media to attend the proceedings from the outset, they seek during the course of the proceedings the temporary exclusion of the media in relation to the evidence of a particular witness or witnesses. I do not think that is either practical or necessary. There are likely to be frequent occasions when, either on the application of a party or of its own motion the Court considers it necessary, on one of the grounds set out in Rule 10.28 (4) to direct that accredited media representatives temporarily withdraw while certain evidence is given. To require the parties or the Court to institute the processes provided for in the President's Direction and CAFCASS Practice Note would create undesirable interruptions and produce unacceptable delays in the administration of justice.

[89] The decision as to the necessity to require the withdrawal of such representatives from the courtroom on a temporary basis will call for careful but robust decision making by the Judge who has the task of hearing the proceedings and completing them so far as practicable in the limited time available for the hearing of the case. Whilst the Judge is required to engage in a balancing exercise as between the Article 10 rights of the press and the Article 8 rights of the child, and the jurisprudence describes the exercise to be performed in fairly elaborate terms, the factors to be weighed in the balance as applied to the particular circumstances of the case will be well in the trial Judge's mind. It will not be a difficult task for the Judge to articulate them shortly to any media representative present, inviting him/her to comment and/or make representations before the Judge gives brief reasons for his/her decision (see para 5.5 of the Practice Direction of 20 April 2009).'

PRACTICAL IMPLICATIONS OF *RE CHILD X* FOR THE MEDIA, SOLICITORS AND COUNSEL

A8.17 1. **What is the importance of *Re Child X?*[15]** This case is a definitive statement of the law relating to media access to the family courts, particularly [but by no means exclusively] in the 'celebrity' and child welfare context. (The numbers below in square brackets are the paragraph references from the judgment of Sir Mark Potter P.)

A8.18 2. **The actual decision in '*X*':** Media excluded under Rule 10.28(4)(a)(i) and under 10.28(4)(b); [59].

A8.19 3. **The net effect of the new Rules?** While the press are entitled to report on the nature of the dispute in the proceedings, and to identify the issues in the case and the identity of participating witnesses (save those whose published identity would reveal the identity of the child in the case) they are not entitled to set out the content of the evidence or the detail of matters investigated by the court; [38].

A8.20 4. General principles flowing from *Re Child X*:

(*a*) *The primary issue:* To decide whether or not to exclude the media from the court-room in the welfare or privacy interests of a party or third party; [46].

(b) *'Celebrity' cases*: No different in principle from any other [51].

(*c*) *The issue is not one of 'discretion':* The Art 8 / 10 balancing exercise is **not** a simple issue of '*discretion*' as between two equally legitimate competing rights; it is a test of '*necessity*'[56]. Thus references to the Court's '*discretion*' in *paragraph 3.1* and in the heading to *paragraph 5* of the PD of 20 April 2009 are a misnomer. [48] and [56]. '*Necessary*' is the yardstick for any of the statutory grounds of exclusion [53]. It demands a strong interpretation; *R v Shayler*[16] [54] and [89].

(*d*) *Balancing exercise:* The court must conduct the balancing exercise and process of parallel analysis in respect of the interplay between Articles 8 and 10: see *Campbell v MGN Ltd,*[17] *Re S (A child)*[18] [46]; recognising in this context that the issue is one of statutory '*necessity*' to exclude – as contrasted with '*Campbell*' and '*S*' which concerned issues of what could be reported. Note under Rule 10.28(4): To what extent is the '*watchdog*' function of the court engaged [58] and [65].

[15] [2009] EWHC 1728 (Fam).
[16] [2003] 1 AC 247 at 268.
[17] [2004] 2 AC 457.
[18] [2005] 1 AC 593.

(e) *Burden of proof*: Easier for partial as contrasted with total exclusion [57].

A8.21 5. **Article 8 and adult interests**: Rule 24.28(4) ground 'b' (*'justice will otherwise be impeded or prejudiced'*) is capable of embracing the Article 8 interests of adult parties to prevent the press from hearing and/or reporting allegations of an outrageous or intimate nature before the court's decision as to whether or not they are established [45]. This is without prejudice to the fact, however, that in considering whether or not to exclude the press under Rule 10.28(4)(a)(i), the focus is upon the interests of the child and not the parents [52].

A8.22 6. **Applications against the media**:

(a) *Which court?*
   (i) Injunctions *'contra mundum'* to be heard in the High Court [11]. For service, use Press Association's *CopyDirect* service [83]. The *President's PD* of 18 March 2005 must be particularly used in cases of high media interest [13], together with the OS/CAFCASS Practice Note of the same date.
   (ii) Any relief sought beyond the jurisdiction of *s 12 AJA* and *s 97(2) of the CA* must be founded on Convention rights [11], is subject to s 12(2) of the HRA [79], must be in the High Court [12] & [18], and must be dealt with under the *President's PD* of 18 March 2005 (including its robust provisions as to the demand for service on the media; see [11] and [76] and in particular *para 3*).

(b) *The impact of s 12(2) and the demands for 'service'*: Section 12(2) of the HRA emphasises the extent, breadth and depth of the Convention right to freedom of expression (including the need for *'service'*); [76].

(c) *What if case is in the county court?* If the need for an order arises in existing proceedings in the County Court, Judges should either transfer the application to the High Court or consult their FDLJ [12].

(d) *Foreign journalist:* The issue of reporters from out of the jurisdiction, out of the reach of the court, is relevant [67].

(e) *What can the media be shown when injunctive relief is being sought?*
   (i) The media must have the opportunity to see any informative material upon which to base any decision: See Official Solicitor/CAFCASS *Practice Note* 18 March 2005 and the *President's PD* of the same date. They give important procedural protection to the media [82].
   (ii) It is sufficient for the justifying statement, without revealing the *detail* of the sensitive or confidential matter, to outline and make clear the *nature* of the matters and issues covered in such reports in a manner sufficient to enable the media to make an informed decision; [84].

A8.23 7. **Revision to para 6.4 of President's Direction of 20 April 2009:** The President gave guidance as to a revision to this paragraph –

(a) *What must be added?* Para 6.4 should end with the following words: 'and should do so by means of the Press Association CopyDirect service, following the procedure set out in the Official Solicitor/CAFCASS Practice Note dated 18 March 2005.'[87].

(b) *What is the effect of that addition in the context of the judgment?* An applicant who wishes to exclude the media from a substantive hearing *ab initio* must raise the matter with the court prior to the hearing for consideration of the need to notify the media in advance of the proposed application and that, if this is done, the court should require the applicant to notify the media via the CopyDirect service [83] and [87].

A8.24 8. **Citations in the judgement from the Press Complaints Commission Editor's Code of Practice:** Passages cited include [74]:

'… editors must not use the fame notoriety or position of a parent or guardian as the sole justification for publishing details of a child's private life.'

'Pupils must not be approached or photographed at school without the permission of the school authorities.'

'In cases involving children under 16, editors must demonstrate an exceptional public interest to over-ride the normally paramount interest of the child.'

Appendix 9

STANDARD FORM PRESS/PUBLICITY ORDERS

STANDARD FORM PRESS AND PUBLICITY ORDERS

A9.01

These standard form press/publicity injunctions issued by CAFCASS Legal Services are based on drafts which have been approved by the Court of Appeal and which have been in circulation for some years.

GENERAL PRESS ORDER

IMPORTANT

(1) This order contains injunctions. You should read it carefully. You are advised to consult a solicitor as soon as possible. You have the right to ask the court to vary or discharge this order.

(2) If you disobey this order you may be found guilty of contempt of court and may be sent to prison or fined or your assets may be seized.

IN THE HIGH COURT OF JUSTICE

FAMILY DIVISION

PRINCIPAL REGISTRY   Case no...........................

BEFORE ....IN CHAMBERS

DATE:

IN THE MATTER of.......................... (A CHILD)

AND IN THE MATTER OF THE INHERENT JURISDICTION

BETWEEN:

..........................[parties]

UPON HEARING..........................

AND UPON READING..........................

AND upon leave being granted to the plaintiff to apply for the exercise of the court's inherent jurisdiction.

Relevant statutes

- Section 12(1) of the Administration of Justice Act 1960.

- Section 97(2) of the Children Act 1989.

Duration of order

(1) This order is to have effect until [*date*] (the eighteenth birthday of the child whose details are set out in the first Schedule) ('the child') or until further order.

Who is bound by this order

(2) This order binds all persons (whether acting by themselves or by their servants or agents or in any other way) and all companies (whether acting by their directors or officers, servants or agents or in any other way) who know that this order has been made.

Restrictions

(3) This order prohibits the publishing in any newspaper or broadcasting in any sound or television broadcast or by means of any cable or satellite programme service or public computer network ('publishing') of:

    (a)   the name or address of:
        (i)   the child;
        (ii)   any residential home or any school or other establishment in which the child is residing or being educated or treated (an 'establishment'); or
        (iii)   any natural person other than a parent of the child having the day-to-day care of the child (a 'carer'); or
        (iv)   the [...] defendants the [foster-] parents of the child ('the [foster-] parents') being the persons whose names and addresses are set out in the second Schedule;
    (b)   any picture being or including a picture of either (i) the child or (ii) either of the [foster-] parents;
    (c)   any other matter.

(4) This order only prohibits publication in a manner calculated to lead to the identification:

    (a)   of the child either as being subject of proceedings before the court or as being the child [...];
    (b)   of an establishment as being an establishment in which the child is residing or being educated or treated;
    (c)   of any [foster-] parent or any carer as being the [foster-] parent or a carer (as the case may be) of the child.

(5) Save for service of this order in accordance with para 8 below, no publication of the text or a summary of any part of this order (or any other order made in the proceedings) may include any of the matters referred to in para 3 above.

(6) This order prohibits soliciting any information relating to the child (other than information already in the public domain):

    (a)   from the child;

(b)   from the staff or the pupils or residents of any establishment;

(c)   from any carer;

(d)   from the [foster-] parents or either of them.

What is not restricted

(7)   Nothing in this order shall of itself prevent any person:

(a)   publishing any particulars of or information relating to any part of the proceedings before any court other than a court sitting in private;

(b)   publishing anything which at the date of publication by that person has previously been published (whether inside or outside the jurisdiction of the court) in any newspaper or other publication or through the Internet or any other broadcast or electronic medium to such an extent that the information is in the public domain (other than in a case where the only publication was made by that person);

(c)   inquiring whether a person is protected by para 6 above;

(d)   seeking information from any person who has previously approached that person with the purpose of volunteering information;

(e)   soliciting information relating to the child while exercising any function authorised by statute or by any court of competent jurisdiction.

Service

(8)   Copies of this order endorsed with a penal notice be served by the plaintiff:

(a)   on such newspaper and sound or television broadcasting or cable or satellite programme services as the plaintiff may think fit in each case by fax or first class post addressed to the editor in the case of a newspaper or senior news editor in the case of a broadcasting or cable or satellite programme service; and

(b)   on such other persons as the plaintiff may think fit in each case by personal service.

Further applications about this order

(9)   The parties and any person affected by any of the restrictions in paras 3–6 above are at liberty to apply on no less than 48 hours notice to the parties.

First schedule

THE CHILD'S FULL NAME:

BORN:

ADDRESS:

Second schedule

FULL NAME:

ADDRESS:

A9.02

PERSONAL PUBLICITY ORDER

IMPORTANT

(1)   This order contains injunctions. You should read it carefully. You are advised to consult a solicitor as soon as possible. You have the right to ask the court to vary or discharge this order.

(2)   If you disobey this order you may be found guilty of contempt of court and may be sent to prison or fined or your assets may be seized.

IN THE HIGH COURT OF JUSTICE

FAMILY DIVISION

PRINCIPAL REGISTRY   Case no..........................

BEFORE..........................IN CHAMBERS

DATE:

IN THE MATTER of.......................... (A CHILD)

IN THE MATTER OF THE INHERENT JURISDICTION

AND IN THE MATTER OF THE CHILDREN ACT 1989

BETWEEN:

..........................[parties]

UPON HEARING..........................

AND UPON READING..........................

Relevant statutes

- Section 12(1) of the Administration of Justice Act 1960.
- Section 97(2) of the Children Act 1989.

Duration of order

(1)   This order shall remain in force until [*date*] (the eighteenth birthday of the child whose details are set out in the Schedule) or until further order.

Restrictions

(2)   [*Name*] be restrained and an injunction is hereby granted restraining him/her from discussing or otherwise communicating (otherwise than for ordinary social and domestic purposes) any matter relating to the education, maintenance, financial circumstances or family circumstances (including any proceedings before any court) of the child whose details are set out in the schedule ('the child') other than with:

    (a)   any legal adviser whom he/she may consult or instruct;
    (b)   the other parties;
    (c)   the medical and educational advisers of the child;

(d) any person to whom information is communicated for the purpose of enabling that person to exercise any function in relation to the child which is authorised by statute or by a court of competent jurisdiction; and

(e) any other person the court may permit.

What is not restricted

(3) Nothing in this order shall of itself prevent [*name*] from:

(a) discussing, communicating or publishing any matter relating to any part of the proceedings before any court other than a court sitting in private; and

(b) discussing, communicating or publishing ('disclosing') anything which at the date of disclosure by that person has previously been disclosed (whether inside or outside the jurisdiction of the court) in any newspaper or other publication or through the Internet or any other broadcast or electronic medium to such an extent that the information is in the public domain (other than in a case where the only disclosure was made by that person).

Further applications about this order

(4) The parties and any person affected by this order are at liberty to apply on no less than 48 hours' notice to the parties.

Schedule

THE CHILD'S FULL NAME:

BORN:

ADDRESS:

INDEX

References are to paragraph numbers.